Common Core Curriculum: United States History, GRADES 3–5

JOSSEY-BASS
A Wiley Brand

Cover design by Chris Clary
Cover image: White Cloud, Head Chief of the Iowas by George Catlin | © Corbis

Published by Jossey-Bass
A Wiley Brand
One Montgomery Street, Suite 1200, San Francisco, CA 94104-4594 www.josseybass.com

Credits:
White Cloud, Head Chief of the Iowas by George Catlin | © Corbis
A Frigate-Dominic Serres © National Maritime Museum, Greenwich, London
George Washington by Gilbert Stuart | © Christie's Images/Corbis
Valley of the Yosemite by Albert Bierstadt | © Burstein Collection/CORBIS
President Reagan giving a speech at the Berlin Wall. Courtesy Ronald Reagan Library

Jossey-Bass books and products are available through most bookstores. To contact Jossey-Bass directly call our Customer Care Department within the U.S. at 800-956-7739, outside the U.S. at 317-572-3986, or fax 317-572-4002.

The content in this book also can be found online. See "The Alexandria Plan" at commoncore.org.

Wiley publishes in a variety of print and electronic formats and by print-on-demand. Some material included with standard print versions of this book may not be included in e-books or in print-on-demand. If this book refers to media such as a CD or DVD that is not included in the version you purchased, you may download this material at http://booksupport.wiley.com. For more information about Wiley products, visit www.wiley.com.

Library of Congress Cataloging-in-Publication Data

Common Core Curriculum: United States history, grades 3-5/Common Core, Inc. – 1
pages cm. – (Common Core U.S. and world history)
Includes index.
ISBN 978-1-118-52696-5 (pbk.); ISBN 978-1-118-58336-4 (pdf); ISBN 978-1-118-58341-8 (epub)
1. United States–History–Study and teaching (Elementary) 2. United States–History–Study and teaching (Elementary)–Standards.
LB1581.C724 2014
973.071–dc23

2013045498

Printed in the United States of America

FIRST EDITION

PB *Printing* 10 9 8 7 6 5 4 3 2 1

Contents

Introduction: How to Use the Alexandria Plan

The Alexandria Plan is Common Core's curriculum tool for teaching United States and world history. It is a strategic framework for identifying and using high-quality informational texts and narrative nonfiction to meet the expectations of the Common Core State Standards (CCSS) for English language arts (ELA) while also sharing essential historical knowledge with students in elementary school (kindergarten through fifth grade). These resources can be used in either the social studies block or the ELA block during the elementary school day. The curriculum helps teachers pose questions about texts covering a wide range of topics: from the caves at Lascaux to King Tut's tomb, Chief Joseph to Kubla Khan, and the birth of democracy to the fall of the Berlin Wall. These books tell stories that thrill students. Accompanying text-dependent questions (TDQs) will elevate student learning to a level that will help them master the new CCSS for English language arts (CCSS-ELA).

We call these curriculum materials the "Alexandria Plan" because we enjoy thinking about the role that they—and the teachers who use them—play in passing along important knowledge to future generations. In ancient Egypt, the Library of Alexandria, along with a museum, was part of a grand complex that sought to collect and catalog "all the knowledge in the world." It became a center of learning, attracting scholars, philosophers, scientists, and physicians from all corners of the earth. Though it fell to fire, the spirit of Alexandria remains. Some twenty-three hundred years later, a new library stands near the site of its ancient ancestor, and the story of Alexandria and its great library inspires our efforts to help teachers illuminate the future by inculcating in their students an understanding of the past.

The Alexandria Plan is the second in a suite of curriculum materials Common Core is developing to help educators implement the CCSS. In 2010, Common Core released its Curriculum Maps in English Language Arts. The Maps are a coherent sequence of thematic units, roughly six per grade level, for students in kindergarten through twelfth grade. Now known as the Wheatley Portfolio, these resources connect the skills delineated in the CCSS with suggested works of literature and informational texts and provide sample activities that teachers can use in the classroom to reinforce the standards. The Wheatley Portfolio will soon grow, with resources to help educators enact the instructional shifts while cultivating in students a love of excellent books—all based on featured anchor informational and literary texts, poetry, and the arts. In summer 2013, we began rolling out a comprehensive, K–12, CCSS-based mathematics curriculum known as Eureka Math, with embedded professional development. Please watch our website, commoncore.org, for future releases.

HOW WILL THE ALEXANDRIA PLAN HELP ME, MY SCHOOL, MY DISTRICT, OR MY STATE IMPLEMENT THE CCSS-ELA?

The CCSS-ELA emphasize the importance of literacy across the curriculum. Indeed, CCSS architect David Coleman has said, "There is no such thing as doing the nuts and bolts of reading in kindergarten through fifth grade without coherently developing knowledge in science, and history, and the arts—period." Unfortunately, research has illustrated that history is one in a group of core subjects that have been squeezed out of many classrooms. The Alexandria Plan guides educators through the process of reprioritizing the teaching of history in the classroom and will assist teachers in addressing key CCSS-ELA while also meeting state social studies standards.

HOW ARE THESE RESOURCES STRUCTURED?

The print editions of the Alexandria Plan, each organized by subject and grade span, present essential content knowledge in United States and world history. United States history is separated into eighteen eras, and so is world history. To make this knowledge accessible to students in elementary school, we established two grade spans: lower elementary (kindergarten through second grade) and upper elementary (third grade through fifth grade). Each book contains one subject area (United States or world history) as well as the resources for teaching to one grade span (lower or upper elementary). Learning expectations articulate the key ideas, events, facts, and figures to be understood by students in a particular grade span. Suggested anchor texts; text studies (comprising TDQs and exemplar student responses, and accompanied by performance assessments based on one or more featured anchor texts); and more select resources flesh out the content for each era. The following is a detailed breakdown of what is contained in a given era of the Alexandria Plan as well as in the accompanying collection of era summaries that provide additional historical content for teachers.

Overview

Each overview captures the essence of the history presented in a given era. The paragraph concludes with a brief description of what students will learn and be able to do after completing the associated text study.

Learning Expectations

This section describes what our teachers have identified as being appropriate and necessary for students to know in each grade span. It is this knowledge that students need to master so that they will be prepared for later grades. Teachers can break down the content indicated into grade-specific expectations that fit their classroom.

Suggested Anchor Texts

For each era of U.S. and world history, we provide a well-vetted list of suggested anchor texts that can be used to impart essential knowledge found in the "Era Summaries" and "Learning Expectations." So that educators can select the book that is best suited to their classroom, we provide text recommendations covering an array of topics in the era. These carefully curated selections include exceptional works of narrative nonfiction, informational texts, and historical fiction. The texts are rich in historical content, well written, fair in their presentation of history, and often beautifully illustrated, allowing for the development of text-dependent questions that illuminate both the historical content and the authors' and illustrators' craft. These texts may also serve as mentor texts for students' own writing.

Featured Anchor Text

Teacher-writers selected one or two of the suggested anchor texts to illuminate in a text study aimed at the higher end of a particular grade span. Although all of the suggested anchor texts are worth exploring with students, each featured anchor text captures a particularly pertinent aspect of the era in which it is featured. Occasionally, the featured anchor text is paired with a supporting text to provide additional content to support student understanding.

Text Study

Each text study provides teachers with detailed guidance about how to lead students through a close, patient reading of a featured anchor text. Using a carefully crafted sequence of TDQs, teachers can effectively guide students through a detailed reading of a complex text. The questions lead students to use evidence directly from the text to explain and support their answers. Such close reading leads students to absorb key historical knowledge while honing essential CCSS-ELA skills. Answers are provided for each question. These TDQs are followed by at least one comprehensive performance assessment for each study. Both the TDQs and the performance assessments require students to support conclusions or opinions about the text with specific text evidence.

Performance Assessments

Each text study is followed by at least one performance assessment that allows students to demonstrate (typically, through a CCSS-based writing assignment) their understanding of the key ideas, historical events, and figures discussed in the featured anchor text. These performance assessments flow naturally from the progression of TDQs about the featured anchor text. Suggestions of activities that can be used to extend or expand instruction, labeled as extensions, are often included.

Connections to Common Core State Standards for English Language Arts

Each text study also includes CCSS-ELA citations for nearly every one of the TDQs, performance assessments, and extensions, along with explanations of how each of these items helps address the CCSS-ELA. Please note that our citations for the standards follow the established CCSS format: strand.grade.number.

More Resources

We include a list of related resources, including works of historical fiction, art, poetry, music, primary sources, and multimedia resources, that teachers can incorporate into lessons, use to extend or enrich instruction, or simply use to build their own content knowledge. Teachers often ask for quality primary sources that they can use in elementary grades, so Common Core sought out engaging, relevant, and accessible primary sources for teachers and their students. Sources of essential geographic knowledge are also incorporated where appropriate. Like our suggested anchor text selections, these resources have been carefully curated to save teachers countless hours of searching for resources to extend students' knowledge of history.

Era Summaries

Each of the eras in the Alexandria Plan also contains a concise and compelling summary of the history of that era—all collected together at the end of each print edition—highlighting the people, events, places, and ideas that constitute essential knowledge for teachers to share with students. The content of the summaries was guided by exemplary state social studies standards, written by a historian with expert knowledge of those standards. Nationally recognized historians vetted each summary and meticulously reviewed them for accuracy. These easy-to-read summaries contain what college- and career-ready high school graduates should know about each era. The summaries also make it convenient for teachers to review the history of the era in preparation for lesson planning and deeper research.

HOW WERE ANCHOR TEXTS SELECTED?

Teacher-writers with decades of classroom experience reviewed hundreds of historical fiction, narrative nonfiction, and informational texts, selecting the most engaging and content-rich among them. Each anchor text conveys an essential aspect of the history addressed in the "Learning Expectations" for each era. The list of texts is neither comprehensive nor exhaustive. In other words, a text has not been selected for every aspect of the history contained in the era summaries, nor do we imagine that we have identified all of the great texts available that are relevant to an era. The list represents a great start—a set that we look forward to building over time.

We were looking for rigorous, accurate, well-written, and wonderfully illustrated texts, considering the following criteria:

- *The text should enliven historical events in ways that nurture children's innate curiosity.*

  We sought texts that bring to life the historical setting, events, and story being told. Although our focus was on the selection of complex, content-rich texts, we also recognized that the texts needed to be age appropriate. Much consideration was given to readability, and whenever possible, we have placed texts in appropriate grade bands, based on their Lexile level. Where Lexile levels may pose ostensible challenges for teachers, we have explained how teachers might approach instruction (for example, reading the text aloud or scaffolding the amount of text students are expected to read).

  In addition, we have geared our questions and answers to the upper level of each grade band. Teachers will have to use questions that are appropriate for their students and look to the answers provided as guides for where to lead students, building understanding over time. Teachers who have piloted these materials have often reported being surprised at how successfully students mine and appreciate these texts, even when the texts were at first considered "too hard." They have told us—and we believe—that it is important not to underestimate what students can do when they are presented with compelling, high-quality texts.

- *The text should make teaching more fun, by engaging the teacher in compelling history.*

  One of the key instructional shifts called for in teaching to the CCSS-ELA is the significant increase in the amount of time and attention students are asked to devote to evidence-based analysis of what they are reading. Instead of focusing on metacognitive reading strategies at the expense of content, teachers can now focus on the content of the text, confident that it lends itself well to the kind of analysis demanded in the CCSS-ELA, but also giving students a chance to immerse themselves in the content, making learning more interesting for students and teachers alike.

- *The text should serve, in its quality and complexity, as an exemplar for teaching the literacy skills defined in the CCSS-ELA.*

  The third criterion for text inclusion was that the text should be significantly complex enough to support the rich text study, including the focus on important English language arts standards. If the texts weren't well written and compelling, they simply would not lend themselves to the kind of analysis that the CCSS-ELA demand—and that teachers and students enjoy. These texts, by celebrated authors including Peter Sis and Diane Stanley, exhibit the power of narrative history, the efficacy of great illustrations, the effect of figurative language, and the strength of arguments that are supported with clear evidence.

HAS THE ALEXANDRIA PLAN BEEN PILOTED?

Yes, extensively. We asked teachers from rural, urban, charter, and private schools across the country to pilot a selection of the materials and to share their experience. Nearly one hundred teachers participated, including new teachers, National Board Certified teachers, and veterans who have been recognized by their respective districts for excellent teaching. Their generous feedback helped us both improve these materials and explain more clearly how to use the features of the curriculum. Rather than speak for them, here are two testimonials from pilot users:

> The Map made it very easy for the teacher by giving information about the book as well as historical information. The direction of the lesson was centered around the character of Christopher Columbus and the vocabulary used to describe him—*brave, studious, curious, patient, dreamer*. The students described Columbus and were able to defend their answers. I never really thought about the character of Columbus and all that he went through to make his dreams come true. He was a true leader. Our school is a "Leader in Me" school, and this lesson illustrated several of the habits (character traits) we want our students to exhibit.
>
> —Trudy Phelps, kindergarten teacher, Dolby Elementary School, Louisiana

> The text was the core of the social studies lesson. I worked from the text out. In most social studies lessons you start from the outside and move in. Students related to the characters and seemed to feel they were there. They simply had a better understanding of the history behind the text. The text, with a well-balanced set of questions, made the experience easier as they developed an understanding of the history.
>
> —Jayne Brown, kindergarten teacher, Avery's Creek Elementary School, North Carolina

WHY ARE THERE SO MANY TEXT-DEPENDENT QUESTIONS?

It is important to note that we do not expect teachers to ask *all* of the questions we've provided. Our rather exhaustive sets of questions are intended to support teachers in the scaffolding that will be necessary to meet the needs of all learners. Further, careful study of these questions, including how they are constructed, will help teachers craft text-dependent questions for other high-quality texts on their own. Indeed, the curriculum can be used as a professional development tool and as a means of understanding what is expected of students according to the CCSS-ELA. Please contact Common Core through commoncore.org if you would like to learn about our professional development services.

DOES THE ALEXANDRIA PLAN REQUIRE ME TO ADOPT A PARTICULAR METHOD OF INSTRUCTION?

No. The way teachers choose to prepare students to approach the study of a text depends on their teaching style and the needs of students. A teacher may choose to have students read short sections of text with a few assigned questions, preparing students to participate fully in discussion. Or a teacher may choose to have students work in pairs or small groups to read and to discuss questions, preparing to pull their ideas together for a rich whole-class seminar discussion. Or a teacher may want students to grapple with the text independently at first. During their first reading of the text, students might circle passages where they are confused and/or underline points that they thought were interesting. Students might annotate the reading selection with questions and notes. As the teacher circulates during the independent reading time, he or she might note themes of questions that students generate as they read. The teacher could then use the TDQs, as needed, to clarify misunderstandings and to go deeper into the text than the students were able to go on their own. We offer these questions for teachers to use as they see fit.

HOW CAN I SCAFFOLD UP TO A TEXT?

If a teacher wishes to use one of the suggested anchor texts but feels it is too difficult for his or her students, using more accessible texts to build background knowledge might be considered. This strategy involves reading aloud less challenging texts to prepare students to tackle the more difficult text. Following is an example of how to build skills and rigor up to the featured anchor text for U.S. era 11, *Abraham Lincoln: Lawyer, Leader, Legend* by Justine and Ron Fontes, recommended for lower elementary students.

At a Lexile level of 790L, this text is certainly at the upper range for the age level, and we are not suggesting that K–2 students read this book independently. Instead, we suggest that they follow along (with their own copy or using a document camera) as the teacher reads it aloud. Even still, it might be best to first introduce some of the vocabulary and concepts through easier books on the same topic, such as the following:

- *Abe Lincoln's Hat* by Martha Brenner: 330L
- *Mr. Lincoln's Whiskers* by Karen B. Winnick: 420L
- *Looking at Lincoln* by Maira Kalman: AD480L
- A. *Lincoln and Me* by Louise Borden: AD650L
- *When Abraham Talked to the Trees* by Elizabeth Van Steenwyk: 670L

Each of the books tells interesting stories about Abraham Lincoln as a person and a leader, creating a whole reservoir of background knowledge. This mounting knowledge arouses curiosity in the children, prompting a desire for more information. By the time the teacher is ready to share the more challenging *Abraham Lincoln: Lawyer, Leader, Legend*, the students know that Lincoln stored important things in his hat, grew whiskers because a young girl thought it would make him more dignified, stood tall to make hard decisions, and practiced his speeches on stumps in the woods. This background knowledge will make the complex text easier to understand.

Across Beringia: Original People of North America

(ca. 20,000 BCE to ca. 1600 CE)

GRADES: 3, 4, 5

OVERVIEW

The first humans to settle on the American continents twenty thousand years ago eventually developed complex cultures with sophisticated political, economic, and religious systems. Native Americans adapted to very different landscapes and climates, from arctic to tropical, and this influenced all aspects of their behavior and customs. The featured anchor texts for this era, *Native Homes* and *The Discovery of the Americas: From Prehistory through the Age of Columbus*, explore how the first Americans lived. Students in lower elementary grades will report informed opinions on how native people lived. Upper elementary students will produce informed essays about the effect of European exploration on the native people of the Americas.

○ ○ ○

Interested in learning more about this time period? Read a more complete history in the "Era Summaries."

LEARNING EXPECTATIONS

Lower elementary: Students should be familiar with the major Native American cultural regions and civilizations—especially those cultures indigenous to what would become the United States, and to students' own state in particular. Students should understand the human impact of early European contact and conquest.

Upper elementary: Students should be aware of the tribal cultures and advanced civilizations that existed in the Americas before European contact. They should understand the environmental impact of both Native American and European arrivals, and the profound effects of European contact and conquest, both on indigenous civilizations and on Europe itself through the discovery of new foods and resources.

SUGGESTED ANCHOR TEXTS

The Discovery of the Americas: From Prehistory through the Age of Columbus by Betsy and Giulio Maestro
The First Americans: Prehistory–1600 by Joy Hakim
First People: An Illustrated History of American Indians by David C. King
"The Cliff Dwellers," *Cobblestone*, September 1999
The Earth under Sky Bear's Feet: Native American Poems of the Land by Joseph Bruchac
The Girl Who Helped Thunder and Other Native American Folktales by Joseph Bruchac
Tikta'liktak: An Inuit-Eskimo Legend by James Houston
Tools of Native Americans by Kim Kavin

FEATURED ANCHOR TEXT

THE DISCOVERY OF THE AMERICAS: FROM PREHISTORY THROUGH THE AGE OF COLUMBUS BY BETSY AND GIULIO MAESTRO

This book was selected because the beautiful illustrations and text invite students to consider how the Native Americans may have originally come to North America, the settlement of various nations over North and Central America, and the impact of the European explorers on those peoples.

TEXT STUDY

These text-dependent questions allow teachers many openings to support the Common Core State Standards for English language arts while also emphasizing essential historical content. Many questions highlight the ways in which informational text features (such as illustrations and maps) complement the text to ensure readers' understanding of essential concepts or details. The questions also give students practice in comparing and contrasting information (for example, about the various groups) within the text, promoting close rereading and therefore comprehension of key concepts.

1. **What were the two continents connected by the natural land bridge during the last Ice Age?**
   - According to page 3, the two continents of North America and Asia were connected by a natural land bridge.
2. **Why did people cross the land bridge connecting Asia and North America? Where did they settle?**
   - According to pages 4 through 7, Ice Age nomads were hunting with "weapons made of stone." They were searching for animals, such as mastodons and mammoths. Because they had already eaten what they could find, they moved on. Eventually, they crossed a land bridge onto a new continent that was later known as the New World, or the Americas.
3. **How do the authors illustrate that different Native American groups found food in varied ways as time passed?**
   - The illustrations on pages 8 and 9 show the Native Americans fishing and planting crops.
   - The text on pages 8 and 9 describes how large animals died out with the Ice Age or because too many of the animals were killed. Different groups of people chose different ways of living. Some groups settled in homes and small settlements, living as farmers. Others continued to move, hunting herds of buffalo for part of the year.

4. **How do the authors use illustrations and text to prove that the Mayan culture was impressive?**
    - On pages 10 and 11, the illustrations show irrigated fields and shelters. The images also show great temples and pyramids. The text supports the illustrations by describing the "sixty cities in the area that is now Mexico and Central America." It describes the people as "master builders." The Mayan people "were skillful in math and astronomy and created a calendar that was highly accurate," and "the Maya artists created pottery, sculpture, and jewelry."
5. **The book says that other groups (including the Japanese, Phoenicians, and Chinese) may have sailed to the Americas before the Europeans came. Describe what you notice on the chart on page 12. How does this chart prove that the Asians probably arrived in America before the European explorers?**
    - The authors show the pieces of craftsmanship and art from the Asian "Old World" juxtaposed with similar pieces found in the "New World." For example, the string cross from India is very similar to the string cross from Central America. The elephant on wheels from India is very similar in structure to the dog on wheels found in Central America.
    - The similarity of those pieces could indicate that the artists and craftspeople came from Japan, India, the South Pacific, Indochina, and Phoenicia.
6. **What do the Hopewell people and the Inca Empire have in common?**
    - According to pages 18 and 19, both the Hopewell people and the Inca Empire were examples of Native American nations that were short-lived. We know about them because of archaeological digs. Although descendants survive, these groups did not last a long time. The Hopewell were around for about six hundred years, and the Inca Empire was in power for about one hundred years.
7. **According to page 20, what sparked European interest in exploration in the fifteenth century?**
    - The people in Europe were busy at home with wars, disease, and religious crusades to the Middle East. They didn't really know much about exploration because of poor communication between distant places, but when Marco Polo and other traders brought back silk, spices, and other goods to Europe from the Far East, the Europeans wanted more of these goods—and therefore wanted to explore the lands that produced them.
8. **On pages 23 through 33, the authors describe the discovery and exploration of the New World by explorers. What were the important discoveries of Christopher Columbus and John Cabot? How did their discoveries serve to encourage *more* exploration?**
    - According to page 29, Columbus "opened up a new world for all of Europe" by discovering sea routes between the two continents.
    - According to page 30, Cabot "began the English exploration and settlement of North America."
    - On page 33, the authors tell of "a promise of vast riches" that was the motivator for the continued exploration of the New World, soon to be called America.
9. **The authors tell of the explorer Vasco Nuñez de Balboa's coming to America. What motivated his exploration, and how did he affect the Native Americans he met?**
    - According to pages 34 and 35, Balboa was motivated by the desire for land, gold, and riches. He didn't care who owned the land and gold. Balboa was brutal and cruel, forcing his Christian beliefs and his customs on the native people. The Native Americans often attacked in response.

10. At the end of the book, the authors write more about the effects of the Europeans on the Native Americans. How do the authors convey the Native American gains and losses due to European exploration?

- On pages 42 and 43, the text describes Native American interest in the new knowledge, skills, and materials that the Europeans brought, using words like *wonderful* and *fascinating*. The authors then note the losses Europeans brought: loss of life due to diseases and weapons, loss of freedom, loss of customs, and loss of pride.

PERFORMANCE ASSESSMENTS

1. Three of the Native American groups highlighted in this book were the Mayan, Inca, and Hopewell peoples. Have students choose one of those groups to feature in an informative/explanatory essay. Give students the following writing task:

- Choose an ancient Native American group that lived in the Americas. Tell about their geographic location, their civilization, and the effect of European exploration on their culture.

2. Direct the students to focus on these research questions:

- In the days before European exploration, what Native American nation lived closest to where you live now? What are some aspects of that group's culture?

List the specific features of culture your class should research. Ask students to use a variety of sources (texts, multimedia sources, speakers, field trips, primary sources) to learn about the Native American nation. Assign students an informative/explanatory essay describing the early culture of the Native American nation.

Note: The focus in this era is on the Native Americans, so the sections on explorers in the featured anchor text are read but only focused on in relation to their effect on the Native Americans.

CONNECTION TO COMMON CORE STATE STANDARDS FOR ENGLISH LANGUAGE ARTS

- Questions 1, 2, 6, 7, 8, and 9 ask students to note important details and ideas in an informational text, citing evidence to support their answers (RI.3.1,2,3,8; RI.4.1,2,3,8; RI.5.1,2,3,8).
  - Question 7 also allows for a discussion of how authors of informational texts draw inferences and synthesize information that they have researched and presented (RI.3.8; RI.4.8; RI.5.8).
- Questions 3, 4, and 5 are opportunities to discuss the role of informational text features, such as illustrations and charts (RI.3.5; RI.4.5; RI.5.5).
- Question 10 addresses the authors' craft, in particular how the authors juxtapose two different sets of information (RI.3.3,8; RI.4.3,8; RI.5.3,8).
- The first performance assessment gives students a chance both to research a topic that builds on their understanding of what they read and to write an informative/explanatory essay (RI.3.3,5,8; RI.4.3,5,8; RI.5.3,5,8; W.3.2,7,9; W.4.2,7,9; W.5.2,7,9).

- The second performance assessment gives students a chance to research a topic related to what they have just read (using a variety of media–including primary sources, interviews, and field trips) and use the research to write an informative/explanatory essay (RI.3.3,5,8; RI.4.3,5,8; RI.5.3,5,8; W.3.2,7,8; W.4.2,7,8; W.5.2,7,8).

MORE RESOURCES

PRIMARY SOURCES

Native American fishing practices (Library of Congress)

Eskimo portrait (Library of Congress)

Eskimo arrowhead shapes (Library of Congress)

Mayan sun god (Metropolitan Museum of Art)

Pueblo mesa architecture (Denver Public Library)

Photo taken in 1899

POETRY AND MUSIC

Inuit throat singing, video (*National Geographic*)

ART AND ARCHITECTURE

Personal pendant, carved during the Ice Age (British Museum)

USEFUL WEBSITES

Native American legends organized by group name (First People)

Native American legends of the Northwest

Caribou migrating across the present Beringia (Encyclopedia Britannica)

UNITED STATES HISTORY, ERA 2

Driven to Discover: Europeans Establish the New World

(Late 1400s to Late 1600s)

GRADES: 3, 4, 5

OVERVIEW

Such explorers as Christopher Columbus, Hernán Cortés, and Amerigo Vespucci were compelled by the attraction of discovering the unknown. Their discoveries of the New World sparked intense competition between European kingdoms, even though journeys were fraught with peril. Still, the imperial nations were consumed by the desire to possess these new lands and their riches. The experiences of noted explorers and those who followed in their trails, and their complex relationships with native people, illustrate the beginnings of North American communities as we know them today. Reading *Follow the Dream: The Story of Christopher Columbus* or *Exploration and Conquest: The Americas after Columbus, 1500–1620* will give students the essential background on these global pioneers. Younger students will dissect Columbus's adventurous spirit, whereas older students will weigh the effects of Europeans' encounters with native people.

○ ○ ○

Interested in learning more about this time period? Read a more complete history in the "Era Summaries."

LEARNING EXPECTATIONS

Lower elementary: Students should understand that European explorers set out seeking "God, gold, and glory" (including the profits to be had from the spice trade). They should know that the Europeans found already peopled lands, met the native peoples with much tension, and settled the Americas for a variety of reasons.

Upper elementary: Students should understand the different aims of the major European empires in the Americas (particularly in the areas that would become the United States) and the consequences of those differing aims in their contact with indigenous peoples. They should understand that European settlers had different aims in different regions, contributing to the creation of very different new societies.

SUGGESTED ANCHOR TEXTS

Exploration and Conquest: The Americas after Columbus, 1500–1620 by Betsy and Giulio Maestro
Where Do You Think You're Going, Christopher Columbus? by Jean Fritz
Explorers News: 1500 B.C. to Today by Michael Johnstone
Who Discovered America? by Valerie Wyatt
Explorers Who Got Lost by Diane Sansevere-Dreher
The World Made New: Why the Age of Exploration Happened and How It Changed the World by Marc Aronson and John W. Glenn

FEATURED ANCHOR TEXT

EXPLORATION AND CONQUEST: THE AMERICAS AFTER COLUMBUS, 1500–1620 BY BETSY AND GIULIO MAESTRO

This book was selected because it is rich in information related to European empires and the eventual colonization of the Americas. It can be read aloud by the teacher or read by students independently. It is filled with detailed illustrations and informative maps that complement the text. The book contains so much information about the many explorers from 1500 to 1620 that it could be used as a core text for an entire unit on explorers.

TEXT STUDY

The text-dependent questions that follow give students a chance to use structural features, such as illustrations and maps, to examine and appreciate a rich informational text about early explorations of the Americas. The questions also contain opportunities for students to practice inferring skills, focus on key vocabulary, and offer evidence of understanding through informative/explanatory and opinion writing.

1. **Which explorer opened the door to European exploration of the New World?**
   - According to pages 3 and 4, that explorer was Columbus. His goal was to reach the "Orient," and he thought he was successful. But the other explorers who came later found that his was a new discovery, inviting further exploration.
2. **Early in the book, the authors point out a treaty made by Spain and Portugal over the control of the seas and the "unclaimed" world between them. Why was it important to note this at the beginning of the text?**
   - According to page 5, this treaty would be the cause of the Spanish domination of exploration in the New World. This treaty would keep the French, Dutch, and English from exploring until courageous explorers were willing to break through the dual control of these two nations.

     Note: Later, on page 28, the book explains that the treaty had a great impact on early exploration and conquest of the New World.
3. **According to evidence in the text, why did Spanish explorers take Native American land, riches, and lives?**
   - According to page 6, the Spanish "considered the natives heathens, or nonbelievers, because they did not worship the Christian God" and thought of them as "uncivilized savages—barely human." Because the Spanish devalued the native peoples, they felt "perfectly free to take their land, their riches, and often their lives."

4. **Which key words do the authors use to summarize Spaniards' change of focus as they turned their attention to searching for gold?**
   - According to page 8, the Spaniards' focus changed from a "search for a passage to a search for gold"—from "exploration" to "conquest."

5. **How do the illustrations of weapons on page 9 enhance the authors' text?**
   - The authors write about how Cortés and hundreds of his soldiers arrived in Mexico to take the land from the Aztecs. Although the Aztecs were greater in number, their weapons were less sophisticated. The illustrations make clear the differences between the gun, crossbow, and poleax of the Spanish, on the one hand, and the club, darts, spears, and bow and arrow of the Aztecs, on the other. It is easy to see that the Spanish weapons were more powerful.

6. **As told on pages 12 through 14, how does the story of Francisco Pizarro exemplify the motivation and ruthlessness of the conquistadors?**
   - As we have already read, the "explorers-turned-conquistadors" became focused on searching for gold and goods, as well as on converting "heathens" to Christianity. They didn't care whom they had to displace or destroy in the process. Pizarro's army killed the Inca emperor when he refused to convert to Christianity. They killed most of the Inca in the attack and stole "immense quantities of gold and silver," which they shipped back to Spain. Pizarro's story is typical of the other conquistadors' stories.

7. **How were the Native Americans in Florida affected by Hernando de Soto's search for gold?**
   - According to page 16, their villages were burned; their food was stolen; and many of the Choctaw, Creek, and Chickasaw were killed or captured.

8. **As the authors summarize the adventuresome journey of Francisco Vasquez de Coronado and his crew, they tell of their bitter disappointment. Why is such a great expedition described as a failure?**
   - According to page 17, although Coronado traveled for thousands of miles from Mexico to the Colorado River, Grand Canyon, and Great Plains, he really only wanted gold. When he came back to Mexico without the gold, he felt as though the expedition had failed.

   Note: *This account exemplifies how notable Spanish explorations were overshadowed by the explorers' sense of defeat as treasure hunters.*

9. **After all of the Spanish expeditions, what was Spain's lasting accomplishment in North America?**
   - According to page 18, the Spanish set up permanent settlements in Florida and in the southwestern part of what is now the United States, sharing a rich culture of schools, churches, and missions.

10. **How did Spain's loss of interest in North America affect exploration by other countries?**
    - According to page 19, the New World was opened up to other countries for exploration and settlement. England, France, and Holland no longer had to worry about challenging the Spanish at sea. They now "felt free to explore there and to claim land for themselves."

    Note: *See the connection between this information and the discussion of the treaty in question 2.*

11. **Examine the description of Giovanni da Verrazano's notes taken as he explored for the French. What do Verrazano's observations say about him as an explorer for France, as compared to the Spanish approach to exploration?**
    - According to pages 21 and 22, he described peaceful encounters with "Indians, finding most of them approachable and helpful." He also noted the value of natural resources and sources of beauty, such as good harbors, fertile farmland, and fresh lakes. The Spanish might have written more about the search for gold and the "heathen" natives standing in

the way of that gold. The land held very little interest for the Spanish explorers, as seen in the previous account of Coronado's expedition in the southwestern part of North America.

12. **What were the real riches of the northwestern part of North America? What is the irony of this reality?**
    - According to page 23, the real riches of northwestern North America were the natural resources–lumber, furs, and fish. The irony is that the French explorers didn't realize the value of these natural resources until much later. They continued to focus on finding pathways to the riches of the Orient or gold and silver in North America. They were missing the riches that were all around them as they explored.

13. **According to this text, how did slavery come to America? How do the illustrations and captions help convey the horror of slavery?**
    - According to pages 25 through 27, John Hawkins, an English explorer and smuggler of goods into Spanish ports, traded goods with plantation owners in the New World. They needed laborers for the tobacco farms, so Hawkins would go by the African coast for slaves before coming back to the plantation owners. The illustrations show the abusive leg irons and shackles used to hold the slaves on ships and the branding iron for branding them as owned. Illustrations show the slaves being marched with yokes on their necks to the boat, headed to a fort where they were to be held.

14. **How did the explorations of Francis Drake help bring an end to the "Spanish Main"? How does the map on page 29 enhance the telling of one of Drake's explorations?**
    - According to pages 28 through 31, Drake's explorations were partially motivated by his hatred of the Spanish control of the seas. He made six voyages to the Spanish Main, raided Spanish ships for treasures and supplies, and proved that Spain could be challenged for control of the seas. The map on page 29 shows the location of the Spanish Main and traces Drake's third voyage, following the path first sailed by Ferdinand Magellan. It shows how he began in England, traveling around the tip of South America, up the coast of South America, to North America, and into the Pacific Ocean.

15. **Using evidence from the text on pages 31 through 37, create a timeline tracing English efforts to establish a colony in the New World.**
    - 1576–Martin Frobisher explored and noted the value of natural resources, such as timber, furs, and fish.
    - 1584–Sir Walter Raleigh settled Roanoke Island, but was not successful due to the settlers' inability to farm and feed themselves.
    - 1587–John White arrived and established what is now known as the Lost Colony.
    - 1606–Captain John Smith arrived in Jamestown and established a settlement.
    - 1609–Jamestown began to thrive due to the leadership of John Rolfe and Pocahontas.
    - 1619–Colonial life began with the arrival of women, tobacco farming, slaves, and colonial self-government. Native Americans moved inland as the colonists took over the coastal lands.

PERFORMANCE ASSESSMENT

Following a close reading of the last three pages of the text (pages 40 through 42), lead a discussion in which you ask students to agree or disagree with the ending statement in the text: "The great gain of one people was the great loss of another." Be sure to ask students to use evidence from the text to support their assertions.

Assign the following writing task:

- Choose one of the explorers cited in this text to research. Write an informative/explanatory essay describing both the gains made by his exploration and the consequent losses to the native peoples with whom he came in contact.

Ask students to be sure to introduce the topic clearly; develop the topic with facts, details, and examples; link ideas; use precise language and domain-specific vocabulary; and provide a concluding statement. At earlier levels, students may write a coherent paragraph that summarizes the main topic and key details. See standards for more details.

EXTENSION

Have students write an opinion essay on one explorer in which they argue one of the following points:

a. The outcomes of his explorations were more **positive** than **negative**.

b. The outcomes of his explorations were more **negative** than **positive**.

Students should cite evidence from sources (either the anchor text or primary sources consulted for research) to support their claims. Ask students to be sure to introduce the topic clearly; provide logically ordered reasons for their opinion that are supported with facts and details; link the opinion and reasons; and provide a concluding statement related to the opinion. At earlier levels, students may write a coherent paragraph that summarizes the opinion and provides some logically ordered reasons as well as a concluding statement. See standards for more details.

CONNECTIONS TO COMMON CORE STATE STANDARDS FOR ENGLISH LANGUAGE ARTS

- Questions 1, 7, 9, and 10 ask students to identify key details in the text (RI.3.1; RI.4.1; RI.5.1).
- Question 2 encourages students to consider the authors' purpose in including a certain factual detail early in the book (RI.3.5,8; RI.4.5,8; RI.5.5,8).
- Question 3 asks students to cite evidence from the text to explain a key detail in the text (RI.3.1; RI.4.1; RI.5.1).
- Question 4 focuses students' attention on the use of words and phrases that are significant to the historical content being conveyed (RI.3.4; RI.4.4; RI.5.4; L.3.5; L.4.5; L.5.5).
- Question 5 helps students understand how illustrations can provide a deeper level of understanding about important content (RI.3.7; RI.4.7; RI.5.7).
- Question 6 asks students to identify how one account in the text typifies the greater story of exploration and conquest described throughout the text (RI.3.1,2,3; RI.4.1,2,3; RI.5.1,2,3).
- Question 8 asks students to make simple inferences from details explained in the text (RI.3.2; RI.4.2; RI.5.2).
- Question 11 requires students to compare one account in the text with others and draw conclusions about the differences between them (RI.3.2,3; RI.4.2,3; RI.5.2,3).
- The first part of question 12 asks students to recall an important detail in the text; the second part allows them to note an important irony about that detail (RI.3.1,2,3; RI.4.1,2,3; RI.5.1,2,3).

- The first parts of questions 13 and 14 ask students to recall important details in the text. The second parts allow students to examine the relationships between the information in the illustrations, in the captions, and in the text itself (question 13), and the relationship between a map and the text (question 14) (RI.3.1,7; RI.4.1,7; RI.5.1,7).
- Question 15 requires students to create their own timeline based on information gleaned from the text (RI.3.1,2,3; RI.4.1,2,3; RI.5.1,2,3; W.3.9; W.4.9; W.5.9).
- The performance assessment gives students a chance to discuss their opinions about the positives and negatives of post-Columbian explorations of the Americas, and then to use this discussion to craft an essay detailing one exploration in detail (SL.3.1; SL.4.1; SL.5.1; W.3.2; W.4.2; W.5.2).
- The extension builds on the performance assessment by having students defend an opinion in an essay about a chosen explorer, using evidence from the text to support their claims (W.3.1; W.4.1; W.5.1).

MORE RESOURCES

PRIMARY SOURCES

Items from a Spanish treasure ship (Library of Congress)

Four faces of Pocahontas (Smithsonian Source: Resources for Teaching American History)

1629 Seal of the Massachusetts Bay Colony (Smithsonian Source: Resources for Teaching American History)

Spanish Settlement at St. Augustine, Florida (Library of Congress)

British gold coin used at Jamestown, Virginia (British Museum)

A *Briefe and True Report of The New Found Land of Virginia*, 1590 (Project Gutenberg)

Letter from Hernán Cortés to King Charles V, 1520 (Fordham University)

POETRY AND MUSIC

"Columbus" by Joaquin Miller

"Sonnet" by J. C. Squire

Uniquely American: The Beginnings of a New Nationality

(1607 to Late 1600s)

GRADES: 3, 4, 5

OVERVIEW

Great Britain was the most successful of the European nations to settle colonies in North America—but at first, it had its attention focused on matters closer to the home isles. Britain's colonies experimented with local self-government and popular power. When the British turned their thoughts back to North America and the profits they could reap, tension mounted between new North American ways of life and the interests of the mother country that sought to govern there. Through a close reading of *The First Thanksgiving*, students will develop an informed opinion about whether or not the benefits of life in the new colonies were worth the hardships. An informational text exploring the New England, mid-Atlantic, and southern colonies, *We the People: The Thirteen Colonies*, gives older students the essential background to facilitate multimedia presentations in which they compare and contrast regional differences in America.

○ ○ ○

Interested in learning more about this time period? Read a more complete history in the "Era Summaries."

LEARNING EXPECTATIONS

Lower elementary: Students should understand that different kinds of colonial societies arose in different regions in response to different circumstances and goals. They should understand that new and often unprecedented freedoms emerged for many colonists, even as slavery was introduced to the colonies.

Upper elementary: Students should be able to identify the basic cultural differences between the New England, mid-Atlantic, and southern colonies, and should understand the fundamental reasons why these regions emerged with such different ways of life. They should also understand the growing role of political and religious freedoms as well as slavery in the different regions.

SUGGESTED ANCHOR TEXTS

We the People: The Thirteen Colonies by Marc Tyler Nobleman
The New Americans: Colonial Times, 1620–1689 by Betsy and Giulio Maestro
"The Pilgrims Rock the New World," *Cobblestone*, October 2009
"Samoset and Squanto," *Cobblestone*, September 2001
"Rediscovering Jamestown," *Cobblestone*, September 2006
Our Strange New Land: Elizabeth's Jamestown Colony Diary by Patricia Hermes
The Starving Time: Elizabeth's Jamestown Colony Diary by Patricia Hermes

FEATURED ANCHOR TEXT

WE THE PEOPLE: THE THIRTEEN COLONIES BY MARC TYLER NOBLEMAN

This book was selected because it presents an overview of the colonies by region: New England, middle, and southern. Organized by chapters, the book explores the different reasons why colonies were established and the different reasons why settlers came: some by choice and some not by choice. The mix of primary sources (such as maps, portraits, and original drawings) and secondary sources enlivens the book's content. The book also includes structural elements commonly found in an informational text (for example, a table of contents, a glossary, a timeline, and an index), which are useful for instructing students about how to navigate this type of historical text.

TEXT STUDY

The following text-dependent questions require close reading and enable teachers and students also to focus on the structural features of this informational text; the author's craft (for example, diction); and inferring skills.

1. **According to the text, why did Europeans want to establish colonies in the New World?**
   - According to page 4, different countries had different reasons for wanting to have colonies. The title of this section indicates that they came for "fortune and freedom."
     - The Spanish were seeking gold and silver.
     - The French were looking for valuable furs to sell.
     - Some of the English were seeking fortune, but most hoped to find freedom of religion and freedom of government.
2. **Explain why the text on page 6 contains the word *tried* in this sentence: "In 1585, Sir Walter Raleigh tried to create the first English settlement in North America."**
   - The text goes on to explain that the effort failed. The author had to use the word *tried* because although Raleigh had made an attempt, the colony did not last.
   - Raleigh sent a group of people to start a colony on Roanoke Island in the New World in 1585. Although the colonists arrived and settled, the colony did not last. The living conditions were difficult, the colonists clashed with local Native Americans, and the Spanish threatened to attack them. They returned home in 1586 with Sir Francis Drake.
3. **According to pages 7 and 8, what was the "Lost Colony," and why was it called that?**
   - In 1587, John White made an effort to settle more than one hundred colonists on Roanoke Island, Virginia.

- Although the colonists seem to have been settled before White returned to England, they were gone when he returned two years later.
- The only clue left was the word *Croatoan* etched in a tree, the name of a friendly Indian nation and of a nearby island.
- The English people were never found, and historians still do not know exactly what happened. Their settlement has been known to history as the Lost Colony

4. **Explain the other English attempts to create a colony in the New World. Say whether they were successful and why or why not.**
   - Page 8 tells the story of another failure by the Virginia Company of Plymouth.
     - In Plymouth, Virginia, the weather conditions were harsh, and the settlers did not know how to farm the land.
   - Finally, Jamestown, Virginia, was successfully settled in 1607 by John Smith, becoming the first permanent English settlement in the Americas—the first of the thirteen American colonies.
     - Smith "was a hard worker and expected everyone else to work hard too."
     - Smith "tried to create a friendly relationship between the native peoples and the settlers."
5. **Compare the situations of the indentured servants and the African slaves in the colonies. Which of the two groups of people would be more likely to say that America was a land of opportunity? Cite evidence from the text to support your assertions.**
   - According to page 12, plantation owners needed indentured servants to grow tobacco. Indentured servants were those whose travel was paid, but who had to work off the cost of the trip after their arrival in the New World. Many were eventually given freedom to own their own land. They had a choice in coming.
   - According to page 13, slaves were kidnapped by slave traders from Africa and sold to plantation owners. They had no choice in coming and no possibility of earning their freedom.
   - Because they had the choice of coming and the freedom eventually to own their own land, the indentured servants had more opportunity in America.
6. **What was significant about the Virginia House of Burgesses?**
   - According to page 15, it was "the first representative government by Europeans in North America." Having a representative government meant that the people themselves, rather than a distant monarch, would rule the colony. The author says that the Virginia colony "planted the seeds of a new nation."

   Note: Teachers might take this opportunity to analyze the word representative, *as well as its other forms (for example, the verb form* represent), *underscoring this key concept in American government as well as exploring some important language standards.*
7. **New England colonies included Massachusetts, New Hampshire, Rhode Island, and Connecticut. Discuss the reasons why people settled in each colony. Use evidence from the text to show what most of the settlers had in common.**
   - According to page 17, Pilgrims, also called Puritans, came to Massachusetts in hopes of religious freedom. The "Strangers," who traveled with the Pilgrims, came to find adventure and riches. According to page 21, many more Puritans came from England in 1630, also in search of religious freedom.
   - According to page 24, people settled New Hampshire for farmland and religious freedom.
   - According to page 25, Roger Williams settled Rhode Island. Although he was a Puritan, he believed that people of all faiths should be welcome: Puritans, Roman Catholics, Jews, and Quakers.

- Pages 25 and 26 explain that Thomas Hooker led Puritans from Massachusetts to Connecticut for rich farmland along a river.
- Most of the people who settled New England wanted religious freedom and rich farmland.

8. **Why was Thomas Hooker called the "father of American democracy"?**
   - According to page 26, his written plan for government of Connecticut called for the election of a governor and lawmakers, excluding the English king. Connecticut "became the first colony with a written plan of government."

9. **When the Dutch purchased Manhattan from the Native Americans for twenty-four dollars, how did the Native Americans probably interpret the deal?**
   - According to page 28, the Native Americans didn't believe that people could *own* land, so when the Dutch paid money, the Native Americans probably believed the land was only being loaned—as opposed to permanently sold.

10. **Considering the religious roots of two "middle colonies," Maryland and Pennsylvania, which colony would have been more welcoming to people of other religions? Cite evidence from the text to support your assertions.**
    - According to pages 29 through 32, Roman Catholics settled Maryland, where they granted religious freedom only to Christians.
    - Quakers settled Pennsylvania and believed that all people, whatever their race, religion, or gender, were equal.
    - Pennsylvania might have been the more welcoming to people of other religions. On page 32, the text says, "William Penn opened Pennsylvania to people of every religious belief."

11. **When James Oglethorpe founded Georgia, what was his goal for the colony? Use evidence from the text to explain why his plan did not work.**
    - According to pages 34 and 35, Oglethorpe thought that people from debtor's prison in Britain could come to farm in Georgia and work off their debts.
    - Oglethorpe's plan didn't work because the debtors wanted to stay in an English prison rather than come to the wilderness of Georgia. Many of those who did come decided that slaves should do the work.
    - Georgia also encountered problems with Native Americans, pirates, and "other colonists." The text hints at what the problems with other colonists (in South Carolina and Florida) were.

    Note: *This question could become a research topic for an interested student.*

12. **Why did the author choose to include a list of important people at the end of the book on page 45?**
    - Although each person is already mentioned in the book, the author may have wanted to draw more attention to their dates of birth and death and to summarize what makes them important. He may also have wanted to provide an easy way for students to reference all of these prominent historical figures in one place.

PERFORMANCE ASSESSMENTS

1. Using the timeline on page 44, divide the dates (from 1620 to 1732) among the students in class and ask them to create a "retelling" of the settling of the thirteen colonies. Ask them to retell (in a narrative or informative/explanatory essay) their assigned event from the point of view of

one of the colonists in the relevant colony (or colonies). They should add as many details as they can from the text. See standards for more details.

2. Divide students into groups representing the three colonial regions (New England, middle, and southern). Divide each regional group into partners to study a specific colony. Have students conduct research, using both primary and secondary sources, into (1) the most famous early settlers, (2) their motivation for coming, (3) the colony's government and leadership, and (4) the economic strengths of the colony. Colony partners should create a multimedia slide (or slides) for each of the four categories of research. Posters could be made if the technology is not available.

Bundle presentations into colonial regions, presented during three different class periods. As a class, compare and contrast the colonies within each region and the regions as a whole; this last activity could be done orally and perhaps using a class T-chart. See standards for more details.

CONNECTIONS TO COMMON CORE STATE STANDARDS FOR ENGLISH LANGUAGE ARTS

- Questions 1, 3, and 9 ask students to recall key details and concepts and offer evidence of understanding (RI.3.1,2; RI.4.1,2; RI.5.1,2).
- Question 2 requires students to recall key details and make connections to larger concepts; it also focuses students on the author's craft by asking them to think about why the author chose a certain word (RI.3.1,2,3,4; RI.4.1,2,3,4; RI.5.1,2,3,4).
- Question 4 presents students with an opportunity to think carefully about the different types of information presented, comparing and contrasting the reasons why some colonies survived and others did not (RI.3.1,2,3; RI.4.1,2,3; RI.5.1,2,3).
- Question 5 prompts students to extrapolate from given information and make predictions based on what they know from close reading. They must cite evidence from the text when making their case (RI.3.1,2,3,8; RI.4.1,2,3,8; RI.5.1,2,3,8).
- Question 6 not only addresses a key historical detail, as explained in the text, but also offers a chance to explore some essential language standards related to the historical content (RI.3.1,2,3; RI.4.1,2,3; RI.5.1,2,3; L.3.1,4; L.4.1,4; L.5.1,4).
- Question 7 allows students to make comparisons across various sections of an informational text; it requires close reading of the text to ensure that students understand the nuances of the objectives of the various settlers (RI.3.1,2,3,5; RI.4.1,2,3,5; RI.5.1,2,3,5).
- Question 8 focuses on an expression used to describe one of the famous first colonists. Students must read carefully to understand and explain why Hooker is sometimes called the "father of American democracy" (RI.3.1,2,3,4; RI.4.1,2,3,4; RI.5.1,2,3,4; L.3.5; L.4.5; L.5.5).
- Question 10 requires that students compare differences in the details associated with related concepts (in this case, two types of religious freedom in two contiguous colonies). It asks them to think beyond the literal to make inferences and comparisons (RI.3.1,2,3,5,8; RI.4.1,2,3,5,8; RI.5.1,2,3,5,8).
- Question 11 asks students to recall key details and concepts from the text and to use them to answer a more conceptual question (RI.3.1,2,3,8; RI.4.1,2,3,8; RI.5.1,2,3,8).
- Question 12 addresses the author's purpose in providing a timeline at the end of the book, underscoring an important structural feature of an informational text (RI.3.3,5,8; RI.4.3,5,8; RI.5.3,5,8).

- The first performance assessment prompts students to reread the informational text, and then to retell for others the key ideas and concepts from that text. It allows them to do so creatively, if the teacher chooses, by writing a narrative, or in an informative/explanatory essay (RI.3.1,2,3; RI.4.1,2,3; RI.5.1,2,3; W.3.2,3; W.4.2,3; W.5.2,3 or W.3.9; W.4.9; W.5.9).
- The second performance assessment provides an opportunity for students to do further research (using both primary and secondary resources), to make a multimedia presentation, and to focus on key ideas and concepts from the text (RI.3.1,2,3; RI.4.1,2,3; RI.5.1,2,3; W.3.2,6,7,8,9; W.4.2,6,7,8,9; W.5.2,6,7,8,9; SL.3.1; SL.4.1; SL.5.1).

MORE RESOURCES

PRIMARY SOURCES

Teacher's guide: Jamestown, Virginia (Library of Congress)

Pine tree shilling from Massachusetts, 1652 (Smithsonian Institution)

Instructions for the Virginia Colony, 1606 (University of Groningen)

Dance instruction manual, 1711 (Library of Congress)

African captives yoked in pairs (PBS: *Africans in America*)

POETRY AND MUSIC

"A Dialogue between Old England and New," a poem by Anne Bradstreet, 1650 (Poetry Foundation)

ART AND ARCHITECTURE

Portrait of Governor John Winthrop (Smithsonian Institution)

USEFUL WEBSITE

Interactive map of New Amsterdam in 1660 superimposed over a map of Lower Manhattan in 2009 (WNET, New York Public Media)

Taxation without Representation: Tension Mounts

(ca. 1660 to 1763)

GRADES: 3, 4, 5

OVERVIEW

During the seventeenth century, Britain's international and domestic problems had caused it to let the colonies essentially rule themselves. But that soon changed: from 1660 to 1763, the British government stabilized and turned to the business of ruling the colonies—lucrative business, because the colonies had grown into profitable trading posts and commercial centers. Britain's expanded rule changed the colonists, laying the groundwork for some of the most important events in modern history. *If You Lived in Colonial Times* gives younger students a resource to explore what daily life in the colonies looked like; they can then select a topic that interests them to explore further. Older students can read *Making Thirteen Colonies: 1600–1740* to learn how regional differences in the British colonies spurred differing attitudes on slavery, prompting students to research the beginnings of America's "peculiar institution."

○ ○ ○

Interested in learning more about this time period? Read a more complete history in the "Era Summaries."

LEARNING EXPECTATIONS

Lower elementary: Students should understand that Britain began to want more benefit from its colonies in the seventeenth and eighteenth centuries and to take more notice of them, drawing Britain and the colonies more tightly together in a British Atlantic world—while also sowing the seeds of conflict over the colonies' rights.

Upper elementary: Students should understand the role of trade in tying Britain and the colonies together, and they should know that this closer relationship generated tension over local self-rule, even as the culture of the colonies became more British. Students should know that the colonies were drawn into wars for the empire, which showed their loyalty to Britain but also set the stage for new conflict over the wars' costs.

SUGGESTED ANCHOR TEXTS

Making Thirteen Colonies: 1600–1740, chapter 38 "A Nasty Triangle" by Joy Hakim
Early American Culture by Catherine Nichols
"Colonial Slavery," *Footsteps*, May–June 2002
"Contest for Empire: The French and Indian War," *Cobblestone*, September 2005
The Matchlock Gun by Walter D. Edmonds

FEATURED ANCHOR TEXT

MAKING THIRTEEN COLONIES: 1600–1740, CHAPTER 38 "A NASTY TRIANGLE" BY JOY HAKIM

This book was selected because it discusses the colonies' trade with Britain and other countries, as well as the slave trade in Africa. It offers a comprehensive but pithy account of the colonies' economic situation at the time, especially their growing dependency on the slave trade. Filled with compelling primary sources, such as drawings, maps, and journal entries, this chapter provides an excellent example of how eyewitness accounts add to the veracity of historical accounts.

TEXT STUDY

Joy Hakim's text and these text-dependent questions offer students the chance to read a clear, informative, informational text and examine its various features, including the interplay among the text, illustrations, insets, and primary source excerpts. The questions and the performance assessments that follow also address the author's technique, domain-specific vocabulary, informative/explanatory writing, and research.

1. **According to the first two paragraphs on page 142, what were the two foundational differences among the colonies in this "collection of settlements"?**
   - The founders of the colonies were different.
   - The conditions of the land were different.
2. **How does the author characterize the effort to farm in New England compared to the effort to farm in the South?**
   - New England farms had rocky soil and a cold climate. New Englanders were only able to grow enough crops for themselves; they did not typically have enough left over to sell. This type of farming was called "subsistence" farming.

     Note: *Teachers might examine the parts of the word* subsistence *and discuss related words for vocabulary development.*
   - In the South, large farms called plantations could sell their produce.
3. **Describe New England's problems with trade. What evidence does the author provide to describe how New Englanders used natural resources to overcome the obstacles?**
   - According to page 142, New Englanders had small farms, so they could not grow enough produce to trade. The British did not allow the colonists to manufacture any goods that were also manufactured in England.
   - According to pages 142 through 143, the New Englanders began to catch fish, especially cod. They salted it to preserve it and then sold it in Europe and in the Caribbean Islands.

- To transport the fish from New England, they used their natural resource of timber to build the ships. They also began selling the wood and products made from the wood.

4. **How is "triangular trade" described on page 143?**
   - The trade routes were basically in the shape of a triangle. The "Yankees" or New Englanders would trade salted cod in the Caribbean for cane sugar. Then they might go north to Virginia to trade for tobacco. The tobacco and sugar would then go to England to be traded for cash, guns, and cloth. The ships would then go to Africa. Guns and cloth were traded for men, women, and children who would be sold into slavery when they arrived in the West Indies.

5. **In the text on page 144, how does the author further explain the triangular routes?**
   - She asks the reader to imagine a triangle stretched to three different points on a map. She then details different scenarios for how the triangle might be created by trade:
     - New England to Africa to South Carolina to New England
     - England to Africa to Virginia

6. **How does the map on page 145 help explain the triangular trade routes?**
   - The map shows various combinations of trade routes with three points: one in North America, one in Europe, and one in Africa. The arrows show the directions of the trade routes and what was traded at each port.

7. **Why did the author include the words of Olaudah Equiano instead of just writing his story?**
   - The author seems to be asking readers to develop empathy for this African child who was kidnapped and traded into slavery. The author writes, "Imagine that you are Olaudah as you read his words."
   - Using primary sources is a way of making history true. Using the real words of a person who experienced part of history and wrote as an eyewitness to the horrors of slavery helps bring home the terrible truth.

8. **Look closely at the sketch of the slave ship on page 144. How does the sketch relate to Equiano's account on pages 145 and 146?**
   - He saw the slave ship and was put on it. Then, as he was on the ship, he wrote about how he didn't understand how it worked, thinking the white people were spirits. He told of horrors on the ship, seeing someone whipped to death, and he told of the smells, sights, and sounds. His story relates a vivid account of traveling on a slave ship that the sketch of the ship cannot convey.
   - The sketch of the ship adds a visual component to our understanding of the experience. The account and the sketch work together to tell the story.

   Note: *These are both fine examples of primary sources that, when used together, help inform history.*

9. **How did Equiano's slave ship experience end?**
   - According to page 146, he was sold in Barbados. He went to sea as a slave, he had adventures, and he learned to read. He wrote his autobiography (part of which is excerpted in Hakim's book).

   Note: *Because so many slaves from this era were not taught to read or write, Equiano's account is especially valuable.*

10. **According to the inset article on Africa, why did the Europeans know so little about Africa?**
    - The Sahara Desert was a natural boundary that kept the more familiar North Africa separated from areas south of the desert.

- Until the fifteenth century, ships were not able to make the journey down the coast of Africa to explore.
- Strong African warriors kept the Europeans from coming into the region and taking their gold.

11. **What would have been discovered about Africa had the Europeans been able to explore African cultures?**
    - There was contrast between sophisticated and primitive cultures, cities, and villages.
    - Gold was a natural resource.
    - Centers of learning and wisdom were in Songhai during the fifteenth century.
12. **According to the article on Africa, why did the slave trade begin?**
    - Both Europeans and Africans were interested in trade.
    - Africans wanted guns, iron, cloth, kettles, and mirrors.
    - Europeans needed "healthy, hardy people" to work on the farms in the New World.
13. **Why did the author include the figures and dates at the end of the chapter on page 148?**
    - The number of blacks in American colonies went from seventy-five thousand to more than seven hundred fifty thousand in the years between 1725 and 1790.
    - She may want the reader to infer how trade brought in a huge increase in the number of slaves in the American colonies.
    - The author probably wants to illustrate how quickly and how much the slave population in America grew in sixty years.

PERFORMANCE ASSESSMENTS

1. Ask students to cite evidence from this chapter to write a rich informative/explanatory paragraph in answer to the following question:

- How did the differences in the geographic characteristics of the New England colonies and the southern colonies cause slavery to become an important social and economic issue in the South?

Students should see that the New England colonies simply did not have the opportunity to establish large farms because of the cold weather and the rocky soil. Although they traded the salted cod and built the ships to eventually carry the slaves, they did not supply their own homes and farms with as many slaves. The South established large farms and had a greater need for the "healthy, hardy people" of Africa. See standards for more details.

2. In chapter 36, Hakim writes, "In 1677 some North Carolinians rebelled against England. They didn't like England's Navigation Acts, which forced them to pay taxes to England on goods sold to other colonies. If a North Carolina tobacco grower sold some of his tobacco to a merchant in Boston, he was supposed to pay a tax to England."

In chapter 38, the Navigation Acts are referenced when Hakim writes, "But when it came to industry, the British made things difficult. They wouldn't let the colonists manufacture goods that competed with English goods."

Divide students into teams to have them research the Navigation Acts beginning in 1651. Have them summarize the effect on trade in the colonies that each British act had. Make sure students use specific examples, like the ones in the preceding Hakim quotations, to illustrate the effect of the act on particular colonies.

After students have worked in teams, create a class cause-and-effect chart showing how the Navigation Acts caused events in the colonies. Using the cause-and-effect chart as a starting point, students should write two to three well-organized paragraphs, each describing how one of the Navigation Acts caused problems for the colonists. See standards for more details.

CONNECTIONS TO COMMON CORE STATE STANDARDS FOR ENGLISH LANGUAGE ARTS

- Questions 1, 2, 3, 9, 11, and 12 ask students to identify key details discussed in the text (RI.3.1; RI.45.1; RI.5.1).
    - Question 2 also asks about a domain-specific word (RI.3.4; RI.4.4; RI.5.4).
    - Question 3 also asks about the author's use of evidence (RI.3.8; RI.4.8; RI.5.8).
- Questions 4 and 5 ask about key details, but also raise interesting questions about the author's description of an important historical term (RI.3.1,4,8; RI.4.1,4,8; RI.5.1,4,8).
- Question 6 allows students to glean historical information from a map that accompanies the text (RI.3.7; RI.4.7; RI.5.7).
- Question 7 encourages students to think carefully about the author's technique, focusing in particular on why the author chose to include a primary source account of a slave's journey on a slave ship (RI.3.6,8; RI.4.6,8; RI.5.6,8).
- Like question 6, questions 8 and 10 give students a chance not only to build knowledge from the text itself but also to understand how other features of informational texts (in this case, illustrations and insets) may work together with the text itself to deepen students' understanding of important concepts (RI.3.6,7; RI.4.6,7; RI.5.6,7).
- Questions 11 and 12 prompt students to make inferences from information in the text (RI.3.1,2,3; RI.4.1,2,3; RI.5.1,2,3).
    - Question 12 also asks about the author's purpose (RI.3.8; RI.4.8; RI.5.8).
- Question 13 requires students to examine the author's purpose in including certain information in the text (RI.3.3,8; RI.4.3,8; RI.5.3,8).
- The first performance assessment asks students to use evidence from the text when writing an informative/expository essay summarizing what they have learned (W.3.1,9; W.4.1,9; W.5.1,9).
- The second performance assessment allows students to conduct independent research to deepen their knowledge of this era, discuss it as a large group, and present their findings individually in an informative/explanatory essay (W.3.1,7,9; W.4.1,7,9; W.5.1,7,9).

MORE RESOURCES

HISTORICAL FICTION

My Name Is Phillis Wheatley: A Story of Slavery and Freedom by Afua Cooper

Part historical fiction and part informational biography. This book is further complicated by the fact that it's written in first person.

PRIMARY SOURCES

George Washington's map accompanying his "Journal to the Ohio," 1754 (Library of Congress)

French and Indian War enlistment papers, 1760 (Smithsonian Institution)

Map of British plantations in North America, 1755 to 1760 (Library of Congress)

"Join or Die" political cartoon by Benjamin Franklin, 1754 (Library of Congress)

POETRY AND MUSIC

"School Days in New Amsterdam" by Arthur Guiterman

ART AND ARCHITECTURE

Thomas Smith self-portrait, ca. 1680 (Worcester Art Museum)

USEFUL WEBSITES

Presentation on the Franklin Court Printing Office by a National Park Service ranger (Independence National Historical Park)

French and Indian War timeline (PBS: *The War That Made America*)

Independence: America Gains Its Freedom

(1763 to 1783)

GRADES: 3, 4, 5

OVERVIEW

Britain expected the colonies to help pay for its costly wars abroad—and began taxing them to that end. Efforts to draw more revenue from the colonies outraged the Americans, who had no voice in the British Parliament. Escalating taxes were met with protest, boycotts, and rebellion. Eventually, the flames were fanned until they sparked revolution and full-blown war. *A Picture Book of Paul Revere* introduces younger students to one of America's first patriots and prompts a thoughtful analysis of how Paul Revere forever changed American history. Older students will explore the divisive issue of taxation as they read *A History of US: From Colonies to Country: 1735–1791*, and they will investigate primary sources to learn why paying taxes sparked the ire of colonists who had once pledged their loyalty to Britain.

○ ○ ○

Interested in learning more about this time period? Read a more complete history in the "Era Summaries."

LEARNING EXPECTATIONS

Lower elementary: Students should understand the concept of taking someone else's property without his or her agreement, and why that threatened many Americans. They should understand that Americans were willing to fight against outside control to protect their freedoms. Students should also know that many figures and events from the American Revolution are still remembered in modern holidays and popular culture.

Upper elementary: Students should understand the monetary needs that the French and Indian War created in Britain and the British decision to tax the colonies to help pay for the war. They should also understand both the concept of taxation without representation and why Americans responded so strongly to the new tax laws. They should know that the dispute over their freedoms was so serious that it led to war and independence. They should understand how difficult the fighting was and how determined many Americans were to protect their liberty.

SUGGESTED ANCHOR TEXTS

A History of US: From Colonies to Country: 1735–1791, chapter 11 "A Taxing King" by Joy Hakim
George vs. George: The American Revolution as Seen from Both Sides by Rosalyn Schanzer
Can't You Make Them Behave, King George? by Jean Fritz
Colonial Voices: Hear Them Speak by Kay Winters
When Washington Crossed the Delaware by Lynne Cheney
And Then What Happened, Paul Revere? by Jean Fritz
What's the Big Idea, Ben Franklin? by Jean Fritz
Where Was Patrick Henry on the 29th of May? Jean Fritz
Why Don't You Get a Horse, Sam Adams? by Jean Fritz
Will You Sign Here, John Hancock? by Jean Fritz
The Declaration of Independence: The Words That Made America by Sam Fink
For Liberty: The Story of the Boston Massacre by Timothy Decker
Write On, Mercy! The Secret Life of Mercy Otis Warren by Gretchen Woelfle

FEATURED ANCHOR TEXT

A HISTORY OF US: FROM COLONIES TO COUNTRY: 1735–1791, CHAPTER 11 "A TAXING KING" BY JOY HAKIM

This book was selected because it has a strong narrative detailing the growing crisis between the colonists and King George III prior to the American Revolution. Descriptions of the leading characters, George III and the colonists, pull the students into a study of the revolutionary crisis. The story is also grounded in compelling primary source accounts that are displayed and discussed throughout the chapter.

TEXT STUDY

Correctly answering the text-dependent questions here depends on close reading of this rich, multifaceted text, through which students are exposed to—and must work with—both narrative history and good primary sources. Several questions allow teachers to point out the power of metaphors—and how and why analyzing a metaphor enhances understanding of essential historical content. The performance assessment gives students a chance to analyze primary source documents, exhibit their analysis through an oral presentation, and enhance their understanding through a deeper group discussion of the source.

1. **In the first two paragraphs of the text, how do Benjamin Franklin and William Pitt use a similar metaphor to describe the relationship between England and America? How do their intentions differ?**
   - Franklin and Pitt both describe the relationship as one between a mother and her child.
   - Franklin does it in a joking poem, calling England an "old mother" and the colonists "children" who have "grown up" with "sense of our own."
   - Pitt is not joking when he refers to England as the "mother country" and the colonists as "children." He says that England must "prescribe" and the children must "obey."
   - Although both writers use the same metaphor, they are on opposite sides of the issue. Franklin believes the "children" are grown and should be treated as independent adults. Pitt believes the "children" need to obey the parent.

2. **Explain the use of the other image of American colonists that is mentioned in this selection.**
   - Colonists are described as a "mongrel breed," meaning that they are a mixture of breeds, or "mutts." It was unusual for a country to be made up of people from so many different nations, but America was. The English, according to one London newspaper, meant it as an insult, but the American colonists knew they were a mixture of peoples and were not insulted.
3. **Use evidence from the text to explain how the English citizens had changed by crossing the Atlantic Ocean and becoming American colonists.**
   - Now Americans, they had "risked their lives" and "gone through great hardships" to come to America.
   - They had built homes and farms in a land of thick forests.
   - They were tougher and more self-sufficient than the English back in England, and they "were not going to let anyone tell them how to run their country."
4. **How are the two primary source images on page 51 and the one on the top of page 52 related?**
   - The man depicted on page 51 is the ruler of England, King George III.
   - The image of the ship on page 51 illustrates the rebellion against George III in the form of the Boston Tea Party.
   - The caption draws these two illustrations together by saying, "George was furious when, in 1773, a group of men threw a shipful of tea into Boston harbor rather than pay tax on it."
   - The image on the top of page 51 is a firsthand account from one of the participants in the Boston Tea Party. George Hewes explains how he dressed like a Native American, joined others, cut boxes of tea open with a tomahawk, and threw the tea into the harbor.
5. **What evidence does the author provide to convince the reader that George III was not a competent ruler?**
   - On page 51, the caption of the painting calls George III "stupid, really stupid . . . a clod of a boy whom no one could teach."
   - On page 51, in the text, the author suggests that George III didn't think about how independent and self-sufficient the colonists had become since crossing the Atlantic and settling in America.
   - On page 51, she writes that George III's "pride was more important to him than the valuable American colonies."
   - She mentions that George III didn't read until he was ten and that his mother had to remind him to "be a king."
   - She explains that sometimes George III "raged and screamed and scared his advisors."
   - On page 53, the author mentions that George III didn't explain the need for taxes very well, but kept demanding taxes nonetheless. The increasing taxes caused the colonists to "get nervous and angry" because they recalled "how European kings and barons taxed the peasants and kept them poor."
   - George III is described as stubborn on page 53.
   - On page 54, the author says that George III may have had a disease that caused the temper and raging.
6. **According to the text, why were the colonists being taxed by England?**
   - On page 51, it says the colonists were taxed to teach the colonists a lesson.
   - On page 53, it says the colonists were also taxed to pay for the French and Indian War.

- The Stamp Act was passed to show the colonists that George III's government was "the boss."
- On page 54, the author says the tea tax was levied to show the colonists that Parliament could tax Americans if it wished.

7. **According to page 53, why were the colonists upset by the taxation?**
   - Peasants in Europe had been kept poor by kings and barons.
   - No colonists served in Parliament, and no colonists voted on taxes. The colonists said this taxation was wrong and used "taxation without representation" as the summary of their complaint.
8. **According to the inset article on pages 54 and 55, "John Rutledge Visits a Foreign Country," what was the "foreign country" he visited? Why did the places seem like foreign countries?**
   - John Rutledge had traveled from South Carolina to New York, from one of the southern colonies to a northern colony.
   - The two places were different, mainly because of the volume of slaves in Charleston as compared to New York. Out of about fourteen thousand residents, two thousand of the New York residents were slaves. But in Charleston, eight thousand out of the fourteen thousand residents were slaves.
9. **Rutledge learned about the Iroquois government while he was visiting New York. He learned that the Iroquois nation had an idea for government whereby "each Iroquois nation governed itself but all were linked together in time of war or when there was business affecting them all. It was that linkage that had made the Iroquois the strongest Indians in the land." How does that Native American idea seem similar to our present-day American government?**
   - It can be inferred from this passage that the Iroquois had a model for affording self-government to smaller nations while allowing a union of all the nations in times of war or in light of business issues. This looks very similar to the divisions of power among our state and national governments today.
10. **According to the text on pages 54 and 55, how did the reaction of the other colonies to the closing of Boston Harbor relate to the teachings of the Iroquois?**
    - Traditionally, the colonies had been acting as separate "nations" in the New World. Now they were drawing together in response to the closing of Boston Harbor. They had a common problem and they were banding together to make themselves stronger and more unified. Other colonies sent supplies and encouragement to Massachusetts:
      - Connecticut sent money.
      - South Carolina sent rice.
      - New York sent sheep.
      - Virginia had a prayer day, and Virginians began to talk about independence.

PERFORMANCE ASSESSMENT

For the first part of this performance assessment, have students choose one of the primary sources in the assigned book chapter that relates to taxation. The students should study the source and prepare a short presentation (two to three minutes) describing the primary source in detail. Each student should explain what primary sources are, why primary sources are foundational to historical study, why the source may have been included in this chapter titled "A Taxing King," and how it helps explain an aspect of taxation.

In the second part of this performance assessment, create discussion groups with students who examined the same primary source. Having listened to each other's presentations, students should be able to more deeply appreciate each person's perspective on the same source. Give the students a set of probing questions to use as they analyze the primary source together on a deeper level, such as "Teacher's Guide: Analyzing Primary Sources" from the Library of Congress. See standards for more details.

EXTENSION

Ask students to write an informative/explanatory essay describing the significance of the primary source. Ask students to be sure to introduce the topic clearly; develop the topic with facts, details, and examples; link ideas; use precise language and domain-specific vocabulary; and provide a concluding statement. At earlier levels, students may write a coherent paragraph that summarizes the main topic and key details. See standards for more details.

CONNECTIONS TO COMMON CORE STATE STANDARDS FOR ENGLISH LANGUAGE ARTS

- Question 1 focuses on a comparison between metaphors that helps students understand important historical content (RI.3.4; RI.4.4; RI. 5.4; L.3.5; L.4.5; L.5.5).
- Similar to question 1, question 2 asks students to examine a metaphor used to help explain an essential historical concept (RI.3.4; RI.4.4; RI.5.4; L.3.5; L.4.5; L.5.5).
- Question 3 prompts students to read closely and to recall and describe several related concepts in the text (RI.3.1,2,3; RI.4.1,2,3; RI.5.1,2,3).
- Question 4 allows students to compare several primary sources (both images and text) pertaining to related topics. It also helps students understand the role that captions play (RI.3.6,7,9; RI.4.6,7,9; RI.5.6,7,9).
- Question 5 requires students to reread closely to locate key details that support the author's claim about an important character in this narrative history (RI.3.1,2,3,8; RI.4.1,2,3,8; RI.5.1,2,3,8).
- Question 6 asks students to identify key details (RI.3.1; RI.4.1; RI.5.1).
- Questions 7, 8, and 10 ask students to identify and explain or compare related key details, concepts, and events in the text (RI.3.1,2,3; RI.4.1,2,3; RI.5.1,2,3).
- Question 9 requires that students infer information from the inset text and compare it to what they know about the present-day American government (RI.3.1,2,3,9; RI.4.1,2,3,9; RI.5.1,2,3,9).
- The performance assessment gives students an opportunity to conduct a rich, multistep examination, presentation, and discussion of important primary sources (RI.3.1,2,3,6,9; RI.4.1,2,3,6,9; RI.5.1,2,3,6,9; SL.3.1; SL.4.1; SL.5.1; W.3.2; W.4.2; W.5.2).

MORE RESOURCES

HISTORICAL FICTION

My Brother Sam Is Dead by James Lincoln Collier

Johnny Tremain by Esther Forbes

Dear America: The Winter of the Red Snow by Kristiana Gregory

PRIMARY SOURCES

Medal commemorating the Treaty of Paris, 1783 (British Museum)

Stamp from the Stamp Act of 1765 (Smithsonian Institution)

Paul Revere's artwork, used as war propaganda, 1770 (Gilder Lehrman Institute of American History)

Revolutionary War enlistment form (Library of Congress)

Broadside announcing the sale of slaves, 1769 (PBS: *Africans in America*)

Treaty of Paris, 1783 (National Archives)

Black soldier in the American Revolution, ca. 1780 (Virginia Foundation for the Humanities and the University of Virginia Library)

ART AND ARCHITECTURE

Engraving of Patrick Henry before the Virginia House of Burgesses on May 30, 1765 (Library of Congress)

Washington Crossing the Delaware, December 1776, painting by Emanuel Leutze (National Archives)

USEFUL WEBSITE

Resources for teachers: political cartoons (Library of Congress)

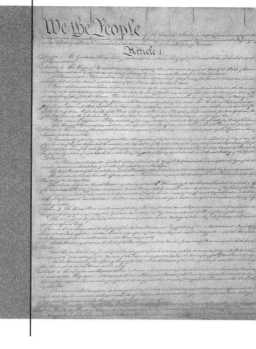

We the People: Building an American Republic

(1776 to 1789)

GRADES: 3, 4, 5

OVERVIEW

Americans fought a long and costly war to gain independence. After a decade of experimentation, they built a system that divided rights, duties, and responsibilities between the state governments and a new federal system. But the new Constitution left some questions unanswered, including the ultimate fate of slavery—an institution that would come to divide the nation. *D Is for Democracy: A Citizen's Alphabet* introduces younger students to the basic principles of our government and encourages them to write and illustrate examples of the importance of these principles. Older students will explore the drafting of the Constitution in *We the People: The Story of Our Constitution* and then synthesize what they've learned in a timeline that they can share with others.

○ ○ ○

Interested in learning more about this time period? Read a more complete history in the "Era Summaries."

LEARNING EXPECTATIONS

Lower elementary: Students should understand that American democracy took years of trial and error before the systems were developed as we know them today. They should also learn the basic role of citizens in our republic under the Constitution, and they should understand that a constitution lays out the basic rules for a system of government.

Upper elementary: Students should understand why the ideas of the American Revolution led the states to make Congress's powers so limited under the Articles of Confederation. They should then understand how different the Constitution's approach is, and why experience had changed so many minds about how powerful government needed to be. Students should learn how the Constitution lays out the structure of the U.S. government, how the different branches check and balance each other, and what fundamental rights are guaranteed by the Bill of Rights.

SUGGESTED ANCHOR TEXTS

We the People: The Story of Our Constitution by Lynne Cheney
Washington Irving's Rip Van Winkle by Thomas Locker and Ashley Foehner
Electric Ben: The Amazing Life and Times of Benjamin Franklin by Robert Byrd
We the Kids: The Preamble to the Constitution of the United States by David Catrow
"Our Constitution: The Road to a More Perfect Union," *Cobblestone*, December 2007
The New Nation: 1789–1850 by Joy Hakim
"Congress: Government of the People," *Cobblestone*
So Said Ben by Michael McCurdy

FEATURED ANCHOR TEXT

WE THE PEOPLE: THE STORY OF OUR CONSTITUTION BY LYNNE CHENEY

This book was selected because it traces concisely and beautifully the writing and ratification of the Constitution. The voices of the participants are "heard" in relevant quotations included on each page of text.

TEXT STUDY

Answering these text-dependent questions requires close reading and rereading. The majority of the questions focus on extracting key details and ideas from the text, ensuring students' understanding of essential historical content.

1. **After reading the text on page 5 and closely viewing the illustration, describe the setting of this time in history.**
   - The setting is October 19, 1781, in Yorktown, Virginia.
   - The Revolutionary War has just ended, and the defeated British are leaving the continent in shock.
   - It is a new beginning for the emerging United States.
2. **America's first rules for government were called the Articles of Confederation. According to page 6, what were the problems with the Articles of Confederation?**
   - Congress didn't have enough power.
   - States could still print their own money.
   - Congress couldn't rally the states to defend the country or pay off debts.
   - Britain didn't feel it had to follow orders to leave.
   - There was so much unrest over unclear leadership that Americans began to kill other Americans in Springfield, Massachusetts.
3. **According to page 9, what were two ways in which James Madison's idea about government differed from the principles in the Articles of Confederation?**
   - He was convinced that America needed a much stronger government than the one outlined by the Articles of Confederation.
   - He believed that people should choose who would represent them, instead of state legislatures' choosing the members of Congress.

4. **Why did the author choose to devote all of page 10 to one particular delegate, George Washington, who came to Philadelphia for the convention? How does the quotation at the bottom of the page support the notion of Washington's importance?**
   - He was an important figure, proven by how Philadelphia celebrated when he arrived at the convention.
     - He was remembered for his persistence during the dark days of the Revolutionary War.
     - He was remembered for giving up power after the war when he could have seized it by being king.
     - He gave the decisions of the convention credibility because he was there.
   - The quotation reinforces the idea of Washington's importance because it refers to him as "the man who unites all hearts." He had united American hearts through his leadership during the Revolutionary War and through his resistance to grabbing power after the war was over. The text describes how Americans as a whole loved and respected him.
5. **Using page 12 of the text, describe the proposed three branches of government.**
   - The legislative branch consists of Congress. It would have two houses, with people elected from each state.
   - The judicial branch would be the courts.
   - The executive branch would be the third.
6. **According to page 15, what was the biggest problem with the proposed Constitution? Why?**
   - Population would determine how many representatives would be in the lawmaking (legislative) branch.
   - Under the Articles of Confederation, each state held one vote. Under the new proposed system, the larger states, such as Virginia, Pennsylvania, and Massachusetts, would have more power. Small states hated the idea of large states' being more powerful due to larger populations.
7. **Describe the Great Compromise.**
   - According to page 18, the Great Compromise was a change in an idea originally thought of by Roger Sherman. He had proposed (page 16) that one house of the legislature have representation according to states' populations and the other have equal representation across the states.
   - The Great Compromise, as suggested by the committee, stipulated that all of the legislation concerning money would begin in the first house, where the big states had more power.
   - Finally, after weeks of heated discussion, the Great Compromise was adopted (page 22).
8. **According to pages 21 and 22, how did the disputed topic of slavery enter into the discussion about small states' and large states' representation?**
   - Southerners wanted to count the slaves for purposes of determining population so they would have more representatives and more power.
   - Northerners rejected the southerners' proposal.
   - But the North and South finally compromised, counting each slave as three-fifths of a person for the purposes of determining population.
   - As an aside, they also decided that the slave trade could not be banned for at least twenty years. Morris and Mason spoke out against slavery.

9. **How did the Committee of Detail finally design the branches of government?**
   - According to page 24, the different components within the branches of government were given official titles.
     - The first house of Congress was named the House of Representatives, with the Speaker of the House serving as its leader.
     - They named the highest court in the land the Supreme Court.
     - They "named the head of the executive branch of government the President of the United States."
10. **According to page 27, what were the two important decisions made before the Constitution was finally written in final form?**
    - The delegates agreed that the president would be chosen by the people, but through electors.
    - They also decided that the people should ratify the Constitution.
11. **Who was the first to sign the Constitution?**
    - According to page 28, it was the president of the convention, Washington.
12. **Describe how Benjamin Franklin saw the two-headed snake and the painted sun on Washington's chair as metaphors in this process of setting up a plan for government.**
    - As described on page 18, the two-headed snake represented the need for compromise in a process such as the convention.
    - On page 28, the text explains that the painted sun represented a new beginning for America as the Constitution was signed.

      Note: There is a quotation at the bottom of the page spoken by Ben Franklin: "At length I have the happiness to know that it is a rising and not a setting sun." Teachers may want to connect this quotation to the text and accompanying illustration on pages 28 and 29.
13. **In the author's note on page 32, why does the author use the words *growing in justice* when she discusses adding amendments to the Constitution?**
    - Over the years, amendments have added more important laws to the original Constitution as our country has seen the need for changes. The Bill of Rights was quickly added in 1789, guaranteeing individual rights of free speech, freedom of religion, and freedom of the press. Later amendments brought the end of slavery and the right to vote for all people, regardless of race or gender.

PERFORMANCE ASSESSMENT

For the first part of this performance assessment, lead a discussion on the overall chronological structure of this text. Have the students strip the text down to a series of eight to ten historical events and discussions and put them in order to create a timeline. For each event, instruct a team of two or three students to create a narrative, using ideas from the text and other sources to tell the story of the writing of the Constitution. See standards for more details.

For the second part, discuss as a class the author's choice to post significant quotations from historical figures at the bottom of each page and how this is an excellent example of the use of primary sources. Assign quotations from the book and the Preamble to the Constitution for students to memorize and dramatically perform.

For the third part, combine the narration and the quotations from the previous two performance assessments to tell the story of the Constitution to parents or other classes in the school.

EXTENSION

Have students read another text that tells the story of the writing of the Constitution, such as *Shh! They're Writing the Constitution* by Jean Fritz. They should compare the two accounts of the same period of history either in an informative/explanatory essay or an oral presentation in which they cite two to three pieces of evidence from each text to support their assertions about the similarities and differences between the two accounts. See standards for more details.

CONNECTIONS TO COMMON CORE STATE STANDARDS FOR ENGLISH LANGUAGE ARTS

- Questions 1, 2, 3, 5, 6, and 8 ask students to identify key details and main ideas from the text, citing evidence from the text to support their answers (RI.3.1,2,3,8; RI.4.1,2,3,8; RI.5.1,2,3,8).
  - Question 1 also asks students to extract information from an illustration (RI.3.7; RI.4.7; RI.5.7).
  - Question 3 also asks students to compare two different ideas presented by the author (RI.3.8; RI.4.8; RI.5.8).
- Question 4 addresses the author's craft, in particular why the author chose to focus on one delegate. It also asks about the purpose of a quotation inserted by the author (RI.3.2,3,5; RI.4.2,3,5; RI.5.2,3,5).
- Questions 7, 9, 10, and 11 ask students to identify key details and main ideas from the text (RI.3.1,2,3; RI.4.1,2,3; RI.5.1,2,3).
- Questions 12 and 13 offer opportunities to discuss the use of figurative language and imagery in an informational text, especially as they relate to the understanding of essential historical content (RL.3.4; RL.4.4; RL.5.4; L.3.5; L.4.5; L.5.5).
- The first part of the performance assessment is designed to help students recognize the order and significance of the events that led to the establishment of the Constitution by extracting these events when rereading the text. In addition, creating the narratives (or "annotations") for the timeline forces students back into the text. The second part of the performance assessment has students memorize the enduring words of some of the Founding Fathers, helping them internalize events and principles essential to a lasting understanding of the American republic (RI.3.2,3,5; RI.4.2,3,5; RI.5.2,3,5; SL.3.1,4; SL.4.1,4; SL.5.1,4).
- The extension gives students the opportunity to compare and contrast two different accounts of or perspectives on the same historical events by reading another text and writing, or presenting orally, an informative/explanatory comparison between the two texts (RI.3.9; RI.4.9; RI.5.9; W.3.3; W.4.3; W.5.3 and/or SL.3.4; SL.4.4; SL.5.4).

MORE RESOURCES

HISTORICAL FICTION

Rip Van Winkle by Washington Irving

Sign of the Beaver by Elizabeth George Speare

Illustrates other historical events in other regions of the United States

PRIMARY SOURCES

Resources for teachers: the Constitution (Library of Congress)

U.S. two-dollar bill, printed in 1776 (Smithsonian Institution)

Thomas Jefferson's notes on writing the Articles of Confederation, 1776 (Library of Congress)

Bill of Rights primary documents (Library of Congress)

POETRY AND MUSIC

"George Washington" by Rosemary and Stephen Vincent Benet

ART AND ARCHITECTURE

Portrait of George Washington holding Pierre Charles L'Enfant's plan for Washington, DC, 1793 (British Museum)

Sculpture of James Madison (Smithsonian Institution)

USEFUL WEBSITES

Creating the Constitution, interactive website (Library of Congress)

Resources for teachers: Constitution Day (National Archives)

Democracy Made Real: America Passes the Torch

(1789 to 1800)

GRADES: 3, 4, 5

OVERVIEW

America's sights would soon shift to westward expansion. But first, the young nation and its fledgling government had to show that the new republic could govern effectively and that power could be transferred from one political party to another. The United States indeed created a working federal government, navigated a potentially poisonous party schism, and it successfully handled the difficult election of 1800. *George Washington: Soldier, Hero, President* gives lower elementary students the biographical knowledge to persuade others that our first president was a great American. Upper elementary students will explore the ideological tension between the Founding Fathers in *The Revolutionary John Adams* and produce essays that evaluate both sides of an argument, paving the way for students' participation in debates about government that continue to this day.

○ ○ ○

Interested in learning more about this time period? Read a more complete history in the "Era Summaries."

LEARNING EXPECTATIONS

Lower elementary: Students should understand what a government is and why we need one. They should know what a constitution is and does, and how it lays out the basic rules that a government follows. Students can then understand not only the importance of George Washington in making the new government work but also Washington's iconic role in American culture. They should also understand that people quickly and inevitably split over what direction the new nation should take, resulting in political debate.

Upper elementary: Students should know that the Constitution left much unsaid, and that the first U.S. Congress and president were left to set up the actual government. They should understand Washington's central role in making the new system function in its early, formative stages. Students should also understand that the first party schism was sparked by different ideas about what kind of country the United States would be—either controlled, European-style, by the wealthy, who would help bolster U.S. military power, or based on a society of relatively equal farmers. Students should also recognize the great achievement of the new system in respecting elections and transferring power between the parties.

SUGGESTED ANCHOR TEXTS

The Revolutionary John Adams by Cheryl Harness
Fever, 1793 by Laurie Halse Anderson
"Hamilton vs. Jefferson: The Rise of Political Parties," *Cobblestone*, September 2008
Tricking the Tallyman: The Great Census Shenanigans of 1790 by Jacqueline Davies
"A Visit to Mount Vernon: George Washington's Home," *Cobblestone*, January 2012
George Washington by Cheryl Harness

FEATURED ANCHOR TEXT

THE REVOLUTIONARY JOHN ADAMS BY CHERYL HARNESS

Covering the political and personal life of John Adams, this narrative history provides a review of America's past and how the colonies became a new country. It traces the establishment of government from the viewpoint of Adams: the first vice-president; the second president; and the "sometimes friend" of the third president, Thomas Jefferson.

TEXT STUDY

1. **Closely read the author's note on page 3. How does the author describe each of the first three presidents?**
   - She describes the first three presidents as follows:
     - Washington: one of the "tall and glamorous Virginians," "reserved, heroic," "first in the hearts of his countrymen," "father of our country"
     - Adams: "stout, stubborn, New Englander," second president, leader of Congress, Founding Father, imagined our checks-and-balances government, kept the nation at peace, built up the navy, brave, brilliant, "intense, cranky, warm, heart-on-his-sleeve," "America's champion"
     - Jefferson: one of the "tall and glamorous Virginians," "cool, complicated genius of Monticello"

   Note: *Teachers could note that good narrative history often exhibits the same qualities as good literary text.*

2. **What are some examples of the use of alliteration in the author's description of the presidents on page 3?**
   - To describe Adams, the author uses "stout" and "stubborn"; "Founding Father"; and "brave and brilliant."
   - To describe Jefferson, the author uses "cool" and "complicated."

3. **What does the author mean by "eternally bookended and overshadowed" in this sentence on page 3: "There stands John Adams, the stout, stubborn New Englander eternally bookended and overshadowed by tall, glamorous Virginians"?**
   - She uses an image of two tall heroes as books on a bookshelf with a stout and stubborn book sandwiched between. The two outer books (Washington and Jefferson) are the

famous ones with the monuments and reputations, but Adams also made contributions. This selection will be about the "book" in the middle.

Note: *The painting on page 28 depicts the three presidents standing together, resembling her imagery.*

4. **In the second paragraph on page 4, the author uses the word *changed* five times. What point is the author trying to prove with this use of repetition?**
   - The author wants to show that Adams had a part in how the world changed by describing all of the changes that happened in the years following his birth. She proves her point that the world was changing by saying that Adams's birth date shifted from October 19 to October 30 because of a calendar change, his house became part of the town of Quincy rather than Braintree because of the change in the village border, and his country changed from being a collection of British colonies to a new nation comprising thirteen states—the last of these being a change in which Adams played a vital role.
5. **What was Adams's work assignment during the Second Continental Congress?**
   - According to page 14, Adams was supposed to make a navy; fortify fifteen hundred miles of coastline; raise, feed, uniform, train, arm, and pay a Continental Army; issue Continental currency; and find a commander for the army (he nominated Washington for the job).
6. **Describe the two illustrations on page 17. What is the purpose of including these two illustrations?**
   - This page is focused on the writing of the Declaration of Independence. The illustration on the top of the page shows the five men who were involved in writing it. This illustration emphasizes that the Declaration of Independence was the work of many men, despite the fact that Jefferson wrote it. The illustration at the bottom of the page is a handwritten copy of the Declaration of Independence. This image reminds us that the declaration was short and written by hand.
7. **Go back and reread page 7. Use text evidence from the passage to show that Adams and his wife, Abigail, were important to each other.**
   - According to page 7, during the first five years after meeting, many letters passed between them. She was called "dear girl". He called her "Diana" after a goddess of the moon. He called her "Portia," a heroine from Shakespeare. He was her "dearest friend." The inset quotes one of Adams's letters from August 1763, in which he expresses his admiration for her: "I lay in the well-known Chamber, and dreamed I saw a Lady, tripping it over the Hills . . . Spreading Light and Beauty and Glory all around her." The reader can assume that the "Lady" he describes is his beloved wife.
8. **How does the author use the early description of John and Abigail's relationship on page 7 to deepen the reader's understanding of the "terrible goodbyes" of 1777 as described on pages 22 and 23?**
   - The author first establishes the closeness of their relationship and then shows throughout the book how often they had to be separated. Knowing about their closeness gives a stronger connotation to the idea of terrible good-byes—it shows the sacrifices they made. The quotation from Adams at the bottom of page 22, from a letter written to Abigail in April 1777, also speaks poignantly of the sacrifice they made: "Posterity! You will never know how much it cost the present Generation to preserve your Freedom! I hope you will make good Use of it. If you do not, I shall repent in Heaven that I ever took half the Pains to preserve it."

9. **On pages 28 and 29, how does the author use the word *machine* as it relates to government?**
   - The word is used to describe the U.S. Constitution as a "beautiful machine of laws and ideas."
   - The word is used in discussing the differences in opinion among Jefferson, Hamilton, and Adams when they disagreed about how the "machinery of government would work."
   - The image of a machine is alluded to in the description of the government working effectively even when there was disagreement. As laws were passed and decisions and deals were made, "the wheels turned."
10. **How does the author describe the 1796 "passing of power" between Washington and Adams? Why was it unique as compared to the colonies' former English rule by kings?**
    - On page 30, the author describes the passing of power as "peaceful and a huge historic step for mankind."
    - The election of Adams was a result of the vote of the citizens, the people; it was peaceful; it worked in spite of politics. This "still unbroken line of leaders" continues through today. Before this, Americans were under British rule, with a permanent line of leadership determined by birth running through royal families, meaning that English leaders were not chosen by choice and election.
11. **How does the author show that Adams and Jefferson had a difficult relationship from the early days of Adams's presidency?**
    - According to page 31, Jefferson wanted to help the French in a war with England, disagreeing with Adams.
    - According to page 31, when Adams wanted to stay neutral in regard to the affairs of France and England, Jefferson said, "Mr. Adams is vain, irritable, stubborn."
    - The race of 1800 between Adams and Jefferson was a first for tenuous party politics.
12. **According to this text, how did Adams and Jefferson resolve their differences?**
    - According to page 36, they wrote 158 letters over fourteen years, from 1812 until their deaths on July 4, 1826. They discussed memories, ideas, sadness, and triumphs. Their friendship was renewed by their fond memories of fighting for the same cause.

      Note: *The quotation from one of Jefferson's letters at the bottom of the page reinforces this point: "A letter from you calls up recollections very dear to my mind. It carried me back to the times when beset with difficulties and dangers, we were fellow laborers in the same cause, struggling for what is most valuable to man, his rights of self-government."*

PERFORMANCE ASSESSMENTS

1. After rereading the text and reviewing the content highlighted by the guiding questions, ask students to respond to one of the following opinion tasks:

   a. In your opinion, what was John Adams's greatest contribution to the United States?

   b. In your opinion, what was John Adams's most significant character trait?

Based on appropriate grade-level expectations, have students write a well-developed essay on the chosen topic. Require students to write a well-developed topic paragraph and then choose specific examples from the text to illustrate the contribution or character trait in the body of the essay. Students should provide a conclusion that summarizes the ideas in the essay. See standards for more details.

If time is available, students could do further research by reading an additional biographical book on Adams to gather more information in the form of real-life examples of that contribution or character trait.

2. The author describes the last years of Adams's life as including lots of correspondence with Jefferson: "You and I ought not to die before we have explained ourselves to each other" (page 26). Continue as a class to discuss the correspondence between them. Discuss the actual day of their deaths, their last words, and the irony of the date.

Then, give the students this writing task:

- Choose one life lesson that can be learned from the relationship between John Adams and Thomas Jefferson. Support your lesson selection by providing text evidence from this anchor text and from other research sources, if time permits. Write an essay that includes a clear topic paragraph, support paragraphs, and a strong concluding paragraph.

For example, a student might choose to write about how important it is to resolve a conflict. The student could use as evidence the way in which Adams reached out to Jefferson after many years by means of a letter, the 158 letters that passed between them, and the fourteen years they spent corresponding. See standards for more details.

3. Different types of media give us different information. View the two online History.com videos dealing with Adams's early life and politics. Discuss the following questions with the class, encouraging students to note closely what familiar book topics are discussed in each video clip.

c. What does Cheryl Harness's book teach us about the same period of John Adams's life or career?

d. How do the bits of information seem similar?

e. How do they show us different sides of the same issue?

For example, in a comparison of the book and the video about Adams's early life, each discusses Adams's hatred of school and love of the farm, but the video goes into more detail about the way the father teaches his son about the hard work of farming and the value of an education.

In regard to the video about Adams's political career, when students compare the latter part of the book dealing with his politics and the film clip, they will note that the video is much more critical of Adams than the book. The video calls Adams "bullheaded." The book says that "Mr. Adams is vain, irritable, stubborn" (page 31) but presents it as only Jefferson's opinion. See standards for more details.

Note: *Teachers may want to address how discussing politics often entails a consideration of two different opinions on one issue.*

CONNECTIONS TO COMMON CORE STATE STANDARDS FOR ENGLISH LANGUAGE ARTS

- Questions 1, 2, and 3 highlight the author's use of figurative language, such as metaphors and alliteration, to illuminate important characteristics of significant figures in American history. (RL.3.4; RL.4.4; RL.5.4; RI.3.4; RI.4.4; RI.5.4).
- Questions 4 and 9 offer opportunities to discuss word choice, analyzing the significance of particular terms, the effect of figurative language, and/or the author's purpose in using or emphasizing specific words (RL.3.4; RL.4.4; RL.5.4; RI.3.4; RI.4.4; RI.5.4).

- Questions 5, 10, 11, and 12 highlight the author's descriptive techniques and ask students to track them when identifying the key details of important historical content (RI.3.1,2,3; RI.4.1,2,3; RI.5.1,2,3).
- Question 6 helps students look critically at how history is presented in written versus visual text, comparing two different historical interpretations of the same topic (RI.3.6; RI.4.6; RI.5.6; RI.3.7; RI.4.7; RI.5.7).
- Question 7 prompts close rereading and gives students a chance to identify evidence in the text to support their assertions (RI.3.1,2,3,8; RI.4.1,2,3,8; RI.5.1,2,3,8).
- Question 8 allows students to note the relationships among different parts of the text and to see how one idea may be revisited in another part of the book (RI.3.8; RI.4.8; RI.5.8).
- The performance assessments require students to formulate and defend an opinion based on key details from a text. Students are also asked to compare and contrast at least two texts (including multimedia sources) and articulate how the texts propose and support comparable arguments (RI.3.9; RI.4.9; RI.5.9; W.3.3,7,9; W.4.3,7,9; W.5.3,7,9; SL.3.1; SL.4.1; SL.5.1).

MORE RESOURCES

PRIMARY SOURCES

George Washington's handwritten inaugural address, 1789 (Library of Congress)

Letter in which John Adams orders relocation to Washington, DC (Library of Congress)

Thomas Jefferson election campaign banner, 1800 (Smithsonian Institution)

Washington's Rules of Civility (Library of Congress)

Adams's audience with King George III, 1785 (National Archives)

Report on the Seal of the United States, 1782 (National Archives)

ART AND ARCHITECTURE

Portrait of James Madison, ca. 1792 (National Portrait Gallery)

USEFUL WEBSITES

"John Adams: The Early Years," video (History Channel)

Information on Washington's Rules of Civility (National Public Radio)

The Great Seal of the United States (U.S. Department of State, Bureau of Public Affairs)

Going West: Opportunity and Peril on America's Frontier

(1800 to 1830s)

GRADES: 3, 4, 5

OVERVIEW

Although America was still mostly a nation of farmers in the early 1800s, the temptation to expand the western border was compelling. This period saw rapid growth in economic and industrial development as urban factories sprang up and delivered goods to markets both at home and abroad. At the same time, the first modern roads and canals allowed Americans to move easily between busy trading ports and once-isolated inland communities while continuing the drive westward into new territory. Younger students will take a journey in *How We Crossed the West: The Adventures of Lewis and Clark* and analyze the relationship between the explorers and the native people they encountered along the way. After reading the chapter on the Erie Canal in *A History of US: The New Nation: 1789–1850*, students in upper elementary grades will be prepared to analyze primary sources or to glean the insight of a civil engineer to construct their own multimedia presentations showing how new modes of transportation change life in a community.

○ ○ ○

Interested in learning more about this time period? Read a more complete history in the "Era Summaries."

LEARNING EXPECTATIONS

Lower elementary: Students should understand that the growing American nation quickly pushed westward in pursuit of opportunity and began to make itself felt in the world. Students should understand that Americans' way of life was quickly changing as commerce brought people closer together.

Upper elementary: Students should know that America began to expand dramatically, both commercially and physically (to the West, with new territory and settlement), and to take a more assertive place in the world. They should understand that commercial development moved with the expanding population, and they should grasp the importance of "internal improvements"—chiefly roads and canals—in allowing people and commerce to expand. They should also realize that commercial expansion created new dangers as well as new opportunities, and that people disagreed strongly about the federal government's involvement in promoting commercial development.

SUGGESTED ANCHOR TEXTS

A History of US: The New Nation: 1789–1850, chapter 22 "Going Places" by Joy Hakim
The Journals of Lewis and Clark by Darlene R. Stille
"On the Frontier with George Rogers Clark," *Cobblestone*, November 2004
Lewis and Clark: Blazing a Trail West by John Burrows
Heading West: Life with the Pioneers; 21 Activities by Pat McCarthy
The Amazing Impossible Erie Canal by Cheryl Harness

FEATURED ANCHOR TEXT

A HISTORY OF US: THE NEW NATION: 1789–1850, CHAPTER 22 "GOING PLACES" BY JOY HAKIM

This chapter was selected because it concisely describes the causes and effects of road building and canal construction in America in the early to mid-1800s. Primary sources, including diagrams, photographs, and quotations, are used to provide evidence of the transportation that characterized this period of American history.

TEXT STUDY

The following text-dependent questions provide students and teachers with opportunities to examine both the structure and the content of a rich historical text. They ask students to consider important vocabulary; the author's technique; and the relationships between the main text and other text features, such as sidebars, illustrations, and captions. The performance assessments help students to summarize and convey their understanding of informational text, as well as to extend their understanding through the study of additional resources—both human and material. Finally, they receive practice in developing strong informative/explanatory essays, as well as multimedia presentations.

1. **Study the primary source pictures and captions on page 110. Describe the transportation used at this time in American history.**
   - The top picture shows a mail stagecoach led by two horses. The caption says that it took two days to go two hundred miles if the weather was good. If the weather was bad, it might have taken seven days.
   - The bottom picture shows a horse and rider traveling on a road made of logs. The caption describes the road as a "corduroy road," an improvement over dirt roads that were either swampy or dusty, depending on the season.
2. **Why does the author begin the selection on page 110 by saying, "One thing leads to another"?**
   - She is making the case that better transportation was needed for trade. She is using a commonly understood expression to make an observation that begins an argument. She then cites a relevant example: "If you grow grain in New Jersey . . . you need to find ways to get your products to people who want to buy them." She is introducing the need for "canals, steamboats, railroads, and improved roads."

3. **What is the definition of *ingenuity*? Why is it featured as a key word in this chapter?**
   - In the inset on page 110, the author defines the word *ingenuity* as "inventiveness–finding a way to get things done."
   - In the text on pages 110 and 111, the author writes in response to the stated need for modern transportation, "Americans–who were becoming known all over the world for their ingenuity–soon came up with some answers." The answers came in the form of creative solutions to the problem of getting goods out to all of the geographic areas of the young country.
4. **How does the quotation in the margin of page 111, by Fortescue Cuming, support the text related to the need for good roads?**
   - The text notes how terrible the roads were. They were often dirt paths that washed away, or they were made of rounded logs or planks that rotted.
   - The quotation tells how badly the roads were needed in western Pennsylvania. Cuming states the need based on the fact that people were traveling all over during each season of the year.
5. **When it came to building the National Road, the people of the West, East, and South all had different opinions. According to the text, how did each group think the road should be financed?**
   - The people in the West wanted the road, and they wanted the national government to pay for it.
   - The people in the East didn't think their tax money should pay for it.
   - The people in the South were focused on states' rights, asking why their tax money should pay for a road they wouldn't use.
6. **After the National Road was finally built from Baltimore to St. Louis, how much time did it save travelers?**
   - According to page 112, the trip originally took four weeks. After the road was built, the trip took four days. People saved twenty-four days of travel by going along the National Road. (If it was a round trip, the travel would be eight days, saving forty-eight days of travel–almost two months of time.)
7. **How do the nicknames for DeWitt Clinton's project tell the story of people's opinions from the beginning of the building of the Erie Canal to the completion of the project? Why did the author choose to include the nicknames for the project?**
   - When the Erie Canal was begun in 1817, some people, such as Thomas Jefferson, thought Clinton was crazy for starting it. They called the canal "Clinton's Ditch." It would span 350 miles through what was then the wilderness.
   - After the Erie Canal was successfully built, it had eighty-three locks; it had been completed in eight years. The Erie Canal connected the Atlantic Ocean and the Great Lakes. Because the project worked, Clinton was ultimately a hero. As the canal opened, the people called it the "Grand Canal" or "Clinton's Wonder."

   Note: *Answers to the second part of the question will vary, but the author may be trying to show that people, even incredibly bright people, such as Jefferson, cannot always predict the future success or failure of a project. She may be also trying to show the general lack of faith people have in others' ideas, and how they may be proven wrong.*
8. **The author writes about the canal, saying, "It made life better for people." How does the author back up that claim with evidence?**
   - According to page 115, everybody could ride on it. Some boats were fancy, and some were flatboats with people and cargo jammed together. There were varied speeds and prices for travel.

- Towns were established along the canal.
- People were able to move west to Indiana, Michigan, and Wisconsin, carrying goods on the canal.
- New York grew to be the largest city in the country.
- The cost of shipping went down, from $100 for a ton of grain to only $8 for a ton to be transported on the Erie Canal.

PERFORMANCE ASSESSMENTS

1. Give students the following task:

- Choose three primary source illustrations from the text selection that are directly related to the construction of or travel on the Erie Canal and the inset of song lyrics on page 115.

You might give them a set of guiding questions to examine their primary sources, such as those found in the "Teacher's Guides and Analysis Tool" from the Library of Congress, and review answers with students prior to asking them to write.

Then ask students to write an expository/explanatory essay explaining how each of the primary sources illustrates part of the history of the canal. Ask students to be sure to introduce the topic clearly; develop the topic with facts, details, and examples; link ideas; use precise language and domain-specific vocabulary; and provide a concluding statement. At earlier levels, students may write a coherent paragraph that summarizes the main topic and key details. See standards for more details.

2. Invite a civil engineer to your classroom to discuss the history of building roads, or possibly a canal, in your local region. Use the information he or she shares to begin a class research project on the history of road or canal building in your community, particularly in the early to mid-1800s. As a class, create a multimedia presentation using old photographs and maps to show how a road or canal was built and how it changed life in your local area. Compare and contrast the building of this local road or canal to the construction of the National Road or the Erie Canal, respectively. Invite grandparents or local historians to a presentation, asking them to share old stories of the way life changed as travel changed.

CONNECTIONS TO COMMON CORE STATE STANDARDS FOR ENGLISH LANGUAGE ARTS

- Question 1 asks students to identify and explain key details in the text by examining primary source illustrations and captions (RI.3.1,2,5,7; RI.4.1,2,5,7; RI.5.1,2,5,7).
- Questions 2 and 3 address the author's purpose and craft, asking students to focus on why the author might have chosen to begin this section in a particular way and why she uses a particular expression or key word to catch the reader's attention (RI.3.3,4,8; RI.4.3,4,8; RI.5.3,4,8).
- Question 4 gives students a chance to compare information in a sidebar to that in the main text (RI.3.1,5,7,9; RI.4.1,5,7,9; RI.5.1,5,7,9).
- Question 5 requires students to have read closely to recall significant details from the text, comparing different perspectives on the same topic (RI.3.1,2,3,8; RI.4.1,2,3,8; RI.5.1,2,3,8).

- Question 6 also requires students to have read closely to recall significant details from the text (RI.3.1; RI.4.1; RI.5.1).
- Question 7 prompts students to explain how the use of figurative language (here, nicknames) helps explain historical content in this text; it also asks students to explain why the author chose to include this information (RI.3.1,2,3,4,8; RI.4.1,2,3,4,8; RI.5.1,2,3,4,8).
- Question 8 helps students understand how the author builds an argument; it encourages them to explore whether or not the author has supported her claim with sufficient evidence (RI.3.8; RI.4.8; RI.5.8).
- The first performance assessment allows students to compare information about important historical content using related but distinct primary sources. It also asks them to discuss primary sources using guiding questions and to write an informative/explanatory essay (RI.3.1,2,3,7,8; RI.4.1,2,3,7,8; RI.5.1,2,3,7,8; SL.3.1; SL.4.1; SL.5.1; W.3.2,9; W.4.2,9; W.5.2,9).
- The second performance assessment gives students a chance to expand their understanding of important historical content by conducting further research on similar phenomena and making comparisons between the researched events and those described in the text. It also allows them to develop a multimedia presentation to convey their findings (RI.3.1,2,3; RI.4.1,2,3; RI.5.1,2,3; SL.3.1,2,3; SL.4.1,2,3; SL.5.1,2,3; W.3.6,7,8,9; W.4.6,7,8,9; W.5.6,7,8,9).

MORE RESOURCES

PRIMARY SOURCES

"Westward Expansion: Encounters at a Cultural Crossroads" (Library of Congress)

Includes a teacher's guide with additional primary sources, related lesson activities, and explanations of concepts

Resources for teachers: Marco Paul's travels on the Erie Canal (Library of Congress)

The Star Spangled Banner, photograph (Smithsonian Institution)

POETRY AND MUSIC

Francis Scott Key's handwritten lyrics to "The Star Spangled Banner," 1840 (Library of Congress)

ART AND ARCHITECTURE

Wagon Train to the West (Library of Congress)

Relief of Meriwether Lewis, William Clark, and Sacajawea (Smithsonian Institution)

Model for Signing of the Louisiana Purchase Treaty (Smithsonian Institution)

Portrait of Francis Scott Key (Library of Congress)

Freedom for All: American Democracy Begins to Transform

(1820s to 1840s)

GRADES: 3, 4, 5

OVERVIEW

Economic changes had already swept the nation by the 1820s, and democracy had expanded as most white men gained the right to vote. Now a great social transformation began as new ideas about religion, women's rights, and abolition took root. More groups of people demanded rights equal to those of free men, laying the foundation for ideological battles that would forever alter the nation. Differences in the rural and urban economies are highlighted in *The Listeners* and *The Bobbin Girl* in a way that is relatable for lower elementary students. Examining the lives of the two protagonists leads younger students to develop an informed opinion about where they would rather live—a rural or urban setting—and why. *Elizabeth Leads the Way: Elizabeth Cady Stanton and the Right to Vote* and *I Could Do That! Esther Morris Gets Women the Vote* prepare upper elementary students to compare and contrast the accomplishments of two pivotal women's rights activists.

○ ○ ○

Interested in learning more about this time period? Read a more complete history in the "Era Summaries."

LEARNING EXPECTATIONS

Lower elementary: Students should understand that Americans remained divided over what kind of society the country should have—agricultural and rural versus commercial and urban—and that as more men were able to vote, these divisions led to new political parties. They should also understand that many people tried to reform the country to end various injustices, even as expansion to the West increasingly forced out Native Americans. Further, students should realize that slavery, getting stronger in the South, was the focus of new tensions between North and South.

Upper elementary: Students should understand that in the Jacksonian era, white, male Americans achieved a new level of democratic power rarely seen before in the world. But they should also know that the thriving American democracy created a push for westward expansion, with dark consequences for Native Americans. They should understand that reformers, often motivated by religious fervor, tried to improve society and morality (and to control new immigrants whom they feared); they should also realize that slavery became more and more powerful in the South, even as the North turned more heavily against it—setting up the conflict that would dominate the country in coming decades.

SUGGESTED ANCHOR TEXTS

Elizabeth Leads the Way: Elizabeth Cady Stanton and the Right to Vote by Tanya Lee Stone
I Could Do That! Esther Morris Gets Women the Vote by Linda Arms White
Only the Names Remain: The Cherokees and the Trail of Tears by Alex W. Bealer
The Trail of Tears by Joseph Bruchac
You Want Women to Vote, Lizzie Stanton? by Jean Fritz
Rightfully Ours: How Women Won the Vote by Kerrie Logan Hollihan
A is for Abigail by Lynne Cheney

FEATURED ANCHOR TEXTS

ELIZABETH LEADS THE WAY: ELIZABETH CADY STANTON AND THE RIGHT TO VOTE BY TANYA LEE STONE

I COULD DO THAT! ESTHER MORRIS GETS WOMEN THE VOTE BY LINDA ARMS WHITE

These narrative biographical books were selected because they portray the early days of the women's suffrage movement, but on different fronts. *Elizabeth Leads the Way* is set on the East Coast in the United States in the 1800s. *I Could Do That!* is the story of someone fighting for women's rights but out in the rugged western territories of early America. Both stories tell of women who were awakened to their need to have a voice in the way their country was run.

TEXT STUDIES

The following text-dependent questions provide a number of opportunities for educators to support the teaching of the Common Core State Standards for English language arts. These questions all require close reading of the text and ask students to use evidence to support their assertions about what they have learned. This effective pairing of two works about two different women who worked toward the same cause during the same period of U.S. history helps students recognize patterns in history as well as the various ways in which historians and biographers choose to convey historical information. A number of questions help students focus on the power of figurative language in informational texts, the importance of characterization in informational texts, and the necessity of citing evidence when making assertions about texts.

Elizabeth Leads the Way: Elizabeth Cady Stanton and the Right to Vote by Tanya Lee Stone

1. **Look closely at the cover of the book. What can you learn about Elizabeth Cady Stanton from the illustration?**
   - We can see that Stanton is wearing a yellow sash that says, "Vote for Women," which suggests that she campaigned for women to be allowed to vote.

- From the number of stars on the flag, we can tell that she was alive when there were only thirty states in the United States.
- She is wearing a long dress and a bonnet, so we can infer that she lived in the nineteenth or early twentieth century.

2. **According to the quotation on the first page of text, what did Stanton expect of her "way," or her journey in life? What words and phrases support your opinion?**
   - Stanton expected her way to be difficult.
   - Words and phrases in this quotation support this inference:
     - She described her way as a path that would not be "strewn with the flowers of popular applause." This means she did not expect people to support her work or help make her work easy to accomplish.
     - She described the path as being covered with the "thorns of bigotry and prejudice." Bigotry is intolerance or being unwavering in your own point of view. Prejudice is present when you have a negative opinion about something or someone without having actual knowledge of or experience with the subject that you disdain.

   Note: *Teachers could also focus here on the metaphors and the figurative meanings of the words* flowers *and* thorns.

3. **The author of this book begins with a list of questions. What can you learn about life in this era from the questions?**
   - Women were not given wide choices for vocations or work.
   - Women were not allowed to vote in elections.
   - Women's opinions were generally not respected.

4. **According to pages 6 and 7, what were the two issues that infuriated Stanton? How did she respond to these challenges?**
   - Women could not own property. Even if a woman had lived on the land throughout her marriage and her husband had died, she still could not own the property in her name.
   - Women could not help change laws. They would have needed to be able to vote to help change the laws.
   - Stanton decided that she "could do anything a boy could do." She was "horrified by this unfairness." She also said, "The law should be cut out of every book!"

5. **According to pages 8 and 9, why was Judge Cady worried about his daughter?**
   - Judge Cady was worried about Stanton because she did things that boys liked to do. He said her life would have been easier if she had been a boy.
     - She practiced horseback jumping over high hurdles.
     - She rafted alone across "a raging river."
     - She won a prize for her studies in Greek.

6. **How did Stanton's teen years differ from those of most young women in her time?**
   - Stanton chose to attend a girls' school to study religion, math, science, French, and writing.
   - Most other women her age were getting married, having babies, and doing chores at home.

7. **What can the reader infer from the author's repetition of the phrase "he did not laugh" on pages 12 and 13?**
   - When Stanton met her future husband, it was a time when men typically laughed at a woman's desire to be free, to live her life the way she wanted, and to keep her last name as

part of her married name. The reader can infer that Henry Stanton respected his wife's ideas about a woman's rights.

8. **According to pages 16 through 21, what was Stanton's shocking idea that she presented at Lucretia Mott's house?**
   - She presented the idea that women should be able to vote. If women voted, she argued, they could help change the laws that held them back.
9. **From the description on pages 24 and 25, explain the historic event on July 19, 1848, and what Stanton's actions reveal about her character.**
   - Women held a meeting in Seneca Falls, New York. Hundreds of people came.
   - Stanton read a paper that she and a few other women had written. Using the Declaration of Independence as a model, they had written a "Declaration of Rights and Sentiments" concerning the rights of women as they perceived and understood them.
   - People clapped when she was finished, and they discussed opinions on what she had read.
10. **What does the author mean by this sentence on page 29: "Elizabeth had tossed a stone in the water and the ripples grew wider and wider and wider"?**
    - The author is using figurative language to describe the way Stanton's ideas about a woman's right to vote were spreading across America, "from Maine to California."
    - The author also writes on page 28 that "word of the meeting spread like wildfire." This means the news of the meeting in Seneca Falls had spread to other parts of the country.

I Could Do That! Esther Morris Gets Women the Vote by Linda Arms White

1. **From page 1 of the text, what do you learn about Esther McQuigg's character? Support your assertions with evidence from the text.**
   - Esther had spunk and determination.
   - She was just six years old when she was asked to learn to serve tea, a very long process for a six-year-old. Back then, they had to pump the water, boil it on a woodstove, pour boiling water over loose tea in a teapot, and strain the tea as they poured it into the cups.
2. **According to page 2, what was the important bit of knowledge that Esther learned as she was looking out her New York window?**
   - She learned that only men could vote.
3. **What can you infer about Esther's role in her family from the pictures and text on pages 4 and 5?**
   - In the illustrations on these pages, Esther seems to be the one who shows effort, even when she is grieving about the death of her mother. Everyone else is drinking tea and dabbing their eyes as she serves the tea.
   - The text says that when the father gathered the eleven children, Esther was the one who took up his challenge to them to "be brave and to take care of one another."
4. **On pages 6 and 7, what do we learn about Esther's talents?**
   - She was a talented seamstress and milliner (hatmaker) who set up her own business in Oswego, New York.
5. **Using the context clues on page 9, what is the meaning of the word *abolitionist*? What does this page tell us about Esther's character?**
   - The people who wanted to tear down the church were those who "believed in the right to own slaves." An abolitionist was a person who was *against* the right to own slaves.

- Esther believed in standing up for what she thought was right.

  Note: *The word* abolish *means "to put something away forever" or "to end something." The word* abolitionist *has come to refer to a person who is against the right to own slaves—someone who wants an end to slavery, specifically. You may want to discuss with students how a word that has a general meaning sometimes becomes more specific because of a link to a certain historical event (in this case, the abolition of slavery).*

6. **According to pages 10 and 11, how was Esther's experience similar to that of the woman who came to Judge Cady for help?**
   - After their husbands' deaths, neither woman could take ownership of her husband's land. This was a law that affected both of the women, even though the woman who approached Judge Cady was in New York and Esther was in Illinois. Esther moved to Illinois after her first husband died, and then she became Esther Morris when she remarried.

7. **According to page 13, who was given the right to vote according to the amendment signed just after the Civil War? How did the author link the signing of that amendment to the issue of women's voting rights?**
   - African American men were given "all rights of citizenship, including the right to vote."
   - The author mentions that Esther had heard Susan B. Anthony speak, giving Esther hope that women might someday also be allowed to vote.

   Note: *The amendment mentioned on page 13 was the Fifteenth Amendment to the Constitution, ratified in 1870. Women were not given the right to vote until the ratification of the Nineteenth Amendment in 1920.*

8. **According to pages 14 through 17, how did life change for Esther in 1869?**
   - Esther and her two sons moved to the Wyoming Territory, where most of the people living in her community were young men who worked all day and drank in the saloons at night.
   - Esther found her role in opening another hat shop, sewing for people, and caring for their physical needs.

9. **How does the book's repeated sentence, "I could do that," change on page 18? Why is that change significant?**
   - Throughout the book, Esther says to every challenge, "I could do that," and then she does her best to meet the challenge.
   - On page 18, when the male citizens are asked to come out and vote, she says, "It's time I did that."
   - The change to the present tense in the phrase shows how Esther came to believe it was time for her to work to secure the right to vote for women.

10. **How did Esther change history by pouring tea?**
    - According to pages 19 through 25, Esther hosted a tea party for the men who were running for the territorial legislature. She made both of the candidates promise to "introduce a bill in the legislature that would allow women to vote." At this tea party, she was able to secure their promises before other people could; the bill was eventually introduced, the legislature passed it, and the governor signed it on December 10, 1869.
    - This was the first time women in the United States were given the right to vote.
    - According to pages 22 and 23, she also became the first woman in the United States "to hold public office." The justice of the peace had resigned after he found out that the law giving women the right to vote had been passed. Ironically, Esther was able to take his place.
    - According to pages 28 through 30, Judge Morris was among the first thousand women in America to vote in a government election.

PERFORMANCE ASSESSMENTS

1. Run copies of the author's note from each of the books. Give students time to closely read and annotate the biographical sketches of the two women. You may also want to give them additional nonfiction resources to add to their research.

Ask the students to use this information, in addition to the information they gathered in the main text of each book, to compare the lives of Stanton and Morris. Ask students to explain the ways the women's lives were similar—and the ways they were different. For example, students might note that the women lived during the same era, and they both died in 1902. Each spent the early part of her life in New York. The year 1869 was an important one for both women in terms of their contributions to history, even though the women were in different places and had different experiences. Neither of the women lived long enough to vote for the U.S. president.

Ask students to craft an informative/explanatory essay that introduces the topic clearly; develop the topic with facts, details, and examples; link ideas; use precise language and domain-specific vocabulary; and provide a concluding statement. At earlier levels, students may write a coherent paragraph that summarizes the main topic and key details. See standards for more details.

2. Give students the following task:

- In an opinion essay, consider the monuments to Elizabeth Cady Stanton or Esther Morris. Both of these women are memorialized with a monument in the Capitol in Washington, DC. In your opinion, which one of these women did more for women's rights?

Note: *You may want to consult the following links for ideas and details:*

http://www.aoc.gov/capitol-hill/other-statues/portrait-monument

http://www.aoc.gov/capitol-hill/national-statuary-hall-collection/esther-hobart-morris

Ask students to be sure to introduce the topic clearly and state an opinion, provide logically ordered reasons, link their opinion and reasons, and offer a concluding statement related to the opinion presented. At earlier levels, students may write a coherent paragraph that summarizes the main topic and key details. See standards for more details.

CONNECTIONS TO COMMON CORE STATE STANDARDS FOR ENGLISH LANGUAGE ARTS

***Elizabeth Leads the Way: Elizabeth Cady Stanton and the Right to Vote* by Tanya Lee Stone**

- Question 1 asks students to examine a cover illustration and consider what they can learn about the content from that illustration (RI.3.7; RI.4.7; RI.5.7).
- Questions 2 and 10 help students analyze figurative language and its ability to help convey content in a vivid way (RL.3.4; RL.4.4; RL.5.4; RI.3.4; RI.4.4; RI.5.4; SL.3.5; SL.4.5; SL.5.5).
  - Question 10 specifically asks students to analyze the author's use of a metaphor (RI.3.4; RI.4.4; RI.5.4; L.3.5; L.4.5; L.5.5).
- Question 3 focuses on how readers can infer information from a series of questions in the text (RI.3.1,2; RI.4.1,2; RI.5.1,2).

- Question 4 requires to students to recall information and use evidence from the text to support their inferences about the main character, noting how the information supports a central idea of the text (RI.3.1,2,3,8; RI.4.1,2,3,8; RI.5.1,2,3,8).
- Questions 5 and 6 help students to appreciate characterization and to note important details about the main subject's early life (RL.3.3; RL.4.3; RL.5.3; RI.3.1,2,3,8; RI.4.1,2,3,8; RI.5.1,2,3,8).
- Question 7 focuses on the author's craft; it asks students to determine why the author uses repetition as a rhetorical device to make an important point (RI.3.1,8; RI.4.1,8; RI.5.1,8).
- Questions 8 and 9 ask students to recall important details in the text that support central ideas (RI.3.1,2; RI.4.1,2; RI.5.1,2).

I Could Do That! Esther Morris Gets Women the Vote by Linda Arms White

- Questions 1 and 2 help students to appreciate characterization and to note important details about the main subject's early life to enhance their appreciation for the subject's actions (RL.3.3; RL.4.3; RL.5.3; RI.3.1,2,3,8; RI.4.1,2,3,8; RI.5.1,2,3,8).
- Somewhat similar to questions 1 and 2, question 3 also helps students to appreciate characterization and to note important details about the main subject's early life. It also asks students to use illustrations to glean information (RL.3.3; RL.4.3; RL.5.3; RI.3.1,2,3,7,8; RI.4.1,2,3,7,8; RI.5.1,2,3,7,8).
- Question 4 asks students to recall information and use evidence from the text to support their inferences about the main character, noting how the information supports a central idea of the text (RI.3.1,2,3,8; RI.4.1,2,3,8; RI.5.1,2,3,8).
- Questions 6 and 7 ask students to draw comparisons between two different characters' experiences and between two different events, respectively (RI.3.1,2,3; RI.4.1,2,3; RI.5.1,2,3).
- Question 9 asks students to note how a technique employed by the author helps convey important historical information (RI.3.1,2,3,5; RI.4.1,2,3,5; RI.5.1,2,3,5).
- Question 10 helps students analyze figurative language and its ability to help convey content in a vivid way (RL.3.4; RL.4.4; RL.5.4; RI.3.4; RI.4.4; RI.5.4; SL.3.5; SL.4.5; SL.5.5).

Performance Assessments

- The first performance assessment gives students a chance to write an informative/ explanatory essay that compares two different texts on a related topic. In particular, students are able to compare two important historical figures (RI.3.1,2,3,6,9; RI.4.1,2,3,6,9; RI.5.1,2,3,6,9; W.3.2; W.4.2; W.5.2).
- The second performance assessment gives students a chance to write an opinion essay in which they must compare two important historical figures, making an argument for which figure made a greater contribution to the historical area discussed (RI.3.1,2,3,6,9; RI.4.1,2,3,6,9; RI.5.1,2,3,6,9; W.3.1; W.4.1; W.5.1).

MORE RESOURCES

HISTORICAL FICTION

Soft Rain: A Story of the Cherokee Trail of Tears by Cornelia Cornelissen

PRIMARY SOURCES

Letter from James Monroe to Thomas Jefferson seeking foreign policy advice, 1823 (Library of Congress)

Andrew Jackson election campaign article, 1825 (Library of Congress)

House of Representatives plan to extinguish the Cherokee land claim, 1825 (Library of Congress)

Names signed on the "Declaration of Rights and Sentiments" at the Women's Rights Convention of 1848 (Library of Congress)

POETRY AND MUSIC

"From Lovely Erin, Sad I Come," sheet music, 1847 (Library of Congress)

ART AND ARCHITECTURE

Illustration of a bobbin girl by Winslow Homer (Lowell National Historical Park)

A House Divided: North versus South

(1820 to 1859)

GRADES: 3, 4, 5

OVERVIEW

The U.S. Constitution banned the importation of slaves after 1807, but it did not answer the challenge of the Declaration of Independence, which asserted that all men have a God-given right to life, liberty, and the pursuit of happiness. As the country rapidly grew, the unresolved controversy over slavery became a bitter and increasingly violent schism. Most northerners held that slavery belittled all those, regardless of race, who lived by their own labor. Joining their horror at the treatment of African American slaves with a desire to see all men free, abolitionists fueled the conversation by exposing the shocking inhumanity of slavery. Among the abolitionists was the eloquent Frederick Douglass, who himself escaped slavery to find refuge in the North. The southern states pushed back against what they felt was a northern attack on their way of life and a violation of states' right to their own self-government. As new western lands were acquired and settled, the sections split over the status of the new territories: Would they be slave states or free states? The government of the young nation found itself unable to handle the crisis, and the sections began to break apart. Lower elementary students who read "When I Reach the Promised Land . . ." and *Henry's Freedom Box: A True Story from the Underground Railroad* will compare and contrast the experiences of two famous slaves who escaped to freedom in an informative/explanatory paragraph. *Words Set Me Free: The Story of Young Frederick Douglass* and an excerpt from *Narrative of the Life of Frederick Douglass, an American Slave* will give upper elementary students the evidence needed to explore, in an informative/explanatory essay, how learning to read set the famous abolitionist free.

○ ○ ○

Interested in learning more about this time period? Read a more complete history in the "Era Summaries."

LEARNING EXPECTATIONS

Lower elementary: Students should understand that northerners were determined to keep slavery from expanding, both for moral reasons and to serve their own interests. In contrast, southerners were determined to maintain slavery's expansion and to protect it, because they saw it as the basis of their way of life. Students should understand that the democratic government could not handle the collision of these views and that the country began to break apart.

Upper elementary: Students should know that the feud over slavery's expansion dominated the 1850s. They should understand that the morally driven abolitionist movement was quite small, but that most northerners—though not abolitionists, not demanding immediate emancipation in the South, and not focusing on the sufferings of slaves themselves—feared slavery would make anyone who worked for a living inferior to slave-owning aristocrats. Students should realize that the issue was made urgent by the rapid addition of new western territories, which had to be made either slave states or free states, and they should know that the quarrel turned increasingly violent over the course of the decade. The country's elected institutions proved unable to solve the crisis, which increasingly threatened the survival of the country.

SUGGESTED ANCHOR TEXTS

Words Set Me Free: The Story of Young Frederick Douglass by Lesa Cline-Ransome
Narrative of the Life of Frederick Douglass, an American Slave, chapter 7 by Frederick Douglass
Liberty for All? 1820–1860 by Joy Hakim
Escape from Slavery: Five Journeys to Freedom by Doreen Rappaport
Frederick Douglass: From Slavery to Statesman by Henry Elliot
Harriet Tubman: A Photographic Story of a Life by Kem Knapp Sawyer
No More! Stories and Songs of Slave Resistance by Doreen Rappaport

FEATURED ANCHOR TEXTS

WORDS SET ME FREE: THE STORY OF YOUNG FREDERICK DOUGLASS BY LESA CLINE-RANSOME

NARRATIVE OF THE LIFE OF FREDERICK DOUGLASS, AN AMERICAN SLAVE, CHAPTER 7 BY FREDERICK DOUGLASS

Words Set Me Free was selected because it tells the story of Douglass's journey into literacy from the first-person point of view. This fictionalized biography provides students with background information that is helpful for understanding Douglass's own writing, which is antiquated and has a tone that is more formal than what most students at this level will generally read. As students closely read the excerpt from Douglass's beautifully written autobiography, they will appreciate his gifted use of language and understand why his writing was such an important part of the abolitionist movement in U.S. history. In a larger sense, students can come to recognize the importance of oratory and rhetoric in historical movements.

TEXT STUDY

The text-dependent questions pertaining to *Words Set Me Free* offer many chances for students to hone literacy skills delineated in the Common Core State Standards for English language arts. Students are asked to consider the text, illustrations, characterization, and the use of figurative language while they learn essential U.S. history content. Further, students have the chance to compare two texts—one literary and one informational—that chronicle the same events.

1. **Look closely at the cover illustration and title of the book. How do the words seem to have a connection to the details in the illustration?**
   - The boy is reading a newspaper (words) on boxes near a seaport.
   - Full-blown sails seem to suggest freedom in travel, as do the birds flying near him.
2. **According to page 1, what is the evidence that young Douglass's mother loved him?**
   - Although she lived on a plantation twelve miles away, she would walk to see him in the night. She would just sit and watch him as he was going to sleep, too tired to talk. He remembered her "rough hands gently stroking his face."
3. **According to page 3, how were the slave children treated?**
   - They ate out of a trough like animals.
   - They ate only twice a day, consuming meals of cornmeal mush.
   - They were whipped for being "too tired or too sick or too slow."
4. **On page 9, which details the moment when Douglass met his new "Missus," Douglass makes this comment, "I was glad no one ever told her that there is a big difference between a servant you pay and a slave you own." What does he mean by that?**
   - Earlier on that same page, Douglass says that she was the "first friendly white face" he had seen.
   - He also says that she "greeted" him.
   - On page 12, the text describes how she would read to him by the fire in the evenings. She read with a kind smile and voice.
   - When he asked the "Missus" to teach him to read, she immediately took down a book from the library in her house and taught him the letter A.

   Note: *The inference here is that the new "Missus" treated him with respect and kindness, the way he imagined a paid servant was treated. This was in stark contrast to his experience as a slave at the other farm.*
5. **According to page 12, how were some slaves treated if they were caught reading? How do you know that the memories of these stories make Douglass afraid?**
   - Douglass remembers that one slave boy's thumb was cut off and that an old master had warned of whippings if slaves tried to read.
   - Douglass uses two fearful expressions:
     - "The letters I was reciting got caught in my throat."
     - "And my mouth was dry."
6. **According to page 14, why did Douglass's reading instruction end?**
   - His master found out and said that reading would make him "forever unfit . . . to be a slave."
7. **How did the master's words inspire Douglass to read more? What does Douglass mean when he says he wanted to "secure [his] freedom one letter at a time"?**
   - On page 14, Douglass's master had said that if Douglass were taught to read, "there would be no keeping him. It would forever unfit him to be a slave."
   - Douglass interpreted his master's words to mean that learning would make him think that he no longer had to be a slave—that he might escape to seek a better life as a free man.
   - Securing his freedom "one letter at a time" is a figure of speech implying that each bit of progress Douglass made with his reading would make him smarter and more confident; it would strengthen his resolve to find a way to live as a free man.

8. **How did Douglass teach himself to write?**
    - According to page 15, he scratched the letters he knew on brick streets and on the wooden fences.
    - According to page 17, he would bring bread to the wharf to trade and ask the white boys to try to write words better than he could in exchange for the bread. He wrote all of the words he saw, and those he remembered from names and newspapers, into a "copy book" that he had taken from the master's six-year-old son.
9. **What did the ships in the harbor represent to Douglass?**
    - The ships represented the idea of freedom: they were free to go as they pleased.

    Note: *This affirms the connection between freedom and ships in the cover illustration.*
10. **According to page 19, why was *abolition* a dangerous word for Douglass to learn when he read the newspaper?**
    - Abolition "called for ending slavery."
    - In the passage on page 19, the word *abolition* is grouped with the words *liberty*, *justice*, and *freedom*. All of these ideas, along with the newspaper stories of blacks in the North who were free, gave Douglass hope that he would also someday be free.
11. **When Douglass returned to his old plantation, what had changed inside of him? Why was he "free on the inside but not yet free on the outside"? Cite evidence from the text on pages 21 and 22 that describes the change.**
    - Even though it seemed to everyone else that he was still the same slave boy, he could now read and write.
        - On page 21, he says, "Though my copy books and newspapers were long gone, words comforted me in the fields as I chopped cotton . . . And words lay down with me at night, when my body ached with pain and hunger. I knew that words would put an end to my suffering. I just wasn't sure when and how."

        Note: *Teachers might pause to discuss the figurative use of "words" here: they are personified, reinforcing the idea that words (reading and writing, knowledge) are powerful tools. This is also an opportunity to talk to students about the power of memorization: making words your own means that nobody can take them away from you.*

    An extension assignment might be to ask students to memorize a few lines from Douglass's autobiography, one of his speeches, or a thematically related poem.
12. **How did Douglass's words allow him to attempt an escape from slavery?**
    - He wrote a permission note for himself to leave the plantation for an Easter vacation in Baltimore. He signed his master's name to the letter.

    Note: *According to the author's note, his plan did not work, and he was caught.*
13. **According to the author's note, how was Douglass finally freed, and what did he do with his freedom?**
    - He was able to find freedom through the Underground Railroad.
    - He became a well-known abolitionist who wrote a book called *Narrative of the Life of Frederick Douglass, an American Slave* and began an abolitionist newspaper called the *North Star*.
14. **The content of Words Set Me Free runs parallel to the events recounted in chapter 7 of *Narrative of the Life of Frederick Douglass, an American Slave*. After reading and studying**

the fictionalized version of the story, read this challenging primary source aloud to the students. Have students memorize the following excerpt or recite it as a dramatic reading:

> The silver trump of freedom had roused my soul to eternal wakefulness. Freedom now appeared, to disappear no more forever. It was heard in every sound, and seen in everything. It was ever present to torment me with a sense of my wretched condition. I saw nothing without seeing it, I heard nothing without hearing it, and felt nothing without feeling it. It looked from every star, it smiled in every calm, breathed in every wind, and moved in every storm.

PERFORMANCE ASSESSMENT

Ask students to write an informative/explanatory essay in response to the following task:

- How did words set Frederick Douglass free? Use evidence gathered throughout the study of *Words Set Me Free* and from chapter 7 of *Narrative of the Life of Frederick Douglass, an American Slave* to support your assertions.

Ask students to be sure to introduce the topic clearly; develop the topic with facts, details, and examples; link ideas; use precise language and domain-specific vocabulary; and provide a concluding statement. At earlier levels, students may write a coherent paragraph that summarizes the main topic and key details. See standards for more details.

EXTENSION

Divide your students into teams of four to do the following activity:

- Choose an abolitionist from the antebellum era. Research the life of the abolitionist, the driving forces in his or her passion for abolition, and his or her writings and speeches. Create a readers' theater presentation combining the story of the abolitionist with real words from his or her writing.

Have students perform the readers' theater presentation for other classes. Students might also create a photobiography of the abolitionist to show as the readers' theater presentation is performed.

CONNECTIONS TO COMMON CORE STATE STANDARDS FOR ENGLISH LANGUAGE ARTS

- Question 1 asks about the relationship between the title and the cover illustration, prompting students to think carefully about the content to come (RL.3.4,7; RL.4.4,7; RL.5.4,7).
- Question 2 asks students to read closely to understand the relationship between a character's actions and her feelings (RL.3.3; RL.4.3; RL.5.3).
- Questions 3, 6, 7, 8, 10, 12, and 13 require students to recall details that support a central idea of the story (RL.3.1; RL.4.1; RL.5.1).
- Question 4 requires students to compare two parts of the book and different characters' actions to understand Douglass's observation about his new "Missus" (RL.3.1,2,3; RL.4.1,2,3; RL.5.1,2,3).
- Question 5 prompts students to make connections between a character's actions and his memories (RL.3.1,2,3,5; RL.4.1,2,3,5; RL.5.1,2,3,5).

- Question 7 asks students to make inferences from characters' words and to consider how one character's actions inspire actions in another character (RL.3.1,2,3; RL.4.1,2,3; RL.5.1,2,3).
- Question 9 addresses the author's use of a powerful image to represent a central idea in this text (RL.3.5,7; RL.4.5,7; RL.5.5,7).
- Question 11 helps students understand powerful figurative language that underscores a central theme of the text (RL.3.1,2,3,4; RL.4.1,2,3,4; RL.5.1,2,3,4; SL.3.5; SL.4.5; SL.5.5).
- The performance assessment gives students an opportunity to reread closely and render their deep understanding of the text in an informative/explanatory essay—not simply by summarizing events, but rather by explaining the connections between an author's use of figurative language, actual events in the subject's life, and the historic implications of these events (RL.3.1,2,3,4; RL.4.1,2,3,4; RL.5.1,2,3,4; SL.3.5; SL.4.5; SL.5.5; W.3.2; W.4.2; W.5.2).

MORE RESOURCES

HISTORICAL FICTION

My Name is Henry Bibb: A Story of Slavery and Freedom by Afua Cooper

PRIMARY SOURCES

Antislavery meeting poster (Library of Congress)

Abraham Lincoln campaign poster (Library of Congress)

Inauguration of Mr. Lincoln, photograph, 1861 (Library of Congress)

"A Number of Valuable Slaves: Life as an Enslaved People" (Library of Virginia)

Contains many primary source documents within

Advertisement for a slave sale in New Orleans, 1835 (Virginia Foundation for the Humanities and the University of Virginia Library)

Slave auction in Richmond, Virginia, illustration, 1830s (Virginia Foundation for the Humanities and the University of Virginia Library)

"The Atlantic Slave Trade and Slave Life in the Americas: A Visual Record" (Virginia Foundation for the Humanities and the University of Virginia Library)

Contains over twelve hundred images of primary sources, arranged into eighteen categories

POETRY AND MUSIC

Follow the Drinking Gourd: A Cultural History

USEFUL WEBSITE

"The African-American Experience in Ohio: 1850–1920" (Ohio Historical Society)

Blue versus Gray: Civil War and Reconstruction

(1860 to 1877)

GRADES: 3, 4, 5

OVERVIEW

Whether the United States would survive as a nation was at times not altogether certain during the Civil War. The political parties had grown even further apart over the slavery issue. The Democrats' 1860 convention split, with the North and South each nominating its own presidential candidate. The Republicans coalesced behind Abraham Lincoln. Because of the strength of the Republicans in the North, Lincoln became the sixteenth president (without ever being listed on ballots in the South). Convinced that the antislavery radicals had seized control of Washington, South Carolina voted to secede from the Union, and other Southern states soon followed. They formed their own nation: the Confederate States of America. With no common ground to be found between the North and South on the issue of federal and state sovereignty or on the issue of the future of slavery, the nation plunged into outright civil war. What began as a fight to save the Union and uphold democracy would eventually grow, due to Lincoln's own resolution, into a larger battle over the final abolition of slavery. The end of the Civil War left many unsolved questions—how to rebuild the South, how to reincorporate it into the Union, and the rights and protection of freed former slaves. Lower elementary students will read *Abraham Lincoln: Lawyer, Leader, Legend* to uncover the sixteenth president's evolving views on slavery, and they will present his ideological development on an illustrated timeline. *A Civil War Scrapbook: I Was There Too!* gives upper elementary students opportunities to compare and contrast the actions of individuals who were seen as heroes by those on one side of the war and as villains by those on the other, and to then craft an opinion essay defending their conclusion on how one such individual should be remembered.

○ ○ ○

Interested in learning more about this time period? Read a more complete history in the "Era Summaries."

LEARNING EXPECTATIONS

Lower elementary: Students should understand that though the crisis was rooted in slavery, the Civil War began as a battle over the fate of the Union. Yet they should also understand that, as the events of the war spurred people to reconsider their views, it became a war to end slavery as well. Lincoln's role as the Union's leader and his iconic status in American memory should be emphasized. Students should also understand that the end of slavery was just the start of a long fight to establish full civil rights for African Americans.

Upper elementary: Students should understand how the division of the country and the fracturing of the political parties allowed states in the North to elect Lincoln, and how the South's rejection of his election sparked secession. They should know that the North believed the Union must be saved to save democracy, and also that Southerners—most of whom were not slave owners—were willing to fight to protect their states from what they saw as outside control. Students should understand Lincoln's role in deciding to expand the war against slavery; they should realize that hard fighting against the South by black troops and the impressive example they set helped convince most Northerners that slavery must be ended forever. Students should realize that those advocating for "radical" Reconstruction tried to keep ex-Confederates from controlling the South by empowering African Americans, but that northern reluctance to press so far helped southern resistance win in the end. The Reconstruction amendments to the Constitution should be remembered for their later importance as the fight for African American rights continued.

SUGGESTED ANCHOR TEXTS

A *Civil War Scrapbook: I Was There Too!* by History Colorado
War, Terrible War: 1855–1865 by Joy Hakim
Abe's Honest Words by Doreen Rappaport
Bull Run by Paul Fleischman
Civil War Sampler (Harper's Weekly) by Applewood Books
Lincoln and His Boys by Rosemary Wells
Pink and Say by Patricia Polacco
The Brothers' War: Civil War Voices in Verse by J. Patrick Lewis
What Was the Battle of Gettysburg? by Jim O'Connor

FEATURED ANCHOR TEXT

A CIVIL WAR SCRAPBOOK: I WAS THERE TOO! BY HISTORY COLORADO

This book was selected because it is a comprehensive look at the Civil War period in United States history. Using a scrapbook-style compilation of primary sources, such as photographs, maps, and newspaper articles, each short section describes the battles, various important people, and events. The book covers many different aspects of the war, including music, photography, the role of women, and the reporting of news. Repeated features in the book, such as "Hero/Villain" and "I was there too!" encourage students to examine the different perspectives on historical events and to appreciate the words of those who were there at the time. The student activities in the book are well written and connected to the fascinating historical accounts in the text.

TEXT STUDY

These text-dependent questions and the performance assessment and extension that follow them give students many opportunities to examine a book with an innovative structure for conveying information about a series of important and related historical events. They allow students to analyze the usefulness of primary source accounts and other accounts about key figures and events in U.S. history. They also give students a chance to compare, contrast, and compile information about the characters and events in a way that hones their inferring skills and helps them form and support their own opinions.

1. **Read closely the table of contents on page 3 of the text. How have the authors organized the information in this book, which is focused on the four-year Civil War?**
   - The war is covered by topic, such as "Slavery and the Civil War" and "The Beginning."
   - The chapters that cover battles are printed in red to distinguish them from chapters addressing the other topics.
   - Both topics and battles are arranged chronologically.
   - There is a glossary, timeline, bibliography, credit list, and index included at the end of the text.

   Note: *Front-loading instruction by noting the structure of this text is very important because it might otherwise be difficult to follow. Going between topical text and historical accounts of major battles might lead to confusion among students.*

2. **According to pages 4 and 5 of the text, how did the demand for goods lead to the Civil War?**
   - Farming was important to the South because of the warm climate and fertile soil.
   - The South grew such crops as sugar, rice, tobacco, and cotton.
   - As the demand for these goods increased, farmers needed to increase the size of their farms and needed laborers to work in the fields.
   - Slaves provided cheap labor for plantation owners.
   - The individual states were permitted to decide whether slavery was allowed to exist.
   - The South insisted that the demand for goods could not be met unless slavery were allowed to continue.

3. **Explain why the Missouri Compromise was not a lasting solution to the problem of which states were to be slave and which were to be free, according to page 5.**
   - In 1820, the Missouri Compromise divided slave states and free states all the way to the Pacific Ocean.
   - The Missouri Compromise didn't decide every issue involving slavery, such as
     - What to do with slavery in regard to the statehood of California and Oregon
     - How to settle the slavery issue in Nebraska and Kansas
     - How to deal with slave owners who wanted to move with their slaves to places where slavery was illegal

   Note: *There is more information on the Missouri Compromise on page 17 of this text.*

4. **After reading the eight minibiographies on pages 6 and 7, create pairs or groups of people based on commonalities you notice among them.**
   - Dred Scott and Frederick Douglass were both slaves at one time and were involved in the abolition of slavery, either indirectly or directly.

- Harriet Beecher Stowe and Douglass each used writing as a way to bring the slavery issue and need for abolition to the public. Stowe wrote a novel, and Douglass wrote a narrative of his life as a slave.
- Scott, Stowe, Douglass, and Lincoln were all instrumental in bringing the issues of slavery and states' rights to the forefront of people's minds.
- Lincoln and Jefferson Davis were the presidents of opposing sides during the Civil War. Lincoln led the North (the Union), and Davis led the South (the Confederacy).
- Davis and Robert E. Lee were both Confederates. Davis was the president of the new Confederacy, and Lee was the general in charge of the Confederate army.
- Lee and Grant were generals of opposing sides in the war, and they both graduated from West Point.
- Grant and Clara Barton were both on the Union side of the war. Grant was the leader of the army, and Barton was a medical worker during the war.

  Note: *This list will extend as students see more commonalities among the Americans who had to take sides based on convictions and loyalty to their country.*

5. **According to page 9, how did the issue of "state's rights" contribute to the decisions by states in the South to secede?**
   - The slave states believed that it was their "right" to decide what happened with slavery within their borders.
   - The free states in the North believed that if the majority ruled on not allowing slavery, the slave states would have to go along with the ruling. Slave states couldn't leave just because they disagreed with the majority.
   - The slave states believed that they could withdraw from the United States if they decided it was necessary.
   - Eleven slave states "**seceded**" from the United States and formed their own country, the Confederate States of America.
6. **According to page 12, why did citizens from Washington, DC, ride thirty miles by carriage to watch a battle near Bull Run? How does this attitude among Union citizens and soldiers help explain the "lesson learned" on page 14?**
   - Both the soldiers and the citizens thought it would be a "short clash" or an "easy win" for the Union.
   - The "lesson learned" was this: "Never underestimate your opponent's skill, especially when spirit and determination are involved."
   - The citizens of the Union and the soldiers believed that this war would be over after a few battles. The Union felt that with this win and the control of the railroad, they would be able to take over Richmond, Virginia, and the war would be over.
   - The Confederate troops had warning from a spy to be prepared for the battle, and nothing happened as expected.
   - The war would drag on for four long years because both sides were determined.

   Note: *You may want to point out the difference between the Northern and Southern practices of naming the battles, as described in the photo caption on page 13.*
7. **According to page 17 of the text, why did Missouri have such a central role leading up to the Civil War?**
   - Missouri's admission to the Union was all about the balance of slave and free states. Missouri was admitted as a slave state in 1820, and Maine was admitted as a free state to keep the balance.

- The Missouri Compromise and its imaginary line, dividing slave and free states, kept the peace in the United States for about forty years.
- The case involving Scott had to do with Missouri. Scott was a slave, the "property" of a woman who was from Missouri. When she moved to free states, she brought Scott and his family with her. Scott had a daughter born in a free state. When the family returned to Missouri, Scott sued for his freedom because he had lived for such a long time in a free state. The Supreme Court ultimately ruled that Scott "was considered property and not allowed to enjoy the rights and privileges of a US citizen."

  Note: *It should probably be noted that the preceding quotation reflects the language in the book, not that in the actual decision.*
- Abolitionists were angry about the decision, and it intensified their efforts to try to end slavery.

8. **How does the "Hero/Villain" inset on page 25 attempt to show different perspectives on a person's role in history?**
   - John Chivington was considered a hero by some and a villain by others for his various actions.
   - He was a hero because he was the Union major who "discovered and destroyed more than seventy Confederate supply wagons carrying food and ammunition." This discovery and destruction of the supply line caused the Confederacy to lose New Mexico and crippled its capability to expand westward.
   - He was also a villain because he led a massacre in 1864 against "a peaceful village of Cheyenne and Arapaho Indians." He killed 130 Native Americans, including 105 women and children. These Native Americans were under the protection of the U.S. government.
9. **According to pages 28 and 29 in the text, why did women have to be determined and creative to be active in the Civil War?**
   - During this era, women had few legal rights, were not allowed to vote, and were not encouraged to become well educated—nor could they own property, except through inheritance.
   - Because of these limitations, and because they were barred from enlisting in military service, women had to use trickery to be active as soldiers in the war. To enlist, some dressed as men and had to maintain the disguise in battle.
   - Some women went along with their husbands and acted as "vivandières" during the war. These women often supplied comfort to the injured and assisted behind the lines in battle.
   - Other women, such as Belle Boyd and Rose O'Neal Greenhow, served as Confederate spies; others served as nurses, such as Clara Barton.

     Note: *Barton is described on page 7.*
10. **In the first paragraph of page 30, what does "change hands" mean in regard to Harpers Ferry?**
    - Harpers Ferry was an "excellent location for providing power for new industries and transportation." It was also the home of an armory of weapons and supplies.
    - Both the Union and the Confederacy wanted to control the town and its resources.
    - When the authors say "causing the town to change hands repeatedly during the Civil War," they are noting that the town kept switching back and forth between Union control and Confederate control.
11. **Describe how John Brown was a hero to some and a villain to others.**
    - According to page 31, Brown was a hero in abolitionist communities. He gave weapons to slaves so that they could rise up against slavery in 1859. He was later tried for treason and hanged.

- He was a villain to slave owners who were against his tactics of arming slaves and "thought he was an insane and dangerous enemy."

12. **How does the "I was there too!" feature contribute to your understanding of the Harpers Ferry history described on page 31?**
    - Annie P. Marmion's story tells of the stress felt by young children during the Civil War, especially in a central place for battles, such as Harpers Ferry.
    - Because this excerpt is a primary source, the reader can read a firsthand account from someone who lived through the time period or specific event. It gives the reader empathy for families living in this place at this time.
    - It explains how children of that time tried to find food to eat and places dark enough to hide.

    Note: *These excerpts help students understand the power of primary sources and learn more about specific people and events described elsewhere in the text.*

13. **According to pages 36 and 37, why is Antietam a well-remembered battle in the Civil War?**
    - Twenty-three thousand soldiers were killed or wounded in the "bloodiest, single-day battle of the Civil War."
    - It was a battle that could have been a decisive victory for the Union if General George B. McClellan had acted quickly on Lee's battle plans, a copy of which had been found by Union scouts and given to McClellan.
    - If the Confederates had won in this Union state (Maryland), it would have convinced "France and England to officially recognize" the Confederacy, and the United States would have had "to accept the new nation and end the war."

14. **According to page 39, what did the Emancipation Proclamation actually do? What did it *not* do?**
    - The Emancipation Proclamation freed all of the slaves in the states that had seceded from the Union as of January 1, 1863.
    - It did not make slavery illegal. Until the passage of the Thirteenth Amendment in 1865, slavery was still legal.

15. **How did the Battle of Gettysburg begin?**
    - According to the text on page 42, Lee was gathering troops to invade Harrisburg, the capital of Pennsylvania.
    - In the meantime, one of the rebel troops got permission to go into the town of Gettysburg to buy shoes for the soldiers.
    - Union soldiers were there, and the battle began.

16. **According to the text on page 45, why was the Gettysburg Address so powerful?**
    - It helped provide the Union with the will to see the war through to the end.
    - Perhaps it was powerful because it was short, beautifully written, and to the point. The text says that another speech that day—a two-hour speech—has now been forgotten.
    - "The speech honors those who fought to preserve the democratic ideal of one nation governed by the will of its people."

17. **According to the text on page 57, how did Grant show generosity in the terms offered for Lee's surrender?**
    - Grant ordered that food be given to the Confederate troops who were hungry.
    - He allowed the troops to keep their horses and mules.
    - The Union took no prisoners of war, instead allowing all of the soldiers to return home.

18. What was the purpose of the Freedmen's Bureau during the Reconstruction period? What happened to newly freed slaves after it closed in 1872?

- The Freedmen's Bureau was started to help the freed slaves "find jobs, land, housing, and education."
- After the Freedmen's Bureau closed in 1872, southern states passed laws to take away the rights just recently given to freed slaves. They were "forced into low-paying jobs, terrible living conditions, and poor schools."

PERFORMANCE ASSESSMENT

Have students go back through the text and choose one of the people featured in a "Hero/Villain" section. Students should reread the description of the person's positive and negative actions and do further research into the heroic/villainous actions mentioned in the text.

Ask students to complete the following task:

- In your opinion, should this person be regarded as a "hero" or as a "villain" in history? Be sure to support your opinion with evidence from this text and from your research.

Ask students to be sure to introduce the topic clearly and state an opinion, provide logically ordered reasons, link the opinion and reasons, and offer a concluding statement related to the opinion presented. At earlier levels, students may write a coherent paragraph that summarizes their opinion and reasons for it. See standards for more details.

EXTENSION

To make the first battle of the Civil War more real to students, ask them to read Paul Fleishman's book *Bull Run*, the multivoiced telling of the story of the First Battle of Bull Run. Supply students with a Civil War–era map to plot the movement of the characters toward the battlefield from all over the Union and the Confederacy as the story progresses. Allow each student to choose a character to focus on, watching how the character changes by meeting challenges throughout the event. Lead discussions throughout the reading of the book to discuss the role of point of view in the telling of a chronological event. Focusing on heroes/villains profiled in *A Civil War Scrapbook* provides a way to compare and contrast literary and informational accounts.

CONNECTIONS TO COMMON CORE STATE STANDARDS FOR ENGLISH LANGUAGE ARTS

- Question 1 helps students understand the importance of examining and analyzing the structure of an informational text and gives them practice in using a table of contents effectively (RI.3.5; RI.4.5; RI.5.5).
- Questions 2, 3, 5, 7, 13, 14, 15, 17, and 18 ask students to cite evidence from the text when recalling and explaining important details—and cause-and-effect concepts—in an informational text (RI.3.1,2,3,5,8; RI.4.1,2,3,5,8; RI.5.1,2,3,5,8).
- Question 4 encourages students to read closely and compare information in an informational text, requiring them to think critically about the similarities among key

individuals or groups described and use knowledge of these qualities and experiences to evaluate generalizations presented about the people and events (RI.3.1,2,3,6; RI.4.1,2,3,6; RI.5.1,2,3,6).

- Question 6 prompts students to consider similarities and differences among the actions and beliefs of distinct groups of people based on information given in an informational text as well as subsequent inferences drawn from that information (RI.3.1,2,3,6; RI.4.1,2,3,6; RI.5.1,2,3,6).
- Questions 8 and 11 each ask students to analyze different historical perspectives on the actions of a key individual in this text and, by necessity, to examine the structural features (insets, including primary source accounts) of this informational text (RI.3.1,2,3,6,7,8; RI.4.1,2,3,6,7,8; RI.5.1,2,3,6,7,8).
- Question 10 requires students to examine figurative language in the context of important historical content (RI.3.1,4; RI.4.1,4; RI.5.1,4; L.3.5; L.4.5; L.5.5).
- Question 12 focuses on the purpose and efficacy of the recurring primary source feature in this informational text, "I was there too!" Answering this question helps students understand the relationship between the insets and the "main" text (RI.3.1,2,3,6,7,8; RI.4.1,2,3,6,7,8; RI.5.1,2,3,6,7,8).
- Question 16 helps students form opinions about a historic speech (a form of informational text), using the evidence and details provided by the authors (RI.3.1,2,3,7,8; RI.4.1,2,3,7,8; RI.5.1,2,3,7,8).
- The performance assessment asks students to use evidence from the book when writing an opinion essay about one of the characters they have learned about in the text and through further research (W.3.1,7,9; W.4.1,7,9; W.5.1,7,9).
- The extension gives students a chance to read related historical fiction and to compare two texts of different types written on the same subject. Students have the chance to examine character development and to compare points of view both within the literary text and between the literary text and the informational text (RL.3.1,2,3,6; RL.4.1,2,3,6; RL.5.1,2,3,6; RI.3.1,6,9; RI.4.1,6,9; RI.5.1,6,9).

MORE RESOURCES

HISTORICAL FICTION

Forty Acres and Maybe a Mule by Harriette Gillem Robinet

PRIMARY SOURCES

Collection of Civil War images and primary sources (Library of Congress)

Resources for teachers: "The Civil War through A Child's Eye" (Library of Congress)
Fort Sumter, December 9th 1863, View of South East Angle (Library of Congress)

White flag of truce, 1865 (Smithsonian Institution)

Images of military activities and the Civil War (Virginia Foundation for the Humanities and the University of Virginia Library)

POETRY AND MUSIC

"Glory Hallelujah!" (song associated with the Union army), 1862 (Library of Congress)

"Southern Soldier Boy" (song from the Confederacy), 1863 (Library of Congress)

ART AND ARCHITECTURE

Abraham Lincoln's Gettysburg Address, read by Harry E. Humphrey, 1914 (Library of Congress)

Surrender of General Lee, 1865 (Smithsonian Institution)

USEFUL WEBSITE

"Civil War History Center" (Civil War Trust)

Resistance and Recovery: Rebuilding a War-Torn Nation

(1870s to 1890s)

GRADES: 3, 4, 5

OVERVIEW

With casualties on both sides numbering in the hundreds of thousands, the North and the South moved at different paces in their respective recoveries from the nightmare of the American Civil War. At the same time, expansion to the West accelerated as new railroads provided a means to move people and goods into newly opened lands, with devastating consequences for the Native American nations that lived there. Advances in machinery and industry took hold, and cities prospered while, conversely, farming products sank in value. Industrialization, however, often brought even harsher conditions for the working poor. Eventually, new labor movements demanded safer working conditions and fairer wages. At the same time, Europe also was experiencing its own population boom, which led to overcrowded cities and towns and few opportunities for work. America shone as a beacon of opportunity to Europeans, but immigrants often encountered discrimination in America and struggled to make new lives in northern cities. African Americans, too, would face new barriers in their quest for freedom: segregation and sharecropping became the way of the "New South," and northern states were far from free of discriminatory practices. Lower elementary students will read *Journey of a Pioneer* and determine the most important character quality of a pioneer, using evidence from the text to defend their opinion. Chief Joseph's "Lincoln Hall Speech" from 1879 gives upper elementary students the context to articulate, in a well-supported informative/explanatory essay, how Joseph made the case for equality.

○ ○ ○

Interested in learning more about this time period? Read a more complete history in the "Era Summaries."

LEARNING EXPECTATIONS

Lower elementary: Students should understand that late-nineteenth-century America became more diverse, but also more divided. Immigrants began arriving in great numbers, but many already living in America did not want them there. Settlers moved west, but the prices of farm goods fell; work could be hard to find, and some industrialists became very rich while their workers stayed very poor. Students should know that discrimination and segregation became rampant in the South.

Upper elementary: Students should understand the enormous strains that the "Gilded Age" brought to America: industry leaders achieved enormous prosperity, but at the cost of poverty for their workers; opportunity brought masses of new immigrants, who then faced discrimination and exclusion; western settlement brought new hope for settlers, but falling farm prices meant deep debt for many of them; and the Plains Indians were nearly destroyed in the process of westward expansion. Students should realize that although the New South represented a modernization of the region, many remained mired in poverty, working for low wages or sharecropping—especially African Americans, who faced increasing discrimination and the rise of open Jim Crow segregation.

SUGGESTED ANCHOR TEXTS

Chief Joseph's "Lincoln Hall Speech," 1879
Reconstructing America: 1865–1890 by Joy Hakim
"Into the West," *Cobblestone*, January 2008
Liberty by Lynn Curlee
"The Gilded Age," *Cobblestone*, April 2000
The Ledgerbook of Thomas Blue Eagle by Jewel H. Grutman
Thomas Edison: A Photographic Story of a Life by Jan Adkins

FEATURED ANCHOR TEXT

CHIEF JOSEPH'S "LINCOLN HALL SPEECH," 1879

This speech was selected because it eloquently explains the plight of the Nez Perce chief after so many promises were broken between the U.S. government and the Nez Perce tribe. Reading the words of the chief himself gives students an opportunity not only to glean important historical information but also to learn how an orator uses reason and rhetorical devices as he argues an injustice.

TEXT STUDY

Note: To give background for this speech, you will want to read a biography of Chief Joseph or a book on the history of the Nez Perce people's relationship with the white man—beginning with the French traders and then Meriwether Lewis and William Clark, up to the time of the speech in 1879.

Answering the text-dependent questions correctly requires that students read closely. Many of the questions offer teachers opportunities to reiterate the Common Core State Standards for English language arts, particularly those that address how an argument is structured, how evidence may support assertions, and effective rhetorical devices in speeches.

1. **According to paragraphs 1 and 2 of the speech, what is it that Chief Joseph claims he does not understand? How does the chief explain the problem?**
   - Joseph doesn't understand how government officials are allowed to "promise so many different things," but not keep their promises.
   - He doesn't understand how U.S. government officials talk: "While their mouths talk right I do not understand why nothing is done for my people."

2. **How does Chief Joseph support his argument in paragraph 3 that "good words do not last long unless they amount to something"?**
   - The chief uses repetition of sentence structure (a common rhetorical device in oratory) to convey his frustration and to offer supporting evidence for his assertion in paragraph 2 and in the opening sentence of paragraph 3. He says:
     - "Good words do not last long unless they amount to something."
     - "Words do not pay for my dead people."
     - "They do not pay for my country overrun by white men."
     - "They do not protect my father's grave."
     - "They do not pay for my horses and cattle."
     - "Good words do not give back my children."
     - "Good words will not make good the promise of your war chief, General Miles."
     - "Good words will not give my people a home where they can live in peace and take care of themselves."

   Note: *Teachers might use this as an opportunity to teach about this common rhetorical device in oratory, asking students why and how the repetition serves the orator's purpose.*

3. **What solutions for peace does Chief Joseph offer in his speech?**
   - In paragraph 4, he suggests that we "treat all men alike" and "give them the same laws." "Give them all an even chance to live and grow," he says.
     - He reinforces these suggestions in paragraphs 6, 8, and 9.
   - In paragraph 10, he says, "Whenever the white man treats the Indian as they treat each other, then we shall have no more wars."

4. **How does Chief Joseph convince the listener that his people will never prosper in a confined space, such as a reservation?**
   - In paragraph 5, he uses metaphors, other vivid imagery, and a rhetorical question to illustrate the faults in the government's reasoning:
     - "You might as well expect all rivers to run backward as that any man who was born a free man should be contented penned up and denied liberty."
     - "If you tie a horse to a stake, do you expect he will grow fat?"

5. **According to Chief Joseph, why do his people have to move from where they are?**
   - In paragraph 6, he says they are dying where they are.

6. **In paragraphs 6 through 10, what is Chief Joseph asking for?**
   - In paragraphs 6 through 8, he asks for equality—"to be treated as all other men are treated," to "have a home in a country where my people will not die so fast," to have an "even chance to live as other men live," and to be "recognized as men"; he asks that "the same law shall work alike on all men."
   - In paragraph 9, he asks for freedom: "Let me be a free man, free to travel, free to stop, free to work, free to trade where I choose, free to choose my own teachers, free to follow the religion of my fathers, free to talk, think, and act for myself."
   - In paragraph 10, he requests that the white men "[treat] the Indian as they treat each other."

7. **Why do you think that Chief Joseph chose to close his speech using the name "Hin-mah-too-yah-lat-kekht"?**
   - According to the footnote, this was his Nez Perce name, meaning "Thunder Coming Up Over the Land From the Water." In the closing, Joseph says, "Hin-mah-too-yah-lat-kekht has spoken for his people." Because he is speaking for his own Native American nation, he is

probably using the name they would recognize, as opposed to "Chief Joseph," a name recognized by the white men.

- It's possible that he thought that his own people and the white men in his audience might recognize the power of the thunder imagery.

PERFORMANCE ASSESSMENT

In this speech, Joseph is asking that his people be treated as any other people are treated. Work with your students to examine the word *equality*. Ask them to write a well-developed informative/explanatory essay describing how the chief makes his case for equality. Ask students to be sure to introduce the topic clearly; develop the topic with facts, details, and examples; link ideas; use precise language and domain-specific vocabulary; and provide a concluding statement. At earlier levels, students may write a coherent paragraph that summarizes the main topic and key details. See standards for more details.

EXTENSION

In paragraph 4 of Joseph's speech, he says, "Treat all men alike. Give them the same laws. Give them all an even chance to live and grow. All men were made by the same Great Spirit Chief. They are all brothers. The earth is the mother of all people, and all people should have equal rights upon it." Help students compare this quotation from Joseph's speech to other U.S. documents and speeches in which similar "all men are created equal" statements are made (for example, speeches by Thomas Jefferson, Abraham Lincoln, Elizabeth Cady Stanton, Martin Luther King Jr., and John F. Kennedy).

As a class, place these famous documents and speeches in chronological order to show how the country began on the premise of equality but has not lived by it for much of its history. Illustrate the timeline, showing the historical context with such primary sources as photographs, documents, ads, or illustrations from the time. Post the timeline along a school hallway or combine the work of the class into a single multimedia presentation.

CONNECTIONS TO COMMON CORE STATE STANDARDS FOR ENGLISH LANGUAGE ARTS

- Question 1 asks students to identify the main idea of the first two paragraphs of this speech by citing evidence (RI.3.1,2; RI.4.1,2; RI.5.1,2).
- Questions 2 and 4 prompt students to identify and appreciate how the speaker builds his argument. In particular, they ask students not only to recognize and explain common rhetorical devices but also to cite examples (RI.3.1,2,5,8; RI.4.1,2,5,8; RI.5.1,2,5,8).
- Question 3 helps students recognize the organizational structure of the speech, requiring them to note where and how the speaker offers solutions to the problem he has previously described (RI.3.1,2,5,8; RI.4.1,2,5,8; RI.5.1,2,5,8).
- Questions 5 and 6 ask students to cite evidence pertaining to details in the text (RI.3.1,2,3,8; RI.4.1,2,3,8; RI.5.1,2,3,8).

- Question 7 focuses the students' attention on the speechwriter's craft, asking them to predict why Chief Joseph made a choice to use his Native American name in closing (RI.3.8; RI.4.8; RI.5.8).
- The performance assessment asks students to reread the text closely, focusing on its central theme, and then to convey their understanding of the theme (and how the speaker makes his argument) in an informative/explanatory essay (RI.3.1,2,3,8; RI.4.1,2,3,8; RI.5.1,2,3,8; W.3.2,9; W.4.2,9; W.5.2,9).
- The extension gives students and teachers a chance to explore the theme of this speech in other speeches and documents throughout U.S. history and helps students place those speeches and documents in historical context (RI.3.1,2,3,8,9; RI.4.1,2,3,8,9; RI.5.1,2,3,8,9; SL.3.1; SL.4.1; SL.5.1; W.3.7,8,9; W.4.7,8,9; W.5.7,8,9).

MORE RESOURCES

HISTORICAL FICTION

Thunder Rolling in the Mountains by Scott O'Dell

PRIMARY SOURCES

Photographs of Native Americans by Edward S. Curtis (Library of Congress)

Inspection station at Ellis Island (Library of Congress)

Map of immigration routes (Library of Congress)

Young miners (Library of Congress)

USEFUL WEBSITE

Biography of Chief Joseph (Oregon History Project)

The Next Benchmark: America Is a Global Leader

(1890s to 1920)

GRADES: 3, 4, 5

OVERVIEW

The United States grew stronger and more stable as it moved away from the chaos of the Civil War and built economic strength. The time soon came for the nation to take its rightful place as a leader on the world stage. The brief Spanish-American War, America's role in settling the Russo-Japanese War, and the nation's powerful position in world commerce made a forceful global impression. While America's global presence grew, however, there were complex problems that needed to be addressed at home. Progressives challenged the social and economic injustices that still lingered from the Industrial Revolution, and women's rights came to the forefront. But although progress was made on these fronts, racial discrimination continued—and unresolved issues would haunt the growing country for decades to come. Lower elementary students will read *A Weed Is a Flower: The Life of George Washington Carver* and then use evidence from George Washington Carver's biography to explain how Carver was a transformational historical figure. Upper elementary students will read two texts about Ellis Island. They will then explain its significance, drawing on evidence from first-person and historical accounts.

○ ○ ○

Interested in learning more about this time period? Read a more complete history in the "Era Summaries."

LEARNING EXPECTATIONS

Lower elementary: Students should understand that America became more and more powerful in the world as it became more economically important, leading to new engagement as a world power. They should also understand that Americans pressed for bold reforms to address growing social and economic inequality at home.

Upper elementary: Students should understand that American global influence grew steadily as the country became more economically powerful and more closely tied to the rest of the world.

They should know that the Spanish-American War launched the United States as a true world power, and that it sparked debate at home over whether America should build an empire overseas. Students should know that Progressivism challenged the social and economic inequities that had dramatically worsened in the Gilded Age, but they should also see the contradictions that marked the Progressive Era: the racial doctrines behind America's foreign expansion also encouraged further discrimination against immigrants and African Americans, even as great Progressive reforms boosted the rights and welfare of ordinary citizens.

SUGGESTED ANCHOR TEXTS

Ellis Island by Elaine Landau
At *Ellis Island: A History in Many Voices* by Louise Peacock
An Age of Extremes: 1880–1917 by Joy Hakim
Coming to America: The Story of Immigration by Betsy Maestro
Hannah's Journal: The Story of an Immigrant Girl by Marissa Moss
One Fine Day: A Radio Play by Elizabeth Van Steenwyk
The Groundbreaking, Chance-Taking Life of George Washington Carver and Science and Invention in America by Cheryl Harness
Titanic: *The Disaster That Shocked the World!* by Mark Dubowski

FEATURED ANCHOR TEXTS

ELLIS ISLAND BY ELAINE LANDAU

AT ELLIS ISLAND: A HISTORY IN MANY VOICES BY LOUISE PEACOCK

Ellis Island was selected for this lesson to provide a general understanding of what happened at Ellis Island during the prime years of operation, 1892 to 1954. The book is rich with information-filled text, diagrams, drawings, maps, and photographs that tell the story. At *Ellis Island: A History in Many Voices* was selected because it is a hybrid text, mixing primary sources (such as photographs and excerpts from the journals and letters of real Ellis Island immigrants); the account of a fictional girl named Sera, who is traveling alone to meet her father on Ellis Island; and the story of a present-day visitor to Ellis Island. The true and diverse voices of the immigrants make this an interesting, layered text requiring some teacher guidance for comprehension.

TEXT STUDIES

Reading these two texts and answering the text-dependent questions about them help students hone their ability to distinguish between and evaluate different types of texts, even within the same book, noting what kind of information is conveyed in which type of text. The questions help students compare and synthesize information from various sources. They also help students recognize the effect that some unusual text structures may have on the reader and the reasons why the authors chose to organize their respective texts as they did.
The text-dependent questions all promote close reading.

Ellis Island by Elaine Landau

1. **From the photograph on page 6 of the text, what can you observe about Ellis Island?**
   - It is close to the water.
   - Ships can travel close by the island.
   - There is a huge building, with a dome-shaped roof.
   - The Statue of Liberty is in the distance, across the water.
2. **Use the quotation by John F. Kennedy and the text on page 7 to define the word *immigrant*. Compare your definition to the definition in the glossary at the back of the book. Consult a dictionary to see how the dictionary definition compares to the glossary definition.**
   - The immigrants referred to in the text were men, women, and children who came to America "to start a new life in the land of opportunity."
   - The glossary definition of the word *immigrants* is "people who arrive to live in a new country."

     Note: *Students may notice that the definition created from the text applies more specifically to immigrants who arrived in America, because this book is about American immigration. A dictionary definition is more general, as in the following: "An immigrant is someone who migrates to a new country where he or she will permanently live."*

     Note: *You may want to have students look at the relationship between the words* immigrant *and* migrate, *relating it to the biology application. When an organism is found in a new habitat, it is also called "immigration."*
3. **According to page 8, why did people come to America? How do these reasons relate to the Kennedy quotation on page 7?**
   - People came to America to escape poverty, to enjoy freedom to worship as they pleased, and to be safe even when they opposed the government.
   - Kennedy said, "There were probably as many reasons for coming to America as there were people who came." Although people came for the three basic goals mentioned on page 8, every person coming had his or her very own story.
4. **Study the map on page 11 of the text. How does this map add to your understanding of Ellis Island?**
   - Most immigrants, 59 percent, came to Ellis Island from the northern and western parts of Europe.
   - Thirty-three percent of immigrants came to Ellis Island from the eastern and southern parts of Europe.
   - Six percent of immigrants came to Ellis Island from South America.
   - People coming from Asia went through Angel Island, on the West Coast of the United States, or they went through Ellis Island.
5. **From the information in chapter 2 of the text, both words and images, what made the journey to America difficult?**
   - According to the photograph on page 12, the ships were crowded with emigrants from Italy.
   - According to page 13, the trips for emigrants (people *leaving* their country to live in a new place) were long rides on steamships.

- According to page 14, tickets were too expensive for people who were very poor.

  Note: *Point out to students that one of the reasons they were leaving was poverty.*
- According to pages 15 and 16, after 1900, immigrants each needed a visa from the country they were going to enter. Immigrants also had to travel to a port city with all of their possessions before they could board the boat. It took "days, weeks, or even months" for the ship to be ready for boarding. Then, the immigrants were not allowed to board until they had been approved by a doctor, inoculated, and given a disinfecting bath.
- According to pages 18 and 19, the "steerage" compartments were inexpensive, but dark and unclean. The floors were dirty and had vomit on them. Three hundred people had to share two bathrooms. The space was very small and crowded; each person had a very narrow bunk on which to sleep and store belongings. Food was scarce.

6. **After studying the annotated map of Ellis Island on pages 24 and 25, use your own words to tell what happened in each place.**
   - The new immigrants dropped off their luggage in the baggage and dormitory building. They each went to their bunk bed in the dormitory, where they stayed until they were released from Ellis Island.
   - They ate their meals in the cafeteria and took their baths in the bath house.
   - If the immigrants were sick, they went to the hospital to be seen by a doctor.
   - In the main building, the immigrants walked a staircase. While they were climbing, doctors watched to see if anyone appeared to be sick. Those people were sent to see a doctor for a checkup.
   - The Registry Room was where the immigrants were interviewed before being allowed to enter the country permanently.
   - The Kissing Post was where the new immigrants met loved ones already in America who were waiting for them to be released.

     Note: *As students read chapter 4, they can find more detailed descriptions of what happened in each place and how each location represented a step in the immigration process.*
7. **According to chapter 4, how were first- and second-class passengers treated?**
   - The photograph on page 27 shows the wealthy travelers going quickly into New York City.
   - The note on page 26 says that the "first and second class passengers usually did not have to go through an inspection at Ellis Island."
8. **What happened in the Registry Room, as described on pages 31 through 34? How does the photograph on page 30 add to your understanding of what happened in the Registry Room?**
   - There were legal inspectors who met with each immigrant as well as translators to interpret the questions.
   - The immigrants were asked twenty-nine different questions, including their age, job, marital status, and "morality."
   - From 1917 on, immigrants had to prove that they could read and write.
   - After the immigrants finished successfully in the Registry Room, they were free to leave Ellis Island and enter the country permanently.
   - If the immigrants were not allowed to leave, they had to go back to the dormitory or to the hospital until they were released or sent back to their home country.

- Although each interview only took a few minutes, the sheer number of immigrants pictured in the photograph makes the whole process seem longer and more overwhelming.

At Ellis Island: A History in Many Voices by Louise Peacock

Have students spend some time with the book, trying to read for understanding. Ask them what is unusual about the way the book is organized (the structure). After they have had time to orient themselves, you may want to lead a discussion, beginning by saying something like, "Look at the first few pages of this book. How do we read a 'hybrid text' such as this?"

Students will need to sort the parts of the book into Sera's fictional journal entries; the authentic, historic voices of Ellis Island immigrants; and the fictional story of the contemporary descendant's walk through Ellis Island. It will help students if you note the different types of fonts and "boxing" techniques used consistently throughout the text for each type of entry.

1. **During the first read of the text, focus on the quotations from real immigrants. What countries are represented by the immigrant voices? Why are these varied voices important?**
   - The countries represented are Russia, Greece, Germany, Romania, Austria, Hungary, Ireland, Czechoslovakia, Ukraine, Sweden, the Netherlands, Armenia, and Italy.
   - "Hearing" the different voices of people who experienced immigration from different perspectives reminds the reader that history is best told by those who were there.
2. **According to the quotation on page 2, what caused these Europeans to leave their respective homelands to come to America?**
   - C. Razovski writes of an interview with a girl who told of war, bombs dropping, being hungry, and "the horrors of pogroms."

     Note: Pogrom *is a Yiddish word, derived from a Russian word meaning "destruction" or "devastation." Historically, it refers to a mob attack on a certain ethnic group of people, used especially to describe attacks on Jewish people.*

     Note: *There is also a very graphic quotation on page 5, describing the piles of bodies in the streets in Greece. You may or may not want to discuss this with your students. The memories described by the contemporary voice on page 17 contain similar imagery.*
3. **According to the quotation from the seven-year-old girl from Germany on page 4, what do you think the "hold" was, and why did people stay down there?**
   - The girl says, "We were seasick . . . because we were down in the hold. The cheapest possible ticket." We can infer or understand from what she says that the hold was an area near the bottom of the ship, where the ride was rough and living conditions were terrible; many people must have gotten sick from being down deep in the ship.
4. **According to the text, what is an example of an immigrant's inflated perception, or exaggerated idea, of America before he or she arrived?**
   - On page 11, E. Steen is quoted as saying, "I knew so little about America. For me, America was cowboys and Indians and streets paved with gold."
5. **Read the quotation on page 17 by the child who immigrated as a seven-year-old girl. What does she say about the Statue of Liberty?**
   - The child's mother knew the significance of the Statue of Liberty. It signified freedom to those who were arriving from other countries where they were not free.
   - Only later in life did the child grasp the idea of freedom. She believed that those who immigrated knew what the word *free* meant more than did those who had always lived in America.

6. **How does the author use the quotations from Esther Almgren (page 25) and Varan Hartunian (page 37) to lend credibility to the fictional story?**
   - On page 25, Almgren's quotation is about the inspectors' letting her and her husband through with only $1.50 between them. Sera's friends Alberto and Rosa have a similar experience when asked if they have money, but they are waved on through.
   - Hartunian's quotation tells of two thousand Armenians burned alive in a church, and it backs up Sera's very real fear of being sent back to the violence in Armenia.
7. **Describe situations in the text in which certain people were barred from entering the United States once they had arrived on Ellis Island.**
   - Ill people (pages 20 and 28), orphans (page 31), and the poor (pages 24 and 25) were not allowed in unless they had proof of someone to care for them. The inspectors were looking for people who could be independent and not a burden to the country. Therefore, they had to know that immigrants were not bringing in illnesses that would spread, and that provisions would be made for the care of each immigrant, whether old or young. Children had to have a parent to care for them. Adults were also asked if they had ever been in prison.

   Note: This discussion could evolve into one about what might be considered "discrimination" now. Note the author's writing (in the voice of the contemporary girl) on page 38: "How would I vote? Let them come in!"
8. **According to pages 22 through 25, what happened in the Registry Room?**
   - According to the quotation from the interpreter on page 22, immigration officers interviewed from three thousand to five thousand people every day. They interviewed people for twelve hours a day.
   - According to page 23, an immigration officer was dressed in a suit and "sat on a podium like a judge," high above the immigrant. People were waiting in lines "behind iron bars like cattle."
   - According to page 24, immigrants were asked such questions as these:
     - "What is your name?"
     - "What is your nationality?"
     - "How old are you?"
     - "What is your final destination in the United States?"
     - "Who paid for your ticket?"
     - "Do you have any money?"
     - "Have you ever been in prison or a poorhouse?"
     - "What is the condition of your health?"
   - According to the quotation from the German immigrant on page 24, some poor people would hand the same twenty-five dollars from one person to the next as they went through the line. The people would help each other out when they didn't have enough money to enable them to successfully answer the question, "Do you have any money?"
9. **Read through the book one more time, noting the old photographs, the painted illustrations, and the new photographs. Why did the author include a mix of these types of text features throughout the book?**
   - The old photographs enhance the reader's ability to imagine the place and the people during the era of immigration to the United States.
   - The painted illustrations tell the story of Sera; they help convey her emotions and perceptions of her trip.
   - The few modern photographs are taken on a present-day tour through Ellis Island, reminding the reader that Ellis Island still exists.

PERFORMANCE ASSESSMENTS

1. One of the texts is an informational text about Ellis Island, and the other is a hybrid text that includes primary source quotations, a fictional story line, and a contemporary visit to Ellis Island. Have students choose one of the places that was featured in the informational text: the dock, the ship, the dorm, the hospital, the Registry Room, the Separation Staircase, or the Kissing Post. Students should gather first-person information from the primary source accounts in the hybrid text to add to the information from the first book. Have students each write a rich informative/ explanatory essay about the place, using information gathered from the two sources studied. You may also want to encourage students to find information from one other source, digital or print.

Ask students to be sure to introduce the topic clearly; develop the topic with facts, details, and examples; link ideas; use precise language and domain-specific vocabulary; and provide a concluding statement. At earlier levels, students may write a coherent paragraph that summarizes the main topic and key details. See standards for more details.

2. Have students each write a narrative journal entry from the perspective of an immigrant in the place they selected for the first performance assessment. Students should use the sources from which they read to provide background information for their journal entry.

Ask students to be sure to establish a situation; introduce a narrator and/or characters; organize an event sequence; use narrative techniques; use transitional words, concrete words, and sensory details to convey experiences; and provide a conclusion that follows from narrated events. At earlier levels, students may write a coherent paragraph that narrates an event, including a few key descriptive details. See standards for more details.

CONNECTIONS TO COMMON CORE STATE STANDARDS FOR ENGLISH LANGUAGE ARTS

***Ellis Island* by Elaine Landau**

- Question 1 helps students understand how a photograph may provide a deeper level of understanding about important content (RI.3.7; RI.4.7; RI.5.7).
- Question 2 focuses on a domain-specific word, asking students to compare context clues to a glossary definition. Answering the question helps students understand the structural features of an informational text and encourages them to compare word definitions and synthesize ideas (RI.3.1,2,3,4,5; RI.4.1,2,3,4,5; RI.5.1,2,3,4,5; L.3.5; L.4.5; L.5.5).
- Question 3 asks students to recall essential details in the text and to relate them to bigger ideas presented in another part of the text (RI.3.1,2,3; RI.4.1,2,3; RI.5.1,2,3).
- Question 4 helps students recognize how maps can provide a deeper level of understanding in regard to important historical content in an informational text (RI.3.7; RI.4.7; RI.5.7).
- Questions 5 through 8 ask students to recall essential details in the text, drawing on both words and images (RI.3.1,2,7; RI.4.1,2,7; RI.5.1,2,7).
  - Question 6 also calls on students to summarize what they have learned (W.3.2,9; W.4.2,9; W.5.2,9; SL.3.2; SL.4.2; SL.5.2).

At Ellis Island: *A History in Many Voices* by Louise Peacock

- Question 1 focuses on key details in the text and asks students not just to identify them but also to explain their significance. It also highlights the power of primary sources (RI.3.1,2,3,5; RI.4.1,2,3,5; RI.5.1,2,3,5).
- A complete answer to question 2 requires students to recall essential details in the text and to focus on the meaning and significance of a domain-specific word as well as on imagery used by various voices in the text (RI.3.1,2,4; RI.4.1,2,4; RI.5.1,2,4; L.3.5; L.4.5; L.5.5).
- Questions 3 and 5 also ask students to recall essential details in the text and focus on some domain-specific terminology (RI.3.1,2,4; RI.4.1,2,4; RI.5.1,2,4; L.3.5; L.4.5; L.5.5).
- Question 4 requires that students understand the difference between what one primary source account suggests about events described in the text and the reality of the events themselves. Students must know that they are to look for the answer in the sections of the book that are quotations from real immigrants (RI.3.1,2,3,5,6; RI.4.1,2,3,5,6; RI.5.1,2,3,5,6).
- Question 6 requires students to understand the author's purpose—and how and why she chose to organize the text as she did. It also asks students to compare information presented in two different places, and in two different ways, in the text (RI.3.1,2,3,5,6,8; RI.4.1,2,3,5,6,8; RI.5.1,2,3,5,6,8).
- Questions 7 and 8 ask students to recount key concepts and details from the text and cite evidence from the text to support their assertions (RI.3.1,2,3; RI.4.1,2,3; RI.5.1,2,3).
- Question 9 requires students to consider the author's and illustrator's craft in designing the book as they did, taking both the words and the images in the text into account when answering (RI.3.7; RI.4.7; RI.5.7).

Performance Assessments

- The first performance assessment affords students a chance to summarize and explain their understanding of key concepts and details pertaining to the historical content presented in two different texts. It asks them to write an informative/explanatory essay that includes pertinent details from a variety of sources (RI.3.1,2,3,6,7; RI.4.1,2,3,6,7; RI.5.1,2,3,6,7; W.3.2,9; W.4.2,9; W.5.2,9).
    - If students do additional research, they will also be addressing W.3.7,8; W.4.7,8; and W.5.7,8.
- The second performance assessment prompts students to convey—in a narrative journal entry—what they have learned about historical content informational texts (RI.3.1,2,3; RI.4.1,2,3; RI.5.1,2,3; W.3.3,9; W.4.3,9; W.5.3,9).

MORE RESOURCES

PRIMARY SOURCES

Partial list of survivors of the *Titanic*, 1912 (National Archives)

Historic photos of Ellis Island (Statue of Liberty–Ellis Island Foundation)

National Association for the Advancement of Colored People (NAACP) advertisement, 1920 (Ohio Historical Center Archives Library)

"Jailed for Freedom" women's suffrage pin, 1917 (Smithsonian Institution)

Wreckage of the USS *Maine* at the second anniversary, 1900 (Smithsonian Institution)

Procession accompanying Theodore Roosevelt's campaign in Chicago, 1912 (Library of Congress)

Portrait of W.E.B. Du Bois, 1911 (Smithsonian Institution)

Portrait of Al Capone, 1925 (National Portrait Gallery)

POETRY AND MUSIC

"Hungarian Rag," recording, 1913 (Library of Congress)

"The More I See of Hawaii, the More I Like New York," 1917 (Duke University Library)

"Women's Political March," musical score, 1911 (Library of Congress)

Early Tin Pan Alley music recordings (Library of Congress)

ART AND ARCHITECTURE

Architecture from 1880 to 1920 (Library of Congress)

USEFUL WEBSITE

History of Ellis Island (Statue of Liberty–Ellis Island Foundation)

The Great War: Rallying American Patriotism

(1914 to 1929)

GRADES: 3, 4, 5

OVERVIEW

At first a reluctant participant, the United States entered Europe's Great War in 1917 when events forced President Woodrow Wilson's hand. In the decade following the war, prosperity and cultural expansion gave rise to the Roaring Twenties and the Jazz Age. But though post-war prosperity was good for some, the divide continued to widen between those who "had" and those who "had not"; immigrants flooded the country, and the ideas of many Americans of what their country should be were challenged. After reading *Bessie Smith and the Night Riders*, lower elementary students will be asked to determine whether or not the protagonist was a hero and to defend their opinion using evidence from the text. Upper elementary students will explore the accomplishments of the American automaker in *Henry Ford: Putting the World on Wheels* and use the evidence from his biography to articulate and defend their opinion on what character trait was most integral to Henry Ford's success.

○ ○ ○

Interested in learning more about this time period? Read a more complete history in the "Era Summaries."

LEARNING EXPECTATIONS

Lower elementary: Students should understand that the First World War—a devastating global conflict in which the United States became embroiled—ushered in a period of dramatic prosperity and wilder culture (the Roaring Twenties), but that prosperity left many people behind and threatened many Americans' ideas of what the country should be.

Upper elementary: Students should know that America was reluctant to be drawn into the First World War, but that Germany's provocations became more than most were willing to accept. They should understand that the war, once America finally entered it, helped propel the United States to greater global prominence—even though American hopes of a noble and lasting peace came to nothing. Students should be aware of the great prosperity of the post-war decade and of the less restrained society of the Jazz Age, but they should also know that runaway prosperity left many behind and that the Jazz Age sparked a backlash from more traditional forces.

SUGGESTED ANCHOR TEXTS

Henry Ford: Putting the World on Wheels by the editors of *TIME For Kids* with Dina El Nabli
War, Peace, and All That Jazz: 1918–1945 by Joy Hakim
The Letter Home by Timothy Decker
Voices of World War I: Stories from the Trenches by Ann Heinrichs

FEATURED ANCHOR TEXT

HENRY FORD: PUTTING THE WORLD ON WHEELS BY THE EDITORS OF TIME FOR KIDS WITH DINA EL NABLI

This book was selected because the biography of Ford is told against the backdrop of significant events in American history. Ford's life spanned both world wars as well as the Great Depression. His leadership in developing the American automotive industry contributed to the creation of the middle class as we know it today. This engaging and informative chapter book will draw students into learning about the era. Insets, photographs, an interview, and a timeline are among the structural features of this informational text that help students glean more information about the topic from different perspectives.

TEXT STUDY

The text-dependent questions address both important historical content and the authors' craft through exploration of how the text is structured and how the authors support their assertions. Among these are questions that also address how to use structural features of informational texts to enhance understanding.

1. **Look closely at the cover of the book, the title, and the subtitle. What are the hints about who Henry Ford was and what the book will be about?**
    - In the upper left-hand corner, it says, "*TIME For Kids* Biographies," so we know that this is a biography.
    - We can assume that the man pictured on the cover is Ford; he is well dressed; he looks like a businessman.
    - *Putting the World on Wheels* is the subtitle, suggesting that Ford had something to do with making travel possible.
    - Ford is standing next to an old-fashioned car with a license plate that says "demonstration," suggesting that he had something to do with the car's invention or production.
    - The car has a lever in the front that goes around.
    - A "turned-down corner" notes that inside is also the story of the U.S. highway system ("U.S. Highway History").
    - Considering this information together, we may assume that this book is the story of a man who made cars and how his story relates to the growth of the car industry and transportation in the United States.

2. **The biography opens with a paragraph that ends with this statement: "He wanted to create a new kind of car." How does chapter 1 describe that car?**
   - Ford's 1906 idea was to create a car that wasn't hard to build and wasn't so heavy and expensive, so that more people could own cars. In other words, "he wanted to build a lightweight car that everyone could afford" (page 2).
   - Ford and the people who worked with him discovered a lighter and cheaper steel called vanadium. They built a car that was bigger and seated five people. It was also lighter because they built it with the vanadium steel.
   - In 1908, the Model T was introduced to the public; fifteen million Model Ts were sold by 1928.

3. **According to chapter 2, how did Ford show early signs of creativity and curiosity? What can you infer about Ford from all of this evidence?**
   - He liked to "experiment with gadgets," taking watches apart and tinkering with them.
   - He was curious about better ways to do farm chores, such as plowing and hauling.
   - When he was seven, he had his own workbench on which he tinkered when he had free time.
   - When he was thirteen, he saw a steam engine for the first time. "That was the day Henry knew he didn't want to be a farmer. Instead, he wanted to build machines that moved on their own."
   - When he was sixteen, he began working during the day as an apprentice in a machine shop, and at night he repaired watches and clocks.
   - We can infer from these details that Ford was a hard worker who had a deep love for working with machines. He was creative in his thinking, and he was curious about both making machines better and using them for new purposes.

4. **In chapter 3, the authors make the claim that Ford was a hard worker and had talent. How is that idea supported throughout the entire chapter? What other character qualities do you see in these examples of Ford's work?**
   - Even when Ford was a traveling machine worker for Westinghouse, barely twenty years old, he took night classes in accounting, typing, mechanical drawing, and business.
     - These actions illustrate his curiosity and willingness to work hard.
   - During a time when jobs were scarce, Ford was hired as a mechanical engineer for the Edison Illuminating Company.
     - His finding a job when jobs were hard to come by indicates that Ford must have had talent that made him stand out from the others. The text also says that Ford's "experience and determination" helped him get the job.
   - Ford continued to work creatively to satisfy his curiosity by doing experiments in his backyard shed. He built a small gas engine that worked.
     - These activities demonstrate his talent and persistence.
   - Three years later, he had invented the "Quadricycle," a gas-powered vehicle with four big bicycle tires.
     - Ford's experiments led to successful inventions, showing a combination of talent, drive, and an ability to follow through with his visions and ideas.
   - The character qualities of curiosity, discipline, determination, and perseverance are all evident in the way Ford conceived of ideas and followed them through to completion. Each invention spurred more ideas.

5. **In the inset on page 13, the authors write that Ford met his "idol." Who was this man, and why was he referred to as Ford's idol? How did the relationship change throughout their lives?**
   - The man who was his idol was Thomas Edison. The word *idol* is used in this context to refer to someone who was adored and admired–someone to whom Ford looked for inspiration. According to the text, Ford met Edison five years after he landed the job at Edison Illuminating Company. Because Ford had drive and curiosity as an inventor, he probably looked to Edison as someone who had already proven his success as the "father of electricity."
   - The relationship changed from Ford's working for Edison's company, to Ford's meeting Edison in person, to their becoming close friends. They bought side-by-side homes in Fort Myers, Florida. The photograph of the men in older age shows a familiarity between the two, but Ford still seemed to have deep admiration for the man when he held a celebration for the fiftieth anniversary of the light bulb and honored Edison by establishing the Edison Institute in Michigan.
6. **Gather evidence from chapter 4 that shows Ford's perseverance.**
   - Ford's first company, Detroit Automobile Company, failed after two years of work.
   - Ford's second company, Henry Ford Company, failed after only a few months.
   - Ford did not give up. In 1903, he began the Ford Motor Company with money that he raised.
   - He went on to invent the Model A and sold 1,708 cars.
   - He and his designers built nine different models of his car before the Model T came out. He was finally on the road to success because of his perseverance.
7. **Chapter 5 opens with this Ford quotation: "I will build a motorcar for the great multitude. It will be so low in price that no man making a good salary will be unable to own one." How did Ford make this dream come true for Americans?**
   - He created the Model T, a bigger car that was lighter and made with vanadium steel.
   - In 1908, the new car was a basic black color and cost $825, much less than the average cost ($2,000 or $3,000) of other cars on the market.
   - In 1913, Ford invented the "assembly line," making the process of building a car take only ninety-three minutes. The more cars his company produced, the more the price dropped. By 1916, the price was down to $345 for a Model T.
8. **According to chapter 6, why was Ford called a "hero of the working class"?**
   - Ford created the eight-hour workday and more than doubled the workers' pay, from $2.38 a day to $5.00 a day. The workers were working an hour less and being paid twice as much.
   - Even though he became very wealthy and famous, Ford and his wife still lived simply. For example, they fixed their old socks instead of buying the new ones that they could easily afford.
9. **According to chapter 6, was Ford every American's hero? Cite evidence from the text to support your answer.**
   - Ford was *not* every American's hero.
     - During World War I, Ford spoke boldly against the war, even traveling to Europe to do so. There were Americans who disagreed with his views.

   - When Ford ran for Senate in 1918, he lost. Former president Theodore Roosevelt was against him and talked about those antiwar views.
   - During his life, Ford spoke out against Jews, and in 1938, he accepted an honor from Adolf Hitler, a German dictator determined to kill Jewish people. His image and business were hurt by his bigoted ideas.

10. **How did Ford's company stay in business during the Great Depression?**
    - According to page 35, the company had to cut the workers' daily pay and lay off workers.
    - According to page 36, the company began to produce and sell cars all over the world. The Model Y sold for twenty-seven years in Europe.
11. **Although Ford did not want America to go to war, how did he help with World War II? What does that tell us about Ford?**
    - According to page 38, Ford's company built an airplane factory to produce B-24 Liberty Bomber airplanes. They built one airplane a day.
    - Even though Ford was against war, he remained committed to his country, supporting America during World War II.
12. **According to page 39, what is the Ford Foundation? What does this fund tell us about Ford?**
    - The Ford Foundation is a nonprofit that was created in 1936. Ford left most of his fortune to the foundation.
      - The foundation wants to "strengthen democracy, reduce poverty, promote international cooperation, and advance human achievement."
      - In 1969, the foundation offered the money to start *Sesame Street.*
      - The foundation gives to public television and the arts.
      - Money is also given "to reduce poverty and the spread of AIDS."
    - These details suggest that Ford was a generous man who believed in giving back to his community and to his country. He believed in giving to those who had much less money and hope than he had.

PERFORMANCE ASSESSMENTS

1. Give students the following writing task, which requires the use of evidence gathered in the text study questions:

- Of all of the character qualities discussed and implied in this biography, which one do you think was the most important to Henry Ford's success? Choose one quality and support your choice with evidence from Ford's life.

Ask students to be sure to introduce the topic clearly and state an opinion; provide logically ordered reasons; link their opinion and reasons; and provide a concluding statement related to the opinion presented. At earlier levels, students may write a coherent paragraph that summarizes the main topic and key details. See standards for more details.

2. As a class, use the timeline at the back of the book to create a visual chain of the events of Ford's life. Students should focus on the connections between events, and they should consider how a major event would not have happened without a previous link in the chain. Students can present the chain of events to the class or another audience, explaining how each event relates to the next.

CONNECTIONS TO COMMON CORE STATE STANDARDS FOR ENGLISH LANGUAGE ARTS

- Question 1 asks students to consider structural features on the cover of this informational text (the title and subtitle, a photograph, and an inset) to infer information about the subject of this biography and what the book is likely to be about (RI.3.5,6; RI.4.5,6; RI.5.5,6).
- Questions 2 and 7 address the relationship between how the main idea of a chapter is introduced and how the rest of the chapter supports that idea with significant details (RI.3.1,2,3,8; RI.4.1,2,3,8; RI.5.1,2,3,8).
- Question 3, in addition to asking students to identify key characteristics of the subject, asks students to make an inference about the subject's character based on those details (RI.3.1,2,3; RI.4.1,2,3; RI.5.1,2,3).
- Question 4 addresses the efficacy of the authors' argument, prompting students to determine if the evidence in a chapter supports the authors' assertions. This question also asks students to identify key characteristics of the subject (RI.3.1,2,3,8; RI.4.1,2,3,8; RI.5.1,2,3,8).
- Question 5 requires students to understand and explain information from an inset—and how it illuminates characteristics of the biography's subject (RI.3.1,2,5; RI.4.1,2,5; RI.5.1,2,5).
- Question 6 asks students to identify key details that support an assertion in the question (RI.3.1,2,3,8; RI.4.1,2,3,8; RI.5.1,2,3,8).
- Question 8 asks students to identify details about the subject of the biography that led to his being given a popular nickname (RI.3.1,2,3,4; RI.4.1,2,3,4; RI.5.1,2,3,4; L.3.5; L.4.5; L.5.5).
- Question 9 requires students to cite key details from a chapter to support an assertion (that is, to answer yes or no to the question and be able to explain their response) (RI.3.1,2,3; RI.4.1,2,3; RI.5.1,2,3).
- Questions 10 and 11 require students to identify key details and events in the subject's life (RI.3.1,2; RI.4.1,2; RI.5.1,2).
- Question 12 addresses the subject's legacy and asks students to explain why the subject took certain actions, as well as their effect (RI.3.1,2,3; RI.4.1,2,3; RI.5.1,2,3).
- The first performance assessment requires students to reread closely with a focus on the subject's characteristics. They must then write an opinion essay that defends an assertion about which characteristic was most essential to the subject's success (RI.3.1,2,3; RI.4.1,2,3; RI.5.1,2,3; W.3.1,9; W.4.1,9; W.5.1,9).
- The second performance assessment helps students recognize the connections among events and asks them to convey their understanding by explaining the construction of a visual chain that identifies the events in the correct order (RI.3.1,2,3; RI.4.1,2,3; RI.5.1,2,3; SL.3.4; SL.4.4; SL.5.4).

MORE RESOURCES

HISTORICAL FICTION

Archie's War: My Scrapbook of the First World War, 1914–1918 by Marcia Williams

PRIMARY SOURCES

Photograph of a 1920s car assembly line (Library of Congress)

Photograph of the HMS *Lusitania*, taken between 1907 and 1915 (Library of Congress)

Zimmermann Telegram, 1917 (National Archives)

"Your Work Means Victory" poster, 1917 (Smithsonian Institution)

Photograph of Langston Hughes, 1925 (Smithsonian Institution)

POETRY AND MUSIC

"Over There," as recorded by Nora Bayes, 1917 (Library of Congress)

"The Negro Speaks of Rivers," a Langston Hughes poem, set to music, 1949 (Library of Congress)

Warren Harding campaign song, 1920 (Library of Congress)

"Charleston Rag," ca. 1917 (Library of Congress)

"Playlist: Temperance & Prohibition" (Library of Congress)

ART AND ARCHITECTURE

Boston Avenue Methodist church—example of art deco architecture, 1928

Prosperity Has Its Price: Economic Collapse and World War II

(1929 to 1945)

GRADES: 3, 4, 5

OVERVIEW

Much of the prosperity of the 1920s was built on a financial house of cards that collapsed in 1929 and plunged the nation into the worst economic situation in its history, the Great Depression. In those hard times, a new vision emerged for the role of government in American life. President Franklin D. Roosevelt aggressively promoted his New Deal legislation, and when it encountered opposition from the U.S. Supreme Court, he attempted—unsuccessfully—to increase the number of justices in an effort to maintain a majority favorable to his policies. The New Deal ultimately established greater federal control of the economy along with a series of basic economic protections for citizens. The collapse of the world's economies generated a widespread state of despair, leaving some nations vulnerable to rising Fascist extremism—which posed a deadly threat to the concept of democracy. The Fascist regimes drove Europe into renewed conflict, and expansionist Japan pulled America into the growing Second World War. This time, Americans would rally together and support their nation's entrance into what became a defense of human freedom across the globe—even as the home front still presented its own challenges. *Finding Daddy: A Story of the Great Depression* gives lower elementary students a glimpse into the hardships families faced during the Great Depression through the eyes of a young girl named Bonnie. Students will craft well-supported opinions on whether or not Bonnie was strong. The strength of the relationship between a British and an American leader is profiled in *Franklin and Winston: A Christmas That Changed the World*. Upper elementary students will read this narrative description along with an informational text about World War II, writing essays comparing and contrasting the ideological differences between the Axis and Allied forces.

○ ○ ○

Interested in learning more about this time period? Read a more complete history in the "Era Summaries."

LEARNING EXPECTATIONS

Lower elementary: Students should understand that the sudden collapse of the economy caused the new president, Roosevelt, to fundamentally change the role of the government in American life, using federal powers to protect citizens from disaster. They should know that World War II pitted the United States against dangerous enemies that threatened all human freedom, and that the war pulled most Americans together in what they saw as a great cause, even as some minorities were treated unfairly.

Upper elementary: Students should understand that the boom of the 1920s collapsed suddenly, dragging the country—and the world—into the Great Depression. They should realize that Roosevelt's New Deal changed the role of government in American life, authorizing the use of federal power to establish basic economic security and protections for citizens. Students should know that despair over the Depression helped create dangerous political movements in Europe; and they should also know that despite strong reluctance in the United States to become involved in Europe's war, Roosevelt's determination to stop Fascist Germany—and Japan's determination to drive the United States from the Pacific—helped pull the United States into the war anyway. Students should understand that the war united most Americans on the home front, but that some—particularly Japanese Americans and African Americans—suffered from the prejudices of the broader society.

SUGGESTED ANCHOR TEXTS

"World War II: An Overview" by Scholastic
Franklin and Winston: A Christmas That Changed the World by Douglas Wood
Boys of Steel: The Creators of Superman by Marc Tyler Nobleman
Eleanor Roosevelt: An Inspiring Life by Elizabeth MacLeod
Out of the Dust by Karen Hesse
Rose's Journal: The Story of a Girl in the Great Depression by Marissa Moss
When Marian Sang by Pam Munoz Ryan
Why Did the Whole World Go to War? And Other Questions about World War II by Martin W. Sandler
World War II for Kids by Richard Panchyk

FEATURED ANCHOR TEXTS

"WORLD WAR II: AN OVERVIEW" BY SCHOLASTIC

FRANKLIN AND WINSTON: A CHRISTMAS THAT CHANGED THE WORLD BY DOUGLAS WOOD

The Scholastic article on World War II was chosen to give the students a basic background on the conflict. The purpose of the war, the causes of the war, America's participation in the war, and the effects of the war are all briefly summarized in this concise article. *Franklin and Winston: A Christmas That Changed the World* gives the students a peek into the short period of time when Britain's wartime leader, Winston Churchill, spent Christmas with America's wartime leader,

Roosevelt, in the White House. This book was chosen to give students a glimpse of the personal aspects of the formation of the important alliance between Britain and the United States against the Axis alliance during World War II. The book contains fine illustrations and other interesting structural features of an informational text, such as an afterword, an author's note, and a bibliography.

TEXT STUDIES

"World War II: An Overview" by Scholastic

1. **How does the author describe World War II in paragraph 1 of the article?**
    - The author writes that it was "the bloodiest, deadliest war the world had ever seen."
    - "More than 38 million people died, many of them innocent civilians."
    - "It was the most destructive war in history."
    - Fifty nations participated in the war in some way.
    - Because of the global nature of the conflict, "the world was changed forever."
2. **The word *tyrant* refers to someone who uses harsh, cruel power. The word *dictator* refers to someone who rules with complete power without having to follow national or international laws created by the people he or she governs. How does the text's description of Adolf Hitler convey that he was both a tyrant and dictator?**
    - The text describes Hitler as having an "iron grip" as a dictator.
    - The text also says that his Nazis were waging "a campaign of terror" against Jews and other minorities.
    - Both of these descriptive phrases show how Hitler was using his cruel power to rule, without himself being under the control of any government.
3. **According to the article, what caused World War II?**
    - Following World War I, nations remained angry and bitter about what happened after the war had ended.
    - The Germans were especially unhappy with the way the war had ended and how much it had cost them, both financially and in terms of land ownership.
    - Even though the League of Nations had been established to keep international peace after World War I, the United States did not join.
    - Countries were busy trying to solve problems of their own and were not paying attention to what was happening in Germany and "other trouble spots."
    - With a worldwide depression happening, countries had become concerned with finding leaders who would change things.
    - Dictators had risen to power in Germany, Italy, and Japan.
4. **What is the difference between the terms *totalitarian government* and *democratic government*?**
    - According to the section titled "Rise of Dictatorships," a totalitarian government is one that is "controlled by a single political party that allows no opposition and tightly controls people's lives."
    - A democracy is a "government by the people; a form of government in which the supreme power is vested in the people and exercised directly by them or by their elected agents."

- A totalitarian government tightly controls the people through the rule of one political party. In a democratic government, the people are more likely to live freely and to be treated equally.

5. **What did Benito Mussolini, Hitler, and the leaders in Japan all have in common?**
   - They were all dictators or military leaders.
   - They each promised that their country would be restored to its former greatness.
   - They each led a totalitarian government.

6. **Reread the text and identify the author's repeated suggestions that democratic countries, such as the United States, Britain, and France, did not act quickly enough to prevent World War II.**
   - According to paragraph 6, the United States helped form the League of Nations to keep the peace, but Americans were "too busy with their own problems to worry about Germany and other trouble spots."
   - According to paragraph 9, as Germany, Japan, and Italy were conquering nations, "none of the world's democracies did anything to stop them."
   - According to paragraph 10, Hitler moved into Europe, but "again, no one tried to stop him."

7. **What did Churchill mean when he said, "Britain and France had to choose between war and dishonor. They chose dishonor. They will have war." What evidence does the author provide for the truth of Churchill's assertion?**
   - As explored in question 6, Britain and France had chosen not to fight the Italian, German, and Japanese invasions. They had chosen not to defend the people who were being hurt by the military rule in those countries. Churchill felt that the British and the French had been dishonorable by not fighting the totalitarian behavior of the German, Japanese, and Italian governments.
   - By avoiding war, these countries had actually allowed totalitarian rule to spread across Europe.

8. **How did the United States help in World War II?**
   - The United States fought in North Africa, Europe, and the Pacific.
   - It took a leadership role against the Axis alliance of Germany, Italy, and Japan.
   - The Americans at home worked hard to supply warplanes, battleships, and guns for the Allies.

   Note: *Teachers will want to introduce the term* Allies *to use in contrast with the* Axis *alliance.*

9. **Who was the president of the United States during World War II? What did he believe needed to happen for civilization to survive?**
   - Franklin D. Roosevelt was the wartime president in the United States.
   - He believed that people of all kinds had to learn how to live and work together in the same world. He believed that we had to learn how to live in peace.

Franklin and Winston: A Christmas That Changed the World by Douglas Wood

1. **What do you learn about Winston Churchill's character in the first five pages of the text?**
   - He was courageous. Page 2 of the text explains that he was unafraid and calm on the deck of the ship as it was being rocked by forty-foot waves.
   - He was a hard worker. According to page 4, when he was asked to lead the government during wartime, he said, "I have nothing to offer but blood, toil, tears, and sweat."

- He had perseverance. According to the text on page 5, when Britain was fighting the Nazi powers and felt alone in the fight, he said, "We shall never surrender."
- He had pride in his country. According to page 5, he encouraged the people who were afraid of the Nazi bombings to handle the challenge in such a way that people would say later, "This was their finest hour."
- He was fearless and defiant. According to page 5, there were Nazi submarines prowling as he was in a storm at sea, but he jutted out his "bulldog jaw" and walked calmly on the deck.

2. **What event brought Churchill and Roosevelt together?**
   - According to page 7, the Japanese had just attacked a U.S. naval base in Pearl Harbor, Hawaii, in 1941.
   - America was now entering the war it had tried to avoid. Americans would be fighting alongside soldiers from Britain (Churchill's country) and other free nations.
3. **What do you learn about Franklin Delano Roosevelt's character on page 10?**
   - He had a "buoyant spirit." He was able to be cheerful even when things were hard, as when he had polio and was unable to walk again.
   - He was inspirational and encouraging. He had led the people of the United States through the Great Depression.
   - He was reassuring. During the Great Depression, he had said, "The only thing we have to fear is fear itself."
4. **On page 11, the text says, "Together they would decide how to confront a menace that threatened all of civilization." If "menace" is used to signify a threat or potential danger, what menace is being referenced here? Refer back to the "World War II: An Overview" article for context.**
   - According to paragraph 2 of the overview article read previously, the Americans and British were fighting against "tyranny," such as Hitler's rule.
   - According to paragraph 8 of the same article, they were fighting against "totalitarian governments."
5. **Why is it significant that Roosevelt was standing by the limousine when Churchill's plane landed?**
   - Roosevelt's polio kept him in a wheelchair most of the time. He only stood on his own on special occasions. When he stood, it showed his courage and his respect for Churchill.
6. **Why did Churchill and the president meet in the Oval Office after the first night's dinner was over?**
   - According to page 15, they had to make plans for how to fight the war together in Europe.
     - They pored over maps from around the world.
     - Decisions had to be made.
     - Plans had to be laid.
     - Roosevelt toasted to their "common cause."

     Note: In Churchill's speech on page 10, he says, "We are all in the same boat now."
7. **The word *alliance* refers to a partnership. What does the author mean, on page 18, when he mentions the "new alliance"?**
   - Britain and the United States were now working together as partners in the war. This partnership, or alliance, had just formed as the United States declared war on Japan after the bombing of Pearl Harbor.

8. **What did the White House mean by "Winston Hours"?**
   - While Churchill stayed at the White House, he did not keep the "norms" of White House bedtimes. He kept the president up later than normal, and he would wander the halls at night in his nightgown instead of going to sleep at a reasonable hour.
9. **On page 22 of the text, the author writes, "Everywhere, it seemed, tyranny was advancing, freedom retreating." What does he mean in this sentence?**
   - According to the article "World War II: An Overview," the war was caused by the "tyranny," or absolute and cruel power, of dictators. The Nazi leadership was conquering countries with cruelty, killing people and assuming power.
   - As cruel power became dominant, freedom was decreasing in the conquered countries.
   - The war was not going well for the Allies; they needed to make plans that would keep them working together for freedom.
10. **Following a brief break for Christmas, Churchill gave a speech to the U.S. Congress. What evidence is given on page 28 that the American leaders loved the speech?**
    - The congressmen "cheered and stomped their feet."
    - Churchill "made them laugh."
    - At the end of the speech, Congress stood up together.
    - When he showed his "V-for-victory" sign, the crowd "roared."
11. **According to page 30, what was "The Declaration of the United Nations"?**
    - "The Declaration of the United Nations" was a document that solidified the partnership of those in the Grand Alliance who pledged to "work and fight together to defeat the Axis Powers, which sought to enslave the world."
    - They said they would "defend life, liberty, independence, and religious freedom, and . . . preserve human rights and justice in their own lands as well as in other lands."
12. **Why was this meeting of two leaders such an important one?**
    - According to page 32, this Christmas meeting was when the two leaders became friends. From that time on, they could trust each other, even during the very difficult days of the four years of war that followed.

PERFORMANCE ASSESSMENTS

1. Ask students to gather two to three key pieces of information about the Axis forces (probably from the article) and two to three key pieces of information about the Allied forces (probably from the book). Have students write an informative/explanatory essay, comparing and contrasting what each stood for.

Students should introduce the topic clearly; develop the topic with facts, details, and examples; link ideas; use precise language and domain-specific vocabulary; and provide a concluding section or statement. At earlier levels, students may write a coherent paragraph that summarizes the main topic and key details. See standards for more details.

2. Ask students to write an opinion essay about why the meeting between Churchill and Roosevelt was so important. Remind them that America had entered the war only three weeks earlier.

Students should introduce the topic clearly and state an opinion; provide logically ordered reasons for that opinion; link the opinion and reasons; and provide a concluding section or statement related to the opinion presented. At earlier levels, students may write a coherent paragraph that summarizes the main topic and key details. See standards for more details.

CONNECTIONS TO COMMON CORE STATE STANDARDS FOR ENGLISH LANGUAGE ARTS

"World War II: An Overview" by Scholastic

- Question 1 focuses students' attention on the author's use of descriptive details (RI.3.1,2; RI.4.1,2; RI.5.1,2).
- Question 2 asks students to discern the subtle differences in meaning between two academic vocabulary words and to explain how evidence from the text supports the use of these terms (RI.3.1,2,3,4,8; RI.4.1,2,3,4,8; RI.5.1,2,3,4,8; L.3.4,5; L.4.4,5; L.5.4,5).
- Question 3 requires students to recall important details from the text and determine cause-and-effect relationships (RI.3.1,2,3; RI.4.1,2,3; RI.5.1,2,3).
- Like question 2, question 4 asks students to discern the subtle differences in meaning between two academic terms (RI.3.1,2,3,4; RI.4.1,2,3,4; RI.5.1,2,3,4; L.3.4,5; L.4.4,5; L.5.4,5).
- Question 5 requires that students compare central characters in the text. They must draw inferences to make an effective comparison (RI.3.1,2,3; RI.4.1,2,3; RI.5.1,2,3).
- Question 6 asks students to locate related information in various places in the text (RI.3.1,2,3; RI.4.1,2,3; RI.5.1,2,3).
- Question 7 requires students to determine the meaning of a quotation from the text; they must also identify where and how the author supports the gist of the quotation (RI.3.1,2,3,8; RI.4.1,2,3,8; RI.5.1,2,3,8).
- Questions 8 and 9 prompt students to recall details from the text about important events and one of the characters in the historical fiction text (RI.3.1,2; RI.4.1,2; RI.5.1,2).

***Franklin and Winston: A Christmas That Changed the World* by Douglas Wood**

- Questions 1, 3, and 5 focus students' attention on the author's use of descriptive details as an aspect of characterization (RI.3.1,2; RI.4.1,2; RI.5.1,2; RL.3.3; RL.4.3; RL.5.3).
- Questions 2, 6, 10, 11, and 12 prompt students to recall details from the text about important events and characters (RI.3.1,2; RI.4.1,2; RI.5.1,2).
- Questions 4 and 7 each ask students to analyze the meaning of a key vocabulary word and to explain how evidence from the text supports the use of this term (RI.3.1,2,3,4,8; RI.4.1,2,3,4,8; RI.5.1,2,3,4,8; L.3.4,5; L.4.4,5; L.5.4,5).
- Question 8 asks students to examine the use of a phrase, a nickname of sorts, for a phenomenon related to the central idea of the text (RI.3.4; RI.4.4; RI.5.4; L.3.4; L.4.4; L.5.4).
- Question 9 addresses the personification of abstract nouns—key academic vocabulary, as well—and requires students to cite evidence from the text to support the author's choice of words (RI.3.1,2,3,4,8; RI.4.1,2,3,4,8; RI.5.1,2,3,4,8; L.3.1,4,5; L.4.1,4,5; L.5.1,4,5).

Performance Assessments

- The first performance assessment allows students to identify and summarize key ideas concerning two related topics, drawing from two sources, and to write an informative/explanatory essay (RI.3.1,2,3,7,8,9; RI.4.1,2,3,7,8,9; RI.5.1,2,3,7,8,9; W.3.2,9; W.4.2,9; W.5.2,9).
- The second performance assessment requires students to formulate and defend an opinion about the events they have been analyzing in the historical fiction texts. They could easily also draw on information gleaned from the first text (RI.3.1,2,3,7,8,9; RI.4.1,2,3,7,8,9; RI.5.1,2,3,7,8,9; W.3.1,9; W.4.1,9; W.5.1,9).

MORE RESOURCES

PRIMARY SOURCES

New Deal primary sources (Library of Congress)

Anti-Nazi propaganda (Library of Congress)

World War II enlistment poster (Library of Congress)

Photographs of New Deal policies in action (Library of Congress)

Photographs of women and the war effort (Library of Congress)

Enola Gay display (Smithsonian Institution)

Ansel Adams photographs of Japanese internment (Library of Congress)

Portraits of interned Japanese Americans (Library of Congress)

Manzanar Relocation Center from Tower, photograph, 1943 (Library of Congress)

Schoolchildren at Manzanar (Library of Congress)

High school recess at Manzanar (Library of Congress)

Martha Graham, world-renowned dancer and choreographer, declining the Nazi invitation to perform at the Olympics, 1936 (Library of Congress)

Choreographers' protest of Nazism, 1937 (Library of Congress)

The New American Dream: Freedom from Tyranny

(1946 to Late 1950s)

GRADES: 3, 4, 5

OVERVIEW

Energized by the tempo and technology that had characterized wartime production, and with the termination of the emergency supports of Franklin D. Roosevelt's New Deal, America experienced a new burst of post-war prosperity. As a result, the overall standard of living rose markedly for most Americans. Meanwhile, a new foreign enemy emerged: the Soviet Union (U.S.S.R.). Relations between the United States and the U.S.S.R. had been rocky at best both during and in the immediate aftermath of World War II. Their incompatible views of the world gave rise to the long conflict known as the Cold War. America and its allies faced a genuine threat from Soviet Communism, expansionism, and espionage—yet a Red Scare at home led to the violation of basic freedoms of expression and speech in the name of protecting democracy. But this period also saw a renewed, determined, and sustained push for civil rights and racial equality. Lower elementary students will explore what life was like for children in war-torn West Berlin after 1945 in *Mercedes and the Chocolate Pilot: A True Story of the Berlin Airlift and the Candy That Dropped from the Sky*, leading them to craft an evidence-based informative/ explanatory paragraph discussing why the "Chocolate Pilot" was so important to the children he served. *The Wall: Growing Up behind the Iron Curtain* gives older students insight into why author Peter Sis so appreciated the freedom he encountered on the other side of the Iron Curtain.

○ ○ ○

Interested in learning more about this time period? Read a more complete history in the "Era Summaries."

LEARNING EXPECTATIONS

Lower elementary: Students should understand that Americans in the post–World War II world, even as they lived more comfortably at home, saw the new Cold War as a battle between democracy and tyranny and thought that whichever side came out on top would control the future of the world. Students should also know, however, that pursuit of Communists at home led to some people's rights being trampled. They should understand that the 1950s saw the start of a new and dramatic push for the rights of African Americans and other minorities.

Upper elementary: Students should understand that America changed dramatically after World War II. Even as standards of living improved at home, with people moving into suburbs and buying television sets, the United States found itself in a new standoff with a dangerous foreign enemy, the Communist bloc. Students should know that the fear of Communism at home, though not baseless, led to dangerous excesses that for a time threatened the rights of many Americans. But students should also be aware that the 1950s saw the rise of new and determined movements demanding full legal rights for minorities, and that the new civil rights push slowly made crucial gains—in the courts, through legislation, and through social pressure—in the face of harsh opposition.

SUGGESTED ANCHOR TEXTS

The Wall: Growing Up behind the Iron Curtain by Peter Sis
Breaking Stalin's Nose by Eugene Yelchin
Rebekah's Journey: A World War II Refugee Story by Ann E. Burg
John's Secret Dreams: The Life of John Lennon by Doreen Rappaport

FEATURED ANCHOR TEXT

THE WALL: GROWING UP BEHIND THE IRON CURTAIN BY PETER SIS

This autobiography of an American immigrant who grew up behind the Iron Curtain in Czechoslovakia was selected because it poignantly describes how an artist was profoundly affected by government decisions. It contains powerful, symbolic illustrations and clever use of different types of text, including various kinds of informational text (including some that is autobiographical, such as the journal entries); detailed captions; an introduction; and an afterword. The illustrations, text, maps, and journal entries all work together to tell an ever-changing, complicated story of the author's creativity amid the fear and contentious politics during the Cold War.

TEXT STUDY

The following text-dependent questions mine this unusual text for opportunities to consider the author's craft and its relationship to essential content. Answering them requires close reading. The questions highlight distinctive decisions the author made about how to structure and illustrate the book and the ways in which those decisions strengthen comprehension of the content.

1. **Study the illustration, title, and subtitle on the cover of the book. What details do you see in the illustration? What questions do you have that are prompted by the title or subtitle?**
    - The illustration shows a baby playing a drum inside a red, star-shaped wall. It looks like a play yard with boundaries to keep the child inside. There is no gate to get through the wall.
    - The title is simply *The Wall*. Maybe the red star represents the wall.

- Possible questions to ask are, "What does it mean to grow up 'behind the Iron Curtain'?" or "What is 'the wall'?"

  Note: *Because it is likely that students won't know what the subtitle is referring to, it might be a good idea to ask them to speculate about what an "iron curtain" might be, its purpose, and so on.*

2. **Closely read the book's introduction. Why did the author choose to include such a lengthy introduction at the beginning of this particular book? Summarize your understanding of the information in a few sentences.**
   - To understand the historical setting of the book, the reader needs historical background about the end of World War I and the subsequent years through the 1950s. The introduction explains how the world had changed. The author describes how world maps were altered due to the outcome of World War I and the subsequent changes in the governments of participating countries. He also tells of the Eastern and Western blocs in Europe following the end of World War II, and of how Russia ruled the Eastern bloc, eventually bringing Communist rule to that part of Europe.
   - The terms *Cold War* and *Iron Curtain* are explained. The Cold War was the forty-year period during which the United States and the Soviet Union each had nuclear weapons and were therefore in a tense standoff with each other. The Iron Curtain was named by Winston Churchill to describe the parts of Europe that were cut off from the rest of the world by a wall—both a symbolic wall of Communist ideas and a wall that was literally a physical boundary (in Berlin, Germany).
3. **How does the map on the front and back endpapers of the book help readers interpret the use of the color red as a symbol and as a motif in the text?**
   - Red is used to show the Communist countries in the world. In Sis's drawings, red is used to depict the Communist flags, missiles, tanks, and uniforms as well as other symbols of Communism.

     Note: *Students may also notice the use of the color red for the printing of three key vocabulary terms on page 1:* Iron Curtain, Cold War, *and* Communism.
4. **In regard to the structure of this text, how does the writing in italics differ from the writing in a normal, or nonitalic, font?**
   - The writing in italics tells the history in sequence—what was happening in Sis's country. The normal font is telling the story of Sis as he grew up.
5. **According to the text, how did Sis's drawings at home differ from his drawings at school?**
   - According to pages 1 through 4, Sis could draw whatever he wanted to at home. He drew shapes and people.
   - According to pages 5 through 7, he had to draw what he was told to draw at school. At school, he drew tanks and wars.
6. **On pages 4 and 5, the words *compulsory* and *discouraged* are written in bold print and repeated. What do these words mean, and what is the author communicating through the repetition and bolding of these words?**
   - The word *compulsory* means that something is required, not optional. The word *discouraged* means that a person is urged not to do something.
   - Each use of these words illustrates a freedom that is taken away under Communism:
     - He had to join the Young Pioneers.
     - He had to collect scrap metal.
     - He had to attend the May 1 parade to honor workers of the world.

  - He had to take Russian classes.
  - He had to undergo political indoctrination.
  - Religious practice was "discouraged."
  - He had to display his loyalty publicly.
  - He had to participate in group gymnastics to show submission to socialism.

7. **How does the author show the effects of government policy in Communist Czechoslovakia through his narrative and his artwork?**
   - The text at the bottom of the pages and in the journal entries is autobiographical. Sis is explaining how the government affected him and especially his freedom to express ideas through art.
     - For example, even as a young boy, he drew what he wanted at home but was "allowed" to draw only certain things at school. The text describes how although he didn't question things when he was young, he started to realize that he was being brainwashed.
     - Sis then began to express himself secretly through art and music. The twists and turns, advances and setbacks, are conveyed both through the art and through the narrative.
     - His creativity is evident, especially when he uses full color, representing the freedom he felt at the time or in the place where he was.

   Note: The book's afterword explains how drawing was at the heart of the author's eventual settlement in America.

8. **On pages 10 and 11, how does the author convey the "time of brainwashing"?**
   - He created an entire page of red, showing the leaders of Communism: Vladimir Lenin, Joseph Stalin, Nikita Khrushchev, and Leonid Brezhnev. He also shows the Kremlin and heroes of the space race. The only figure on the page in black is the main character. It is striking how he is walking from the red, with his red scarf on, but not included in it. It seems to symbolize that he was not one of the brainwashed, even though the time of brainwashing was overwhelming.

9. **Why did the author choose to include four pages of journal entries within the text?**
   - The author is describing years of personal experiences during the different times of his life.
   - On pages 12 and 13, he tells of the years 1954 through 1963. He tells personal stories to show what life was like in the Communist country, from reporting the victory of putting a cosmonaut in space to describing citizens' fear of trying to escape. He tells how the United States was described to them in films and textbooks as a "capitalistic and decadent" country full of poor people living in the street.
   - On pages 20 and 21, the author tells personal stories to describe how life was changing for the better. He tells how the increased freedom brought the possibilities of greater creativity and even of leaving the country.

10. **How does the author convey the emotions of events of the "Prague Spring" of 1968, described in the text on pages 16 and 17 and illustrated on pages 18 and 19?**
    - A full-color, two-page spread on pages 18 and 19 contrasts dramatically with the black, white, and red sketches in the rest of the book. The full color represents how open it seemed to be in the Eastern bloc with new ideas being allowed in from the United States and elsewhere. The drawing shows the Beatles, Allen Ginsberg, "travel," "art," the Harlem Globetrotters, bell-bottoms, and long hair.

11. **How does the artist convey the crackdown in Czechoslovakia in August 1968?**
    - On pages 22 and 23, he returns to the use of thick black lines and red. He draws a maze to show the confusion of the people when the Russian tanks invaded.

12. **According to the text, what freedoms that we enjoy in the United States were lost in Czechoslovakia as the Iron Curtain fell again?**
    - According to pages 30 and 31, military service became required, phones were bugged, mail was opened, people were watched, Western-style art was banned again, radio stations were jammed, and books were banned.
    - According to pages 34 and 35, borders were closed, artists were told what to paint, professors were required to join the Communist Party before being allowed to teach in the universities, artists and musicians were tricked into signing loyalty statements, films were censored, and everyone was suspected of being an informer.
    - According to pages 36 and 37, people were followed, monitored, harassed, imprisoned, deported, and tortured.
13. **According to the art on pages 38 through 41, what was the boy's dream?**
    - He dreamed of being free. He wanted to fly over the wall to freedom, to the United States. Notice the sketch of New York City and the Statue of Liberty on the bottom right of page 41.
14. **On pages 42 and 43, how does the author communicate the differences between life on either side of the Iron Curtain?**
    - He uses words and color to communicate. The lighter side of the wall seems to be full of living things, whereas the darker side of the wall is lifeless.
    - On the side with freedom, he uses yellow and brown shades of color. The words he records there are *hope*, *justice*, *truth*, *inspiration*, *integrity*, *joy*, *liberty*, *freedom*, *dreams*, *respect*, *dignity*, *wisdom*, *love*, *morality*, *happiness*, *benevolence*, *virtue*, *equality*, *spirit*, *honor*, *knowledge*, *pride*, *trust*, and *art*.
    - On the side behind the wall, he uses blue and gray shades of color. The words he records there are *stupidity*, *terror*, *suspicion*, *fear*, *injustice*, *envy*, *corruption*, and *lies*.
15. **What is communicated in the final drawing on pages 44 and 45?**
    - The boy is still flying toward freedom, and the wings seem to be lifting him over the wall. The writing communicates the idea that dreams come true.
    - The white stars seem to symbolize the collapse of communism in the countries that became free.
    - The countries formerly seen in red are now a beautiful shade of blue.
    - The wall is being broken down by an effort of many people with pickaxes.
    - The caption gives the date when the wall fell down, November 9, 1989.

PERFORMANCE ASSESSMENTS

1. Give students the following task:

- Write an imaginary journal entry (a narrative essay) by Peter Sis, written just after his entry into the United States. Using evidence from the text describing his lack of freedom behind the Iron Curtain, describe what he must have experienced on arriving in a free country.

2. After reading this book, including the afterword, ask students to write an expository/explanatory essay on the ways that Communism affected people's lives during the Cold War.

Ask students to be sure to introduce the topic clearly; develop the topic with facts, details, and examples (for example, students might write a paragraph on each of the effects, citing evidence from the text); link ideas; use precise language and domain-specific vocabulary; and provide a concluding statement. At earlier levels, students may write a coherent paragraph that summarizes the main topic and key details. See standards for more details.

3. Reread the text to glean information from this book about the United States during the Cold War. After students have had a chance to mark pages that have to do with the United States, work as a class to create a timeline of events happening in the Eastern bloc that involved the United States. Choose topics from the chronological timeline for the students to research either independently or in small groups. For example, students might choose to look more deeply into the Cuban Missile Crisis, John F. Kennedy's trip to Berlin, or Cold War bomb drills. Have students write a three- to five-paragraph informative/explanatory essay telling about the key event or key person in the Cold War in the United States.

Ask students to be sure to introduce the topic clearly; develop the topic with facts, details, and examples; link ideas; use precise language and domain-specific vocabulary; and provide a concluding statement. At earlier levels, students may write a coherent paragraph that summarizes the main topic and key details. See standards for more details.

EXTENSIONS

1. Create a class list of questions about living in America during the Cold War. Have students interview grandparents on an audio recorder about their memories of the Cold War. Create a multimedia presentation using voices and photographs of relatives from that time period. Invite grandparents to come and watch the presentation.

2. Read the book *John's Secret Dreams: The Life of John Lennon*. As a class, compare the lives of Sis and John Lennon as they grew up as artists in the age of the Cold War. Note the differences in the ways they were allowed to express themselves and grow in creativity and knowledge. Hold a student-led Socratic seminar discussing their very different childhoods on opposing sides of the Cold War. Discuss how their lives were intertwined because of music and their individual creative contributions to art and music.

CONNECTIONS TO COMMON CORE STATE STANDARDS FOR ENGLISH LANGUAGE ARTS

- Question 1 addresses students' ability to glean information from—and understand the relationships among—the title, subtitle, and cover illustration of an informational text (RI.3.6,7; RI.4.6,7; RI.5.6,7).
- Question 2 helps students understand why the author chose to structure the text the way he did; they must also summarize important information conveyed in this informational text (RI.3.2,5,8; RI.4.2,5,8; RI.5.2,5,8).
- Questions 3, 10, and 11 ask students to explore how the use of color in illustrations reinforces central ideas in the text (RI.3.2,7; RI.4.2,7; RI.5.2,7).
- Similar to question 3, question 4 asks about the author's craft—here, the choice of font to help convey information (RI.3.5,8; RI.4.5,8; RI.5.5,8).
- Questions 5 and 12 ask students to note key details in the text that relate to central ideas (RI.3.1,2; RI.4.1,2; RI.5.1,2).

- Question 6 addresses the author's choice to bold and repeat key words as a method for conveying central ideas (RI.3.1,2,4,5; RI.4.1,2,4,5; RI.5.1,2,4,5).
- Questions 7, 8, 14, and 15 help students recognize how inextricably linked the artwork and the narrative text are in this autobiographical informational text (RI.3.1,2,3,5,7; RI.4.1,2,3,5,7; RI.5.1,2,3,5,7).
    - Question 8 specifically addresses how the author supports an assertion (RI.3.8; RI.4.8; RI.5.8).
- Question 9 asks students to read the journal entries closely and to extract key details related to central ideas (RI.3.1,2,3; RI.4.1,2,3; RI.5.1,2,3).
- Question 13 focuses on what the reader can glean solely from the illustrations on several continuous pages (RI.3.7; RI.4.7; RI.5.7).
- The first performance assessment affords students a chance to demonstrate understanding of the text by writing a narrative journal entry from the point of view of the author (RI.3.1,2,3,6; RI.4.1,2,3,6; RI.5.1,2,3,6; W.3.3,9; W.4.3,9; W.5.3,9).
- The second performance assessment asks students to write an informative/explanatory essay that conveys their understanding of essential events and ideas presented in the text, citing evidence to support their assertions (RI.3.1,2,3; RI.4.1,2,3; RI.5.1,2,3; W.3.2,9; W.4.2,9; W.5.2,9).
- The third performance assessment asks students to write an informative/explanatory essay that conveys their understanding of how essential events and ideas presented in the text relate to events in other parts of the world, citing evidence to support their assertions. It also requires some further research (RI.3.1,2,3; RI.4.1,2,3; RI.5.1,2,3; W.3.2,7,8,9; W.4.2,7,8,9; W.5.2,7,8,9).
- The first extension lets students conduct research, gathering oral histories from those who lived during the time discussed in the text. It also requires them to prepare a multimedia presentation to convey their findings (SL.3.5,6; SL.4.5,6; SL.5.5,6; W.3.2,7,8,9; W.4.2,7,8,9; W.5.2,7,8,9).
- The second extension offers an opportunity for students to read a related text and compare the experience of the author of the featured anchor text to that of another artist who lived during the same time. It also asks students to lead a seminar discussion in which differences between the two artists' experiences are discussed (RI.3.6; RI.4.6; RI.5.6; SL.3.1,2,3; SL.4.1,2,3; SL.5.1,2,3).

MORE RESOURCES

HISTORICAL FICTION

The Composition by Antonio Skarmeta and Alfonso Ruano

Deals with repression under a dictatorship

In the Year of the Boar and Jackie Robinson by Bette Bao Lord

PRIMARY SOURCES

Newspaper article on Joseph McCarthy, 1953 (University of Iowa Libraries)

Julius and Ethel Rosenberg, 1951 (Smithsonian Institution)

Gary Cooper testifying before the House Un-American Activities Committee, 1947 (Library of Congress)

Dwight D. Eisenhower addressing the North Atlantic Treaty Organization, 1963 (Library of Congress)

Political cartoon depicting Mao Zedong and Nikita Khrushchev, 1960 (Library of Congress)

American Ballet Theatre performing in the Soviet Union, 1960 (Library of Congress)

USEFUL WEBSITE

"Mr. Gorbachev, tear down this wall!"

UNITED STATES HISTORY, ERA 17

Communism and Counterculture: The Challenges of the '50s and '60s

(1950s to Late 1960s)

GRADES: 3, 4, 5

OVERVIEW

With the United States and the Soviet Union jockeying for position and fighting to gain allies across the globe, the stakes of the conflict between the superpowers were constantly being raised. As more catastrophic weapons were created, the dance between these two nations became ever more complex, their interaction spilling over into developing nations and fueling the race to space. Though war between the superpowers was narrowly averted in the brinksmanship of the Cuban Missile Crisis, a long and draining war by proxy would fester in Vietnam. While this international theater played out, the home front was seeing dramatic political and social change. From the Civil Rights Act of 1964 to President Lyndon B. Johnson's Great Society, this era would deeply change America's social and economic outlook and practices. *Martin Luther King, Jr. and the March on Washington* gives lower elementary students the context to explore the significance of Martin Luther King Jr.'s leadership by listening carefully to his "I Have a Dream" speech and creating a "found poem" featuring the masterful phrases and words spoken by King. Upper elementary students will explore the historical importance of America's first trip to the moon by reading *Moonshot: The Flight of* Apollo 11 and crafting research essays detailing a topic of interest to them or why the trip was historically important.

○ ○ ○

Interested in learning more about this time period? Read a more complete history in the "Era Summaries."

LEARNING EXPECTATIONS

Lower elementary: Students should understand that the Cold War pitted the democratic West against the Communist East, each attempting to dominate the rest of the world; both sides tried to avoid dangerous confrontations that could end up blowing up the world, but there were still close calls. Students should realize that the 1960s brought dramatic social and political change. The fight for civil rights began to change the country's laws, and the federal government increased its support for the poor and the elderly, but many Americans still fought over what kind of country the United States should be.

Upper elementary: Students should understand that with the invention of the hydrogen bomb in the early 1950s, the Cold War became too dangerous for direct fighting between the superpowers, even though tensions sometimes rose out of control—as in the Cuban Missile Crisis. Students should understand that the United States and the Soviet Union instead struggled to win the support of Third World countries and extend their global influence, as each tried to project the more impressive image, including in the space race. Students should realize that America's determination to block Communist expansion led to a difficult and controversial war in Vietnam, which helped spark a youth revolt against the traditional powers in society. At the same time, the federal government increased its support for social justice causes as civil rights activists won new legal victories and as President Johnson pressed for his Great Society programs. Students should understand, however, that such developments sparked backlash from the white South, and from a growing conservative movement opposed to "big government" programs.

SUGGESTED ANCHOR TEXTS

Moonshot: The Flight of Apollo 11 by Brian Floca
Cracker! The Best Dog in Vietnam by Cynthia Kadohata
Destined for Space: Our Story of Exploration by Don Nardo
John F. Kennedy: The Making of a Leader by the editors of *TIME For Kids*
Little Rock Girl 1957: How a Photograph Changed the Fight for Integration by Shelley Tougas
Marin Luther King, Jr.: A Photographic Story of a Life by Amy Pastan

FEATURED ANCHOR TEXT

MOONSHOT: THE FLIGHT OF APOLLO 11 BY BRIAN FLOCA

This beautifully written informational text about the *Apollo 11* trip to the moon combines a strong narrative with detailed illustrations and helpful text features. It is designated as an exemplary text in the Common Core State Standards for English language arts, and serves as an excellent informational text that is destined to grab the attention of elementary students. The ancillary matter also provides rich informational text and detailed sketches of the rocket, as well as a thorough account of U.S. participation in the space race, beginning with John F. Kennedy's speech of intent in 1961.

TEXT STUDY

The following text-dependent questions elicit close reading of this rich narrative, including the interpretation of such text features as illustrations and original drawings of *Apollo 11*. The questions help students focus on the relationship between illustrations and text, the importance of figurative language, and the author's attention to detail.

1. **Look closely at the diagrams and drawings on the front and back endpapers of the book. How did the artist, in this case also the author, organize his work? Why might the author have included this information?**
   - The annotated diagrams are ordered chronologically, depicting the rollout of the rocket to the launching pad; its launch, transposition, lunar landing, lunar lift-off, and reentry; as well as the quarantine and parades that occurred once the rocket had landed.
   - The author is providing a chronological summary of the *Apollo 11* flight for the reader. He is also showing an illustration to help explain each technical term in the process of launch, orbit, landing, and reentry.
   - The author probably wanted to give an overview of the actual flight from beginning to end that was easy to follow.
2. **Read the Kennedy quotation from 1961 on the flyleaf. What are the key words and phrases in this quotation that show that the United States saw the trip to the moon as part of a "race"?**
   - Kennedy said, "That goal will serve to . . . measure our energies and skills" and "We intend to win." He also used the word *challenge*.

   Note: You may want to extend this into a discussion on Sputnik *and the way it began the space race between the United States and the Soviet Union.*
3. **In the first few pages of text, how does the author describe the two key settings in this account? How does he draw the two contrasting settings together?**
   - On page 1, he describes the moon by saying "high above," "cold and quiet," and "no air, no life, but glowing in the sky."
   - On page 3, he describes Florida by saying "summer," "hot," and "near the sea."
   - On page 3, he draws the settings together by discussing how the astronauts were dressed in "suits not made for Earth," suits made for the "colder, stranger places." Even though they were in hot Florida, they were dressing in preparation for their trip to the moon.
4. **What do you notice about the author's use of "click" on pages 3 through 6 of the text? What does this repetition illustrate for the reader?**
   - At the beginning of the account, "click" is used when the astronauts are donning gloves and helmets, and again when they are being secured by the seatbelts and closed into the hatch.
   - Later in the account, the word is repeated with a prefix, now "unclick," to describe what happens to the gloves, helmets, and straps as the astronauts float around the aircraft.

   Note: The symbolism of being strapped in with a click has a scary element to it—like being locked up. The unclicking seems to bring adventure and a sigh of relief that the astronauts are now safely on their mission.
5. **Why does the author call the rocket "a monster of a machine"? How does he support his statement with facts?**
   - The author is describing the enormous size of the rocket that carried the astronauts' spaceships.
     - It was thirty stories high.
     - It was six million pounds.
     - It was a "tower full of fuel and fire and valves and pipes and engines, too big to believe."
     - It was "mighty and massive."

6. **After reading page 7, summarize the job of Mission Control in Houston, Texas.**
    - Mission Control was monitoring the incoming data on the condition of the equipment (the rocket, ships, fuel, valves, pipes, and engines) and also the condition of the astronauts flying into space ("the beats of the astronauts' hearts").
7. **On pages 9 through 14, how does the author enable the reader to sense the tremendous power of the rocket taking off into space?**
    - On page 9, the illustration shows the flames pushing against the rocket, and the text says, "Flames push hard against the pad, every second pushing harder." It also explains that "mighty arms hold it steady" because it is not liftoff time yet.
    - On page 11, the illustration shows the paint being stripped from the rocket's exterior as the flames push it up from below. The text reads, "It rises foot by foot . . . pound by pound."
    - On page 13, the author writes about the shaking of the earth, the shaking of the air, and the "mighty roar."
8. **On page 17, how does the author describe the direction of the new flights of the *Columbia* and the *Eagle*?**
    - The author writes that the astronauts are "rushing into darkness, flying toward the Moon," and then repeats the description of the moon from page 1.

    Note: *Students may note that the moon is illustrated with the same crescent of light as seen in the drawing on page 2.*
9. **How does the story's setting change on page 19? Why is this setting change important for the reader to note?**
    - The reader is pulled onboard the *Columbia* and the *Eagle*.
    - The reader needs to see what is going on inside the ship: the effects of the lack of gravity.

    Note: *Consider the author's use of repetition on pages 21 and 22 with "Here where everything floats," and discuss what the effect of this repetition is on the reader.*
10. **On page 22, why does the author say, "This is not why anyone wants to be an astronaut"?**
    - He has just explained that the food is not very good, it's not easy to sleep, there is always noise, it is hard to use the bathroom, and it smells bad. With these statements, he suggests that there must be something greater that drives an astronaut to want to go to the moon.

    Note: *Page 23 affirms the astronauts' drive to explore: "But still ahead there is the Moon . . . it takes them in, it pulls them close."*
11. **The text cites American anticipation on the evening of the moonwalk: "And far away, where friends and strangers lean to listen, where friends and strangers lean to hear, there comes a distant voice . . . on Earth they cheer." By studying the illustrations of the family watching the moonwalk, what else can you learn about the emotions of Americans during this evening of history in the making?**
    - In the first illustration, we can see tension and eager anticipation.
    - From the second, we can infer relief, wonder, excitement, and happiness.

    Note: *You may want to lead a deeper discussion here contrasting the parents' reactions and the children's reactions. The parents would know more about what was at stake in terms of the astronauts' safety, and they would know more about the competitiveness of the U.S. and Soviet space programs. The children would be excited about the fairly new ability to see this event in real time on television, experiencing—in a way—the thrill of being on the moon.*

12. **In the final endpaper article, "One Giant Leap," consider carefully Neil Armstrong's famous quotation: "That's one small step for [a] man, one giant leap for mankind." Using all of the background information in the text and in this final article, describe what you think he meant.**

    - His step was a small one when you think about it literally: he stepped onto the moon from the *Eagle*. But the step *symbolized* a huge moment for humankind in general. People from Earth had figured out how to travel to another planet; they had actually reached their goal.

      Note: You might also want to discuss the symbolism involved in the placement of the U.S. flag on the surface of the moon, the plaque, and the call by President Richard Nixon.

PERFORMANCE ASSESSMENT

Have students choose one facet of the *Apollo 11* trip that is of particular interest to them *or* one aspect of the important role this trip played in securing America's place in history.

Use two specific online sources geared toward increasing their knowledge base: one news special on *Apollo 11* from MSNBC and one website that details additional information described on one of the pages of *Moonshot*. After students have chosen a topic and done additional research with at least one more source, have them each write a well-organized, three- to five-paragraph informative/explanatory essay that describes the importance of the topic they have chosen.

The two sources for this assessment activity are as follows:

MSNBC presentation on *Apollo 11*: http://www.msnbc.msn.com/id/21134540/vp/31569056#31569056
Author's notes on *Moonshot*: http://brianfloca.com/MoonshotNotes.html

EXTENSION

As a class or individually, students can reread the book *Moonshot* with the purpose of creating a timeline of events, from sitting on the launch pad to landing back on Earth. Discuss how viewing newscasts from the actual day of the landing and walk on the moon could add to students' depth of understanding about this historic time. Then view the forty-three-minute MSNBC presentation on *Apollo 11*. Stop and start the video to discuss how the video is adding details to those presented in *Moonshot*. After video notes have been added to the class timeline, have each student create a well-illustrated timeline of five sequential events in the journey of *Apollo 11*.

CONNECTIONS TO COMMON CORE STATE STANDARDS FOR ENGLISH LANGUAGE ARTS

- Question 1 helps students understand the efficacy of including a detailed and chronological summary about the book's technical subject matter on the front and back pages of the book. It also helps students understand why the author chose to organize the information as he did (RI.3.1,2,3,7,8; RI.4.1,2,3,7,8; RI.5.1,2,3,7,8).
- Question 2 requires students to focus closely on word choice in a celebrated quotation and explain how it helps illuminate the theme of the text (RI.3.1,2,3,4,6,8,9; RI.4.1,2,3,4,6,8,9; RI.5.1,2,3,4,6,8,9).

- Question 3 prompts students to compare two settings in one informational text and note how the author juxtaposes them (RI.3.1,2,3,5; RI.4.1,2,3,5; RI.5.1,2,3,5; RL.3.3; RL.4.3; RL.5.3).
- Question 4 requires students to determine the emotional effect that the author's diction has on the reader (RI.3.3,4; RI.4.3,4; RI.5.3,4; SL.3.5; SL.4.5; SL.5.5).
- Question 5 asks about the use of an expression that describes the rocket, requiring that students locate the facts supporting the author's metaphor (RI.3.3,4,8; RI.4.3,4,8; RI.5.3,4,8; SL.3.5; SL.4.5; SL.5.5).
- Question 6 requires students to recall important details in the text that support a central idea (RI.3.1,2; RI.4.1,2; RI.5.1,2).
- Questions 7 and 8 draw students' attention to the author's craft in combining illustrations and text with sensory details in a way that conveys the excitement of the rocket launch and the flights of the spaceships (RI.3.1,2,3,7; RI.4.1,2,3,7; RI.5.1,2,3,7).
- Question 9 asks students to note a change in setting and why the author has changed it (RI.3.1,2,3; RI.4.1,2,3; RI.5.1,2,3; RL.3.3; RL.4.3; RL.5.3).
- Question 10 speaks to the author's purpose, asking why the author chose to include certain details about the topic (RI.3.1,2,3,8; RI.4.1,2,3,8; RI.5.1,2,3,8).
- Question 11 helps students examine the impact of illustrations and text together at a critical point in this narrative history (RI.3.1,2,3,7; RI.4.1,2,3,7; RI.5.1,2,3,7).
- Question 12 requires students to think carefully, in both literal and figurative terms, about what they have learned about the *Apollo* 11 mission. They must then convey that understanding to others (RI.3.1,2,3,4; RI.4.1,2,3,4; RI.5.1,2,3,4; SL.3.5; SL.45.5; SL.5.5).
- The performance assessment requires students to reread closely, to do some additional research, and to write an informative/explanatory essay about a critical facet of the history they have learned (RI.3.1,2,3,7,8,9; RI.4.1,2,3,7,8,9; RI.5.1,2,3,7,8,9; W.3.2,7,8,9; W.4.2,7,8,9; W.5.2,7,8,9).
- The extension also allows students to read and/or view one or two additional, related resources on the same topic, building content knowledge and rendering their understanding of events in a detailed timeline (RI.3.1,2,3,7,8,9; RI.4.1,2,3,7,8,9; RI.5.1,2,3,7,8,9; W.3.7,8,9; W.4.7,8,9; W.5.7,8,9).

MORE RESOURCES

HISTORICAL FICTION

Shooting the Moon by Frances O'Roark Dowell

Riding to Washington by Gwenyth Swain

PRIMARY SOURCES

"Soviet Fires Satellite into Space," October 1962 (*New York Times*)

Neil Armstrong's landing on the moon (National Aeronautics and Space Administration [NASA])

John F. Kennedy and Nikita Khrushchev in Vienna (Library of Congress)

Onlookers watching army missiles in Florida (Library of Congress)

United Nations Security Council: meeting on the Cuban Missile Crisis, October 1962 (Library of Congress)

Vietnam War service medal (Smithsonian Institution)

"Nine Rules for Personnel of US Military Assistance Command, Vietnam," 1967 (Smithsonian Institution)

Black Panther Convention, Lincoln Memorial, 1970 (Library of Congress)

Photograph of the Apollo 11 launch, 1969 (Smithsonian Institution)

Draft resistance protest sign, 1967 (University of Washington)

Remains of Bikini Island after nuclear testing, 1968 (Smithsonian Institution)

Space race resources (History Channel)

POETRY AND MUSIC

We Troubled the Waters by Ntozake Shange

ART AND ARCHITECTURE

Hair: The American Tribal Love Rock Musical, 1967 (Official Website)

> *Written during the time period. The official website features photos of the original cast and really showcases the world of the counterculture.*

USEFUL WEBSITES

History of the Apollo 11 mission (NASA)

"October 4, 1957: Soviet Union Launches Sputnik Satellite," article (*New York Times: The Learning Network*)

"The History of Rocketry and Space Travel" (NASA)

The National Security Archive: "The Cuban Missile Crisis, 1962" (George Washington University)

Modern Times: Presidential Scandals, Conservatism, and Unrest

(1968 to Present)

GRADES: 3, 4, 5

OVERVIEW

Winning by a narrow margin, President Richard Nixon, a Cold War conservative, would nonetheless take up the mantle of Lyndon B. Johnson's Great Society, working with a Democratic Congress to push forward even further social reforms. But despite Nixon's successful efforts to reduce Cold War tensions, his inability to end the Vietnam War plagued his time as president—and his paranoid use of power against his political enemies brought about the Watergate scandal that destroyed his presidency. The aftermath found Americans sharply divided about the country's policies; and the nation's politics would follow suit. Conservatism became reinvigorated and found a leader in Ronald Reagan. Reagan worked to shrink the federal government, bolster military spending, and end the Cold War once and for all. But the end of the Cold War did not signal the end of unrest. America itself would sustain a major terrorist assault on its own soil in the September 11, 2001, attacks and a severe economic recession in 2008. Challenges and perils continue to be a part of the American experience. *America's White Table* deepens younger students' understanding of the sacrifices of men and women in uniform. Older students will gain an understanding of a pivotal event in U.S. history that still affects Americans to this day after a close reading of *September 11*.

○ ○ ○

Interested in learning more about this time period? Read a more complete history in the "Era Summaries."

LEARNING EXPECTATIONS

Lower elementary: Students should understand that Americans, in recent decades, have had many different views on how the country should respond to new directions and new challenges. In the 1970s, the war in Vietnam and President Nixon's abuse of his powers divided the country. A new conservative movement pushed to scale back government, wanting to reduce the expensive social role government had taken on in the 1960s, while pushing for a stronger stance against the Soviet Union (U.S.S.R.). The Cold War ended as the Communist world broke up under pressure, but the battle over American domestic policy would continue.

Upper elementary: Students should understand that the United States was badly divided in the 1970s and afterward. The war in Vietnam dragged on, even as Nixon worked to lower Cold War tensions; Nixon angered conservatives by continuing many 1960s government programs; and, finally, he destroyed his presidency in the Watergate scandal, abusing his powers and covering up crimes. Students should understand that a "New Right" movement, led by Ronald Reagan, came to challenge the rapid growth of government social programs and regulations, which they saw as expensive burdens on business that encouraged dependency on welfare benefits. As president, Reagan worked to cut taxes and shrink government, while increasing military spending to pressure Cold War adversaries. Students should realize that the need to match U.S. spending helped force the U.S.S.R. into reform, undermine the Communist bloc, and—boosted by Reagan's swing to diplomacy in his second term—end the Cold War. But that spending also drove up huge U.S. deficits. President George H. W. Bush helped build new alliances as the world changed.

SUGGESTED ANCHOR TEXTS

September 11 by Mary Englar
All the People: Since 1945 by Joy Hakim
America Is under Attack: The Day the Towers Fell by Don Brown
Barack Obama: A Photographic Story of a Life by Stephen Krensky
Who Was Ronald Reagan? by Joyce Milton

FEATURED ANCHOR TEXT

SEPTEMBER 11 BY MARY ENGLAR

This book was selected because it details the story of September 11, 2001, in a way that is both fascinating and appropriate for elementary students. The photographs were chosen with purpose, assembled as a chronology of memorable moments. The text features are varied: they include a map, airport security camera shots with time stamps, a glossary, a "did you know" fact sheet, a timeline of just one day, and important information about four individuals who played pivotal roles on this historic day.

TEXT STUDY

The following text-dependent questions are designed to help students navigate this unusually organized text, which describes a series of related and terrifying events that happened within two unforgettable hours in U.S. history. They also help students understand the causes and effects of the events by asking them to closely examine details, the structural features of the text, the illustrations, and the use of figurative language. Students must cite evidence to support their assertions.

1. **Look closely at the photograph on page 5. What can you learn from the clues in the photograph and the information in the caption about what was happening to the World Trade Center towers?**
   - The people are standing in Times Square viewing a video of the North Tower burning on September 11, 2001.
   - The people are not moving, simply watching the fire and smoke billowing out of the high tower.

- It is morning, as indicated by the *Good Morning America* news show being viewed.
- It was a Tuesday, not hot but warm, as indicated by the people's clothing.

2. **After reading pages 4 through 6, explain the first seventeen minutes of the "surprise attack" (from 8:45 a.m. to 9:02 a.m.), as shared from four different viewpoints in the text. Which of the four viewpoints has the most limited information?**
   - Barry Meier's view came from Greenwich Street in New York City. He was walking at about 8:45 a.m. when he "heard a loud roar." When he looked to see what it was, he saw "a huge silver jet . . . flying closer to the ground than [he] had ever seen."
   - At 8:46 a.m., the head of the Fire Department of the City of New York, Chief Peter J. Ganci Jr., looked out of his window and saw the jet hit the North Tower of the World Trade Center. He shouted to his chief of operations, and they "stared out the window as a fireball burst from the 110-story building." The chiefs jumped into their cars and raced toward the scene.
   - People in the streets saw fire and thick black smoke coming "from a gaping hole between the 93rd and 99th floors. Pieces of steel, airplane parts, debris, and clouds of office papers fell from a huge opening."
   - The people in the North Tower felt "a thud," but didn't know that a plane had crashed into them. Because people in floors below saw the smoke, they rushed to get out of the building as "smoke filled the stairwells, offices, and elevators."

   Note: *The people inside the North Tower seemed to have the least amount of information. The text said that some of the people there thought it was an earthquake. The following paragraph confirms that "most of the 16,000 to 18,000 people in the two towers didn't know that planes had collided into their buildings."*

3. **How does the text describe the second plane hitting the South Tower, and how do the six photographs on page 7 enhance the text in the telling of that story?**
   - The text explains that it was only seventeen minutes between the crashes of the first airplane and the second airplane. It describes how the people only knew to leave because of the smoke filling their workspaces.
   - The first photograph shows the first tower burning in the higher floors and then the second airplane approaching even lower than the first one did. The second photograph shows the impact of the second airplane crashing into the second tower. The explosion erupts into flames. The smoke billows and grows as the photographs progress.
   - The photographs exhibit dramatic details that aren't in the text.

   Note: *The photographs therefore help the reader visualize the sequence of events described in the text, showing how the towers would have looked to an eyewitness at 9:03 a.m. on September 11, 2001.*

4. **Describe the sequence of events that happened in the next hour, between 9:03 a.m. and 10:03 a.m. of that same day. What key word does the author use on page 8 to explain why the Federal Aviation Administration (FAA) order to ground the planes did not work to end the plane crashes?**
   - At 9:25 a.m., the FAA "ordered all airplanes over the United States to land immediately."
   - Despite that order, at 9:37 a.m., another airplane crashed into the headquarters of the Department of Defense at the Pentagon, near Washington, DC.
   - At 10:03 a.m., a fourth "hijacked" airplane crashed near Shanksville, Pennsylvania.

- The airplanes were hijacked, meaning that the pilots of the airplanes could not follow the orders of the FAA. The meaning of the word *hijack* in the glossary is "to take control of an airplane or other vehicle by force."

5. **According to page 8, why are the September 11 attacks so significant for Americans?**
   - It was the "deadliest in U.S. history."
   - A total of 3,379 people died aboard the airplanes, in the World Trade Center, and in the crash at the Pentagon. Among the dead were airline personnel, airplane passengers, World Trade Center workers, police officers, firefighters, and Pentagon personnel.

6. **According to the text, what is al Qaeda, who used to lead them, and what did they seek to do?**
   - On page 10, the text describes al Qaeda as "a group founded in 1988 by [Osama] bin Laden to train Muslims, people who belong to the religion of Islam, to fight against people he called the enemies of Islam." The text goes on to explain that al Qaeda members were expected to "wage war against any government that they thought was harming Muslims."

     Note: *Teachers should point out that the author separates this group from most Muslims by saying that "most Muslims do not agree with bin Laden's ideas and do not believe in killing innocent people for any reason."*
   - Bin Laden was the leader of al Qaeda. He believed that "U.S. foreign policies and American society were harming Muslims in the Middle East and destroying Muslim culture."
   - The nineteen hijackers had a plan to leave on four different planes, each loaded with thousands of gallons of jet fuel, crashing into buildings all at the same time. They did not want America to be able to fight back.

7. **How did the "first responders" react to the emergency situation at the Twin Towers? Why did so many of the emergency workers die?**
   - Within one minute of the first airplane crash, the firefighters and police received the alarm.
   - Over one thousand first responders rushed to the World Trade Center.
   - Evacuations of the buildings were ordered, saving many lives.
   - The New York City fire and police departments set up emergency treatment centers and command centers.
   - Firefighters were sent into the North Tower to rescue people from the danger and to help them get out of the building.
   - Many of the emergency workers, both firefighters and police personnel, died because no one thought the towers would collapse. They had been built to withstand a plane crash, but new planes are bigger and carry more fuel, causing crashes worse than those the towers were designed to sustain. It happened so fast that there was no time to get out. They were doing their job to rescue people who were stranded.

8. **According to page 21, why were the Twin Towers so important to the people of New York?**
   - These two buildings, along with the Empire State Building, "defined the Lower Manhattan skyline" for more than thirty years. They stood "majestically above New York City."

9. **Note the opening statement of page 22. How does this chapter opening demonstrate how difficult this story was to organize?**
   - The opening statement says, "While firefighters were scrambling to help people at the World Trade Center, American Airlines Flight 77 was flying toward the nation's capital."

- This story is difficult to tell because so many different places were involved in multiple events that happened in a short period of time. The author is trying to tell the story chronologically, placing events in the order in which they actually happened, but she has to keep going back to statements introduced by the word *meanwhile*.
    - For example, on page 24, when the author introduces Flight 93, she begins with the word *meanwhile* and then goes back to the 8:42 a.m. departure.

10. **On page 22, the author writes, "Although they worked at the headquarters of the U.S. Department of Defense, none of them knew a plane was headed toward their building." What is the underlying irony of that statement?**

    Note: Teachers will probably need to do a quick minilesson on the word irony.

    - The Pentagon represents "defense" or protection to Americans, yet al Qaeda was so organized and focused on harming America that the group was actually successful at attacking a building created to symbolize defense.
    - People in the Pentagon were watching television coverage of the New York City attack and had no idea that a plane was moments away from hitting their own building, killing everyone on the plane and 125 people in the Pentagon.

11. **How does the map on page 25 help explain the events of September 11, 2001? Which of the four flights did not land in a city?**

    - The map shows the four flights. It shows where each flight began and how each flight was headed west. It shows where each flight turned and headed back east to attack.
    - United Airlines Flight 93 landed southeast of Pittsburgh, Pennsylvania, but not near a city. The text says that it crashed in an empty field near Shanksville.

    Note: This observation is important because it was not the hijackers' intention to crash-land in an empty field. A city was their intended destination also. The courage of the passengers prevented the deaths of many more in an urban area.

12. **Why are passengers on Flight 93 considered heroes?**

    Note: Teachers might discuss the "hero" concept with students if it is a new one to them.

    - It is believed that the hijacking pilots of Flight 93 were heading the plane to attack the White House or U.S. Capitol in Washington, DC. The text explains that the passengers who stormed the cockpit door did so because they knew that they might be able to stop the hijackers or at least divert them from their main targets. Although all of the passengers died, the plane did not destroy the White House or the Capitol; the passengers may have saved many more lives.

13. **The chapter title of pages 28 through 32 is "The Best of America." Where did the author find the title? How do the details that the author included support President George W. Bush's claim that September 11 represented "the best of America"?**

    - The author pulled this phrase from a quotation by Bush. Bush had said it in an 8:30 p.m. address to the nation on September 11, 2001: "Today, our nation saw evil, the very worst of human nature. And we responded with the best of America."
    - The author of this text chose to include many examples of people's willingness to help each other, indicating that they were in fact "the best of America." Some examples are the following:
        - Firefighters, police officers, construction workers, and medics came from all over the United States to help with the search for survivors and to care for the injured.

  - Fighter jets, helicopters, and U.S. warships patrolled the skies or guarded the waters of the eastern United States.
  - All over America, people made efforts to help. They sent money, food, water, ice, socks, and gloves for rescue workers. Restaurants gave free coffee and food to the rescue workers and those clearing debris from Ground Zero.
  - People gave blood to help with the victims' recovery.

14. **What caused the U.S. military to enter Afghanistan in the months following the 9/11 attacks?**
    - According to pages 32 through 35, the Central Intelligence Agency and the Federal Bureau of Investigation learned that al Qaeda and bin Laden led the attacks; they found out that bin Laden was in Afghanistan, but was protected by a group of people called the Taliban. The Taliban agreed with bin Laden that "American foreign policy was hurting Muslim culture."
    - When the Taliban refused to hand over bin Laden to be tried in U.S. courts, the United States sent in military troops to find and capture bin Laden.
    - The goal of the military battles was to remove the Taliban from power and to find bin Laden.
15. **According to the text, how did the attacks of September 11, 2001, change most Americans "in some way"?**
    - According to page 40, many Americans "became more fearful of the world."
    - "Others volunteered more often to help victims of disasters."
    - "Many men and women joined the military to defend the United States."
    - "Countless Americans shared a deep gratitude for the brave first responders who tried to save as many lives as possible."
    - Americans were united, showing "courage and strength in the face of the most deadly and frightening attack in modern American history."

PERFORMANCE ASSESSMENT

Give students the following task:

- Reread the George W. Bush quotation on the plaque pictured on page 37: "Terrorist attacks can shake the foundations of our biggest buildings, but they cannot touch the foundation of America." The word *foundation* is key to understanding this quotation. Write an informative/explanatory essay discussing the literal and symbolic meanings of the word as it is used in the quotation; cite evidence and details from the text that support your assertions.

EXTENSIONS

1. As a class, create a list of interview questions for parents, grandparents, and friends. Students should ask these people questions about where they were on September 11, 2001, and what they remember about that day. They should be sure to ask them, "How has America changed because of September 11, 2001?" Create a class newspaper or class book with the results of students' research into people's remembrances of 9/11.

2. As a class, research heroes of the 9/11 tragedy. Create a wall of heroes to show how this terrorist act resulted in showing off "the best of America."

CONNECTIONS TO COMMON CORE STATE STANDARDS FOR ENGLISH LANGUAGE ARTS

- Question 1 asks students to use information from a photograph and its caption to aid their understanding of events described (RI.3.1,2,5,7; RI.4.1,2,5,7; RI.5.1,2,5,7).
- Question 2 asks students to consider four different points of view and make inferences (RI.3.1,2,3,6; RI.4.1,2,3,6; RI.5.1,2,3,6).
- Question 3 focuses students' attention on examining the ways in which photographs in an informational text enhance their understanding of the events described (RI.3.1,2,7; RI.4.1,2,7; RI.5.1,2,7).
- Question 4 asks students to recall important details in the text and to use context to develop a deep understanding of the meaning of a key word (RI.3.1,2,3,4; RI.4.1,2,3,4; RI.5.1,2,3,4; L.3.4; L.4.4; L.5.4).
- Question 5 asks students to determine the significance of events described in this informational text, prompting them to use evidence from the text to support their claims (RI.3.1,2,3,8; RI.4.1,2,3,8; RI.5.1,2,3,8).
- Questions 6, 7, 8, and 14 require students to recall important details from the text that support their understanding of main ideas (RI.3.1,2,3; RI.4.1,2,3; RI.5.1,2,3).
- Question 9 discusses the author's craft and helps students recognize not only, in general, the importance of how a text is organized but also, in particular, why this text was difficult to organize. Thinking about how to organize the text here reinforces the main ideas of the terror and chaos that ensued on September 11, 2001 (RI.3.1,2,3,5,8; RI.4.1,2,3,5,8; RI.5.1,2,3,5,8).
- Question 10 gives teachers an opportunity to introduce the concept of irony, which here very much enhances students' understanding of the gravity of the events described in this text (RI.3.1,2,3,8; RI.4.1,2,3,8; RI.5.1,2,3,8).
- Question 11 helps students use text features—in this case, a map—to enhance their understanding of the text (RI.3.1,2,3,5; RI.4.1,2,3,5; RI.5.1,2,3,5).
- Question 12 requires students to think about a word with a meaningful connotation and explain how actions described in this text embody that connotation (RI.3.1,2,3,4; RI.4.1,2,3,4; RI.5.1,2,3,4).
- Question 13 prompts students to recognize the relationship between details and evidence in the text and the main ideas that they support (RI.3.1,2,3,8; RI.4.1,2,3,8; RI.5.1,2,3,8).
- Question 15 asks students to cite evidence in support of one of the author's assertions (RI.3.1,2,3,8; RI.4.1,2,3,8; RI.5.1,2,3,8).
- The performance assessment asks students to think deeply about a quotation cited in the text and to write an informative/explanatory essay that conveys their understanding not only of the literal and figurative meanings of a key word but also of the import of the events described in the text (RI.3.1,2,3,4,8; RI.4.1,2,3,4,8; RI.5.1,2,3,4,8; W.3.2,9; W.4.2,9; W.5.2,9; L.3.5; L.4.5; L.5.5).
- The extensions allow students to conduct further research and convey their findings in ways that will enhance their understanding of the events described in the text (RI.3.1,2,3; RI.4.1,2,3; RI.5.1,2,3; W.3.2,6,7,8,9; W.4.2,6,7,8,9; W.5.2,6,7,8,9).

MORE RESOURCES

PRIMARY SOURCES

Antiwar demonstration advertisement in the Washington Post, 1970 (Library of Congress)

Washington Post article covering Richard Nixon's resignation, 1974 (*Washington Post*)

Berlin Wall resources (History Channel)

Ronald Reagan ending the Cold War, video (PBS: *American Experience*)

Camp David Accords, 1978 (Israeli Ministry of Foreign Affairs)

POETRY AND MUSIC

"Hello Ronnie, Good-Bye Jimmy," sheet music, 1980 (Smithsonian Institution)

Era Summaries

ERA 1: ACROSS BERINGIA: ORIGINAL PEOPLE OF NORTH AMERICA (CA. 20,000 BCE TO CA. 1600 CE)

INDIGENOUS PEOPLES ARRIVE

Although scholars disagree on when the first humans set foot in the Americas, recent archaeological work suggests that the first settlers crossed from eastern Asia to the Americas by at least 13,000 BCE—and probably earlier—during the last global Ice Age. The massive amount of water locked up in glaciers lowered worldwide sea levels and created a land bridge called Beringia between Siberia and Alaska (where the Bering Strait now lies).

Until recently, many archeologists had embraced the Clovis model, which stated that the Clovis people—known for their intricate stone tools and spear points—were the first to cross into the Americas from Asia via Beringia. But more recent findings suggest that humans were in the Americas before the Clovis culture, when the land bridge was still blocked by glaciers. One theory posits that early hunter-gatherers came down the Pacific coast, by sea and land that was then exposed by low sea levels, while the land bridge was still ice-locked. Later glacial melt would have submerged their settlements, leaving little evidence of their culture behind.

Around 12,000 BCE, the Ice Age ended, and glacial melt created an ice-free corridor across Beringia. Now larger groups came from eastern Siberia. It is most likely that these groups were the ancestors of the Native American populations that would settle most of North and South America.

DISTRIBUTION, DIVERSITY, AND CULTURAL REGIONS

Across the American continents, climates ranged from subarctic to tropical. These dramatically different environments led to diverse living conditions, animal populations, and natural resources. Settlement patterns and regional cultures were heavily influenced by distinctive opportunities for hunting, gathering, and settlement in each region.

Over thousands of years, the post–Ice Age climate shifted, altering plant and animal life forever. Climate change, possibly coupled with hunting by humans, led to the extinction of the wooly mammoth and other large animals. As resources changed, human communities were forced to change, too; some migrated to other regions, whereas others adapted to new conditions and took advantage of new resources.

Many people in North America lived as hunter-gatherers, divided into diverse language groups and spread across the continent. Peoples settled in distinct climatic zones, such as the Eastern Woodlands, Great Plains, Southwest, and Northwest Coast. Some groups lived in settlements for at least certain parts of the year, farming local plants and exchanging local resources with other groups through broad trading networks.

Farming communities were well established in Central America (also known as Mesoamerica) and South America by 1500 BCE, forming complex societies with social classes, political organization, and ritual practices.

NATIVE AMERICAN CIVILIZATION IN NORTH AMERICA AND BEYOND

In North America from circa 1000 BCE to 500 CE, the Adena and the Hopewell cultures built large ceremonial mounds, first along the Ohio River and later throughout the Mississippi Valley. Many of these mounds, and those of later cultures, can still be seen. The ruins puzzled early European settlers, who refused to believe that supposedly primitive Native Americans could have built them.

After 200 CE, settled farming communities appeared in North America's Southwest, cultivating crops (for example, beans and squash) introduced from Mesoamerica. The climate gradually became very dry, and groups fought over scarce food and water. They developed irrigation systems and, with warfare erupting over limited resources, started building defensible cliffside settlements.

Cultivated maize from Mesoamerica reached the Mississippi Valley after 700 CE. This allowed the extensive Mississippian mound-building cultures to develop and thrive over the coming centuries, with large ceremonial centers surrounded by agricultural communities in the fertile river floodplains.

In Central America, the militant Aztec Empire—centered on the enormous and advanced city of Tenochtitlan, present-day Mexico City—arose in the 1400s and dominated Mexico at the time of Spanish contact. A sophisticated warrior culture, the Aztecs aggressively exploited those whom they conquered for labor, resources, and human sacrifice.

The other major Native American empire that met the Spanish was the Inca Empire, which had come to dominate South America's Andes Mountains—in present-day Peru—by 1500. The Inca built spectacular urban structures and a sophisticated road system, but like the Aztecs, they also extracted labor, resources, and sacrifices from the local peoples they conquered.

THE EFFECTS OF EUROPEAN CONTACT IN THE AMERICAS

North America's southwestern cultures were already under siege by Mexican peoples and Navaho and Apache tribes before Europeans arrived in the sixteenth century. The Mississippian cultures, overcrowded and afflicted by disease, were also in decline before European contact. In Central and South America, the great Maya civilization had long since fallen by the time Europeans arrived, but the powerful Aztec and Inca Empires were both at their height when the Spanish first came.

The Europeans' contact with what they called the New World began when Christopher Columbus's Spanish-financed expedition landed in the Caribbean in 1492 (see era 2). For the native cultures, the consequences of this contact were immediate and dire. The Caribbean islanders were essentially reduced to slaves as the Spanish sought to extract mineral wealth and tighten their hold on their newly conquered territories. Within a few decades, the native island people virtually vanished.

Spanish expeditions soon moved to the mainland, challenging the Aztec and Inca Empires. Spanish forces succeeded by pitting groups of native peoples—whom the Aztecs and Incas had dominated and used for their human sacrifices—against the empires. Although the natives were willing to help Spain, they were soon subjected to the country's harsh rule and forced to convert to Christianity (see era 2).

Europeans' heaviest impact on the Americas was unintentional. The explorers carried pathogens that were common in Europe, Asia, and Africa, but to which the biologically isolated peoples of the Americas had no resistance. Measles, smallpox, and other diseases quickly spread throughout the Americas. Scholars disagree over the death toll, but these so-called virgin soil epidemics may have killed as much as 90 percent of the Native American population within a few generations of contact. Meanwhile, Europeans carried syphilis back to Europe, where it would become a major health scourge.

North America, settled by Europeans well after they conquered Central and South America, had already been devastated by disease before European settlers arrived there—in North America, cultural contact was therefore made with already weakened populations.

Disease, however, was only one part of the vast transfer of plants, animals, peoples, and cultures that began as contact opened between Europe, Asia, Africa, and the Americas—a process that has been called the Columbian Exchange.

Europeans also brought their livestock and crops. The horse, previously unknown in America, would have a profound influence on native ways of life. Many crops cultivated by Native Americans and some animals they had domesticated or consumed were quickly introduced to Europe, Asia, and Africa. These included maize, chilies (called "peppers" by the Spanish to spur competition with prized black pepper from Asia—a trade then dominated by Portugal), chocolate, turkeys, potatoes, and tobacco. The results of this exchange and diffusion would dramatically transform the economies, environments, and cultures of both hemispheres.

ERA 2: DRIVEN TO DISCOVER: EUROPEANS ESTABLISH THE NEW WORLD *(LATE 1400S TO LATE 1600S)*

EUROPE DISCOVERS THE AMERICAS

Europeans had long prized Asian silk and spices. But Central Asia's Silk Road—the ancient trade thoroughfare—was long and dangerous, and made Asian goods scarce and expensive. Europe also lusted after the East's legendary wealth, which was evoked in Marco Polo's hugely popular thirteenth-century account of his travels to China. By the fifteenth century, the Renaissance and its probing intellectual culture had inspired Europeans to look beyond their continent. New shipbuilding technology made long ocean voyages possible, while expanding commerce encouraged bold gambles for new sources of profit. At the same time, Europeans believed deeply in bringing the Christian gospel to new lands. Their quest for new routes to Asia thus began in earnest.

During the fifteenth century, the Portuguese pioneered ocean routes along the African coast and opened access to India. Spain's King Ferdinand and Queen Isabella feared that Portugal, their neighbor and rival, would monopolize trade with Asia. They sponsored Genoese navigator Christopher Columbus, who thought he could reach Asia by sailing west across the Atlantic. Though Viking colonists from Greenland had found Newfoundland around 1000 CE and briefly settled in a colony there, called Vinland, knowledge of their discovery had been long forgotten: Columbus had no inkling that unknown continents lay just where he thought Asia would be.

Columbus's three ships, the *Nina*, the *Pinta*, and the *Santa Maria*, landed in the Caribbean in 1492. In four voyages that spanned a decade, he explored the area's islands and reached South America. He remained convinced that he had found China and Japan (these were then considered part of the "Indies"—hence the name "Indians" for Native Americans). But other explorers like the Florentine Amerigo Vespucci, sailing in the service of Portugal, realized that Columbus had stumbled on a new world. A mapmaker soon honored Vespucci—who claimed to have discovered South America—by calling the new land America.

A 1493 papal decree and the 1494 Treaty of Tordesillas divided the entire non-Christian world between Portugal and Spain. A line down the Atlantic ceded Asia to Spain, and Portugal acquired India and Africa. The nations later learned that the treaty's dividing line actually ran through the newly discovered Americas. Portugal gained Brazil, which was east of the line. Spain gained everything else.

Spanish settlement quickly took hold in the Caribbean, where the native islanders were virtually enslaved. But disease and exploitation soon decimated the native communities, and the Spanish lost their labor supply. Despite early European hopes, the islands also failed to yield much gold or silver. But the Spanish heard rumors of wealthy empires on the mainland (Columbus thought these tales referred to China, which he still believed was just over the horizon).

In 1519, Hernán Cortés led an expedition from Cuba to Mexico. Though his army numbered only five hundred, he found allies in local peoples who had been subjugated by the militant Aztecs. Cortés took the Aztec emperor Moctezuma (or Montezuma) hostage, trying to rule through him; when this failed and Moctezuma was killed, the Spanish rallied their local allies to besiege and conquer the vast Aztec capital city of Tenochtitlan. By 1521, the Spanish had taken control of Mexico, imposing their own strong and often brutal rule in place of that of the defeated Aztecs.

From their Central American base, Spaniards then moved against the other great Native American power, the Inca Empire of the Andes. In 1531, brothers Francisco and Gonzalo Pizarro led an invasion of Inca Peru, again recruiting local allies against the Inca overlords. They defeated the emperor Atahualpa and held him for a massive ransom, before finally murdering him and installing a puppet leader in his place. The region descended into chaos during the ensuing decades of Inca revolts and Spanish infighting (during which both Pizarro brothers were killed by rivals). Spain managed to impose control, but only very slowly.

EUROPEAN RIVALS IN THE AMERICAS

As Spain tightened its grip on Central and South America, its American empire, called New Spain, melted down the gold and silver treasures of the conquered peoples and forced natives to dig for more. Gold and silver from the mines of New Spain filled regular treasure fleets, on which Spain's vast and growing global power soon came to depend. The Spanish state and the Catholic Church worked together to control the conquered peoples. They often imposed harsh government on them and stamped out native religious beliefs, which they viewed as idolatrous superstitions.

Other European powers did not accept Spain's exclusive claim to the New World. In 1497, Italy's John Cabot (who had been commissioned by England) discovered the North American mainland. Spain also claimed ownership of that continent and tried to keep others out, but North America was too large and too far from Spain's Mexican center of power. The Spanish were unable to block others who were also interested in controlling the newly found lands. England and France explored the coasts, and adventurers and entrepreneurs created new settlements. Rival empires emerged and expanded, fighting for ownership whenever they met.

An English group led by Sir Walter Raleigh tried to gain a British foothold on Roanoke Island (in present-day North Carolina) in 1587. A resupply mission, delayed by the Spanish Armada's attempt to invade England in 1588, finally arrived in 1590 and found the colony abandoned. The Virginia Company of London tried establishing the Jamestown settlement as a commercial venture in 1607. This British group hoped to match the Spaniards' success in finding precious metals, but found very little.

Led by John Smith, Jamestown survived disastrous early famine (the "starving time") to become the first permanent British settlement in America. When the settlers' attempts at Spanish-style mining failed, they turned to agriculture. Long-term settlers achieved wealth from commercial crops and valuable land, gradually replacing early gold-seeking adventurers. Over the coming decades, British settlement along the Atlantic coast would focus on farming and fisheries.

France also had its eye on North America and began expanding into Canada in the early seventeenth century. France's aim was always to make money, particularly through its fur trade with Native Americans. Although the French controlled much of Canada and the Mississippi Valley by 1700, they settled the land only lightly, viewing it mainly as a commercial base. France, in any case, quickly shifted its emphasis from North America to the more profitable sugar islands in the Caribbean.

Other European states also tried staking claims in North America, but few succeeded. The most profitable was a Dutch commercial enterprise, which mainly engaged in the fur trade. But the New Netherland colony, established in the 1620s with New Amsterdam as its capital, came under British control in the 1660s and was renamed New York.

AIMS OF BRITISH SETTLEMENT DIFFER BY REGION

After the first settlers in Virginia failed to gain wealth through mining, new communities switched to farming such valuable cash crops as indigo, rice, and tobacco (a North American crop already cultivated by Native Americans but previously unknown to Europeans). Successful planters imported indentured servants, who were bound to serve their masters for a specific term of years. In turn, servants could attain their own wealth after they fulfilled their terms. For a brief period, Chesapeake society was unstructured enough to promote real social mobility, and indentured servants were able to work toward their own economic success.

In contrast, New England was settled by religiously motivated families who abandoned what they saw as a corrupt English church and fled the persecution they faced in England due to their outspoken nonconformity. The Pilgrims arrived first: they were strict Separatists who wanted to sever ties completely with the Church of England. After having tried to settle in Holland, they chartered the *Mayflower* to take them to America, hoping to build a godly community in the "wilderness." Landing at Plymouth in 1620, they rejected the English commercial investors who had backed their venture and created the Mayflower Compact. The document mirrored those compacts on which Separatist churches were founded, in that it created a government based on majority vote.

The number of Plymouth Pilgrims was soon dwarfed by a far larger migration of Puritans to New England. Though less radical than the Separatists, Puritans were strict Protestants who wanted to purify Christianity by restoring its earlier practices. After facing persecution under the strongly anti-Puritan King Charles I, their hopes of reforming the Church of England waned. Thus, some of them aimed to establish a godly society in the New World. The Puritans won a royally approved charter to establish a commercial colony, but they tricked the king and used the charter to establish their own government in Massachusetts: their faith, rather than potential profit for Britain, was what motivated them.

After the Puritans settled Boston in 1630 and began to expand, the Massachusetts Bay Colony became a magnet for further settlement. The Puritans centered their towns on independent church congregations. Their brand of Puritanism thus came to be known as Congregationalism. These colonies spread throughout New England, and each pursued its own form of Puritanism. Whereas the Virginia settlers focused on cash crops and dramatic profits, the Puritans supported their communities through farming and fishing.

As mid-Atlantic settlement grew around the newly won colony of New York, the region shifted its focus to seaborne trade and commerce. The Hudson River Valley was filled with large cash-crop farms, which were often controlled by powerful Dutch families from the earlier New Netherland colony. New York City, formerly New Amsterdam, became a prominent port for trade with Europe and other colonies. These global contacts, in addition to the earlier Dutch settlement in the area, created a dynamic religious and ethnic diversity in New York that was unique among the British colonies.

Most of the early colonies were established by companies that were created with royal consent to run profit-seeking ventures in America. But Britain soon pushed aside this corporate model, the king taking direct charge of many of the colonies. He appointed their governors, and Virginia was given a royal governor in 1624. Britain repeatedly sought to annul New England's almost completely independent charters, but Britain's civil war and the temporary overthrow of its monarchy delayed its efforts to assume control of the New England colonies for decades.

Another model for colony creation soon arose: individual proprietors began to found colonies as their personal ventures. As early as the 1630s, proprietary governments allowed powerful men to create colonies based on their personal beliefs and in the interest of personal profit. For example, Lord Baltimore established the proprietary colony of Maryland partly to create a haven for his fellow Roman Catholics.

THE COLONISTS ENCOUNTER THE NATIVE NORTH AMERICANS

By the time European settlers arrived in North America, the virgin soil epidemics unwittingly unleashed by the Spanish had already spread from the Caribbean and Mexico throughout the Americas. Though the exact death toll is unknown, 90 percent of the native population may have died in some regions. The groups and regional alliances that the Europeans encountered varied greatly, in regard to both their remaining strength and their attitudes toward the newcomers.

The French lightly settled a central region in Canada, using it as a base for trade *with* Native Americans. Though French Jesuits actively tried to convert the Native Americans to Catholicism and were sometimes attacked and killed, the French were more likely to clash with the enemies of their own Native American trading partners and religious converts: France fought with the Great Lakes region's powerful Iroquois Confederacy, an enemy of many French-allied peoples.

British regions were different because their communities often relied on farming instead of trade. Unlike the French colonies, British settlements thus needed land to expand. Although the British settlement pattern offered unique opportunities and personal freedoms to the British settlers, conflict with the native peoples already living on that land was inevitable.

In Virginia, the Jamestown settlers encountered a confederacy led by the powerful Chief Powhatan. Early relations between settlers and the native people were tense, as each tried to gain advantages from the other. Mutual mistrust and strained diplomatic efforts (including the kidnapping of Powhatan's daughter and emissary, Pocahontas, and her diplomatic marriage to settlement leader John Rolfe) escalated into fighting. By the 1620s, Powhatan's successor tried unsuccessfully to wipe out the growing colony. Thus began the long demise of the native peoples there.

In contrast, initial relations between local tribes and the New England settlers were often friendly. The Indians helped settlers survive by teaching them to farm local crops and take advantage of natural resources. The peaceful relations are famously commemorated in depictions of Plymouth's "first Thanksgiving." But New England's farm towns needed space, and settlers came to view the native people as obstacles to their success. Active efforts to convert and "civilize" the Native Americans—that is, to shift their mobile, hunter-gatherer lifestyle to a settled, Christian model—resulted in some groups of "praying Indians'" settling their own towns. Yet expanding colonies ultimately turned against even these groups.

To be sure, New England's early settlers and some tribes formed alliances that lasted for decades. But the settlers found themselves at odds with other groups, including their local allies' own traditional enemies. As early as 1636, tensions erupted into the brutally violent Pequot War between a tribal group and an alliance of New England colonies—with the colonists aided by native allies traditionally hostile to the settlers' Native American adversaries.

Rapidly expanding settlement worsened tensions throughout the colonies. Both sides increasingly abandoned all restraint, killing civilians wholesale in wars and raids. As the frontier moved steadily westward in the following decades, settlers' rapid encroachment threatened to extinguish Native American cultures. Ever-increasing bitterness drove many native groups to ally with Britain's imperial rivals, particularly the less land-hungry French with whom they could much more easily coexist.

ERA 3: UNIQUELY AMERICAN: THE BEGINNINGS OF A NEW NATIONALITY *(1607 TO LATE 1600S)*

THE EARLY COLONIES: REGIONAL DIFFERENCES ABOUND

Early southern colonists were mainly adventurers pursuing quick wealth through mineral exploration. When their hopes of easy fortunes faded, settlers turned to cash crops. Still, their singular aim was money—not the establishment of permanent settlements. Many came to America as indentured servants, serving the master who paid their passage for a fixed term: once free, a former servant could pursue his own fortune. Men far outnumbered women, making conventional married life impossible for most. The low birth rate, coupled with disease and civil unrest, created tremendous social instability in the southern colonies' earliest days.

Over time, the most successful planters gained land and wealth. As a result, opportunities for rapid advancement faded as southern society became more settled and more stratified. Below the great planters were yeoman farmers working small holdings as well as a large laboring underclass. Early on, women had achieved some independence and opportunity as looser rules weakened traditional barriers: there were, for instance, successful female landowners in the early period. But as permanent communities formed, women's opportunities vanished as they were pushed back into traditional domestic roles.

In Massachusetts, Governor John Winthrop invoked the Biblical image of a "city on a hill" (a virtuous beacon for the world) to describe the Puritan mission, a metaphor that would resonate powerfully for later generations of Americans. But the Puritans' true aim was to create a godly community for themselves—as opposed to a model for others. Whereas men led the southern migration, many Puritans arrived as members of nuclear families. The presence of women, a healthy population increase, and long life spans helped ensure social stability. The migration largely ended after 1642, however, when England's civil war offered Puritans an alluring opportunity to create a Puritan Britain. Some settlers returned to England, and the number of new colonial arrivals plummeted.

Compared with Britain, the New England settlements offered people relative equality in wealth, status, and education. Although women did not have official church leadership roles or a voice in government, their opinions often drove community attitudes and directions. And although religion remained central, larger towns that focused on fishing, shipbuilding, and overseas commerce emerged along the coast. Non-Puritans who arrived pursued economic opportunity, as opposed to religious community, and thus created additional tensions. Many Puritans were drawn into wider commercial networks that threatened the religious isolation the founders had envisioned, and children began to drift from their parents' Puritan zeal.

The middle colonies on the mid-Atlantic coast were mainly driven by profit. The Dutch created the most prominent settlement, New Netherland (which would ultimately become New York) as a commercial venture. The British who later took over the colony, and the many Dutch settlers who remained (including such families as the Roosevelts), also embraced a commercial focus as large towns like New York City emerged as powerful centers of overseas trade.

Uneven success led to great wealth and class division in these trading centers, and communities with both great affluence and dire poverty soon mirrored Europe's old and crowded cities. Inland, the great plantations in the Hudson River Valley further promoted stratification, with dominant Dutch families controlling vast stretches of land. At the same time, widespread commerce brought merchants and settlers from many countries and created a mid-Atlantic society with unusual ethnic diversity. In parts of the mid-Atlantic and South, poorer immigrants (including

Scots, Irish, and Germans) were often drawn to the backcountry frontier, where they could take land (frequently from the Native Americans, toward whom they were often very violent) and build communities.

The colonies' rapid expansion worsened tensions with Native Americans, whose way of life was under siege. Early settler wars against the native groups had broken most of the rules that maintained any level of civility between settlers and Native Americans. Now each side was prepared to attack the other with almost unlimited fury. In New England, strain between settlers and several tribes erupted into King Philip's War in 1675. Native American forces were eventually defeated, but only after heavy fatalities and the total destruction of many colonial towns. In 1676, Virginia's governor tried to curb conflict between settlers and Native Americans that had driven frontier settlers from their homes. A frontier uprising against the governor, called Bacon's Rebellion, resulted in further warfare. Native Americans everywhere were losing ground.

RELIGIOUS TENSION AND TOLERANCE

Religion was pivotal in the lives of many Americans—both in New England, where settlements were established for chiefly religious reasons, and throughout the colonies. But colonists' attitude toward those with *different* beliefs and practices was a complex issue—and one that shifted dramatically over time.

Since the English Reformation under King Henry VIII, the Church of England (also known as the Anglican Church) had been an independent national institution led by the king. Some colonies, such as Virginia, the largest and most heavily populated of the southern provinces, simply followed England's model and officially established the Anglican Church. The church was supported by taxes imposed on the colonists. Unlike England, however, America had no Anglican bishops.

The New England colonies were created to provide freedom of worship for Puritans. Prominent Puritan ministers were among the first settlers, and the towns were designed around Congregationalist churches. Puritans had little tolerance for people of other faiths and actively sought to keep them out. Indeed, Massachusetts even executed several Quaker missionaries who dared to return after their banishment from the colony.

In the first few years of Puritan settlement, dissenters fled the New England colonies to establish the settlement that would become Rhode Island. Separatist minister Roger Williams had been cast out of Massachusetts after quarrelling with other preachers and challenging the government's power over religion. Anne Hutchinson and her followers had challenged the authority of the most prominent ministers in Boston, and sparked a major crisis that nearly tore Massachusetts apart. Insisting that government could not favor one faith over another, Rhode Island allowed full religious tolerance and separated church from state. This concept of religious freedom would gain ground through American history to come.

Proprietors of other colonies also pursued their own religious aims. The Catholic Lord Baltimore insisted on religious freedom for Catholics in his province of Maryland, whereas English Quaker leader William Penn established Pennsylvania as a Quaker haven and a proprietary commercial venture. This caused friction with the non-Quaker settlers who resented his political control despite the colony's full tolerance for other faiths.

THE RISE, ENTRENCHMENT, AND REGIONAL PATTERNS OF SLAVERY

Slavery had existed in most human societies from the earliest days. In Africa, forms of slavery had existed for millennia as debtors, criminals, and captives in war were all made slaves. Slave trades from Africa to the Muslim world, across North Africa and the Sahara, had also operated for centuries. As Europe's contact with Africa increased after the fifteenth century, its efforts to conquer African territory largely failed. However, a slave trade with coastal African kingdoms soon emerged.

A small number of African laborers were first brought to Virginia in 1619. At first, they were viewed as indentured servants: that is, potentially free after a fixed term of service. Some Africans achieved freedom and even became wealthy in the economically mobile society of the early South. But a far more rigid system of slavery quickly developed.

As large cash-crop plantations gained a foothold in the southern colonies, the need for labor skyrocketed. Yet as opportunities for rapid advancement diminished in the increasingly stratified colonies, the flow of white indentured workers steadily declined. Planters became highly dependent on African slaves, who were immune to many illnesses that afflicted settlers working in disease-ridden rice and indigo farms. Common racial beliefs of the time encouraged many planters to see black Africans as naturally inferior.

The Western Hemisphere's rapidly expanding labor demand led slave traders from various European nations to buy ever larger numbers of slaves from Africa's coastal states. Slave exports became a major source of those nations' wealth. Wars and raids ravaged the African interior, as people were captured by other Africans and forcibly marched to the coasts. As many as half died along the journey. Powerful African kings rented coastal land to Europeans for slave-trading fortresses, where slaves were sold to European merchants and packed onto ships for the dreadful Middle Passage to the Americas.

The vast majority of slaves went to the sugar plantations of the Caribbean and Portuguese Brazil, where dismal conditions and high mortality required a constant supply of fresh laborers. But slavery took hold throughout British North America, too. The institution was especially important in the South, with its large-scale system of cash-crop plantations. Slavery was not limited to the South, however: it also developed on the large plantations of New York's Hudson River Valley and in parts of southern New England. It also spread beyond plantations to cities, where slaves were trained as artisans or urban laborers, and to towns, where they were held as domestic servants and farm workers.

At first, the legal status of slaves raised hard questions. Would slaves be freed after a certain term of service? If they were indeed "servants for life," what would be their children's status? In the early years, answers varied by place and circumstance. In time, however, the legal status of slaves became more clearly defined. By the end of the seventeenth century, it was firmly established that slaves were permanently unable to be free, and that children would inherit their mother's bondage. Slavery was now an established part of early American society.

THE RISE OF REPRESENTATIVE GOVERNMENT AND POPULAR POWER IN THE COLONIES

One of the crucial developments in the colonies—one that would affect the colonists, the future United States, and ultimately the world—was the rise of local self-government. Because it could take months for a letter to cross the Atlantic, many government decisions had to be made in the colonies themselves. More important, by electing representatives who in turn held strong influence in their respective local governments, American settlers assumed more power than most people throughout the world enjoyed.

In Virginia, a representative body was introduced under the original corporate charter. Reforms introduced to satisfy the growing population created the Virginia House of Burgesses in 1619, elected by white, male, Protestant, landowning adults, which granted a very wide franchise by the standards of the day. This was the first elected legislature in British America, and it was retained when Virginia received a new charter as a royal colony in 1624. By the late 1630s, the burgesses were ordered to meet at least once per year.

The New England Puritans had planned to govern themselves all along. Though the British government had assumed that Massachusetts would be run from London as an overseas investment enterprise, the settlers brought the charter to America in 1629 and created a local government in Boston. A company head served as the colony's governor, the corporate board its legislature, and the shareholders its voters. The legislature, or the voters themselves, elected all officers. Although the colony accepted the king as head of the British Empire and flew the royal flag over Boston's fort (an important concession because the flag bore a cross, which Puritans considered idolatrous), the king had no role in their internal government.

There were other New England innovations. The town meeting served as the colonies' main means of local government. Local affairs were decided there by majority vote, and town representatives for the colonial legislature were chosen there as well. All adult, male, property-owning church members could vote; in New England's relatively egalitarian society, that included most men (and the property requirement was not always enforced). Tensions rose, however, as the region's commerce expanded and more non-Puritans arrived. Those who were not church members had no voting rights.

As other colonies were founded, colonial legislatures became the universal standard. Outside New England, property requirements excluded many men from voting, and power was confined more tightly to the wealthy elite. Nonetheless, the right to vote was far more widespread in the colonies than virtually anywhere else in the world, even in comparison to the election of Britain's Parliament. In the colonies, the powerful had to win the support of ordinary farmers—a reality that, in those times, was nothing short of revolutionary.

The circumstances of the seventeenth century helped strengthen local governments. Aside from its distance from the colonies, Britain had little time to focus on happenings amid its own more pressing political concerns: a bloody Civil War (1642 to 1649), the overthrow and execution of King Charles I (1649), a Puritan-led commonwealth in Britain (1649 to 1660), and the restoration of King Charles II (1660). Thus, the British government had to divert its attention from the colonies to largely manage its own affairs. After Charles II reclaimed the throne, Britain finally stabilized and turned its attention to the colonies. But Americans would not readily give up the self-governance on which they had come to rely.

ERA 4: TAXATION WITHOUT REPRESENTATION: TENSION MOUNTS *(CA. 1660 TO 1763)*

BRITAIN EXPANDS ITS RULE OVER AMERICA

After the fall of the Puritan commonwealth, which had ruled England after the 1649 execution of Charles I, and the restoration of King Charles II in 1660, the British government began to stabilize and turn its attention to America. During Britain's decades of crisis, its North American colonies had grown from a few scattered and tentative outposts to a rapidly expanding, lucrative network of plantations, towns, and trading ports. Now Britain had to determine how it could reap the highest profit.

In the seventeenth century, European powers increasingly saw colonies as producers of valuable raw materials (for example, food, cash crops, and mineral resources) and consumers of the mother country's own exported goods. Colonies existed to benefit the mother country—a premise that had led Britain to challenge Spain's claim to North America in the first place. This system of economic "mercantilism" viewed colonies as necessary in a nation's struggle for self-sufficiency, wealth, and dominance over its rivals.

Even under the Puritan commonwealth, Britain had tried to block the colonies from trading with anyone else. After the Restoration, Parliament passed a series of Navigation Acts, which mandated that colonial imports from Europe had to be carried on British ships. Meanwhile, America's main cash crops (namely, sugar, tobacco, and indigo) could only be exported to British territories. By the century's end, Britain had even tried to stop the colonies from exporting manufactured goods that might compete with its own products. Enforcement was difficult and erratic, and Britain's customs service steadily increased in power and size (and in the resentment it provoked) as it tried to maintain its authority.

Britain also sought tighter control in the political realm, especially over New England's nearly independent governments. Just after the Restoration, Charles II had in fact confirmed Connecticut's elected government with a new charter. But his brother James, Duke of York, believed in absolute royal authority. Before England's civil war, Charles I had tried to revoke the Massachusetts charter, and now James renewed the attack. In 1684, Charles II finally annulled the charter. A year later, James—now King James II—created the Dominion of New England. This single province included New York and all of the New England colonies. Under direct royal rule, the colonists' freedoms were sharply reduced: the dominion allowed neither elected officers nor assemblies.

Colonists chafed under the dictatorial dominion, but the Catholic James II was tolerated in England so long as his Protestant daughters remained his heirs. When James fathered a male, Catholic heir, the English were unwilling to accept a Catholic successor and deposed him in 1688's bloodless Glorious Revolution. When word of James's overthrow reached America the following year, colonists rebelled in Boston and New York, toppling the dominion. Colonists in Maryland also rose against the Catholic Lord Baltimore, Maryland's proprietor. Although it took twenty-five years, the Baltimore family—whose members were, by that time, Anglican converts—eventually regained power.

After James II was deposed and exiled, Britain's newly installed monarchs, King William III and his wife, Queen Mary II, installed a new government in New York, complete with a royally appointed governor and an elected assembly. Massachusetts failed to win back its old charter but was granted a new one. Although its governor was now royally appointed, the elected legislature held considerable power. The old requirement stating that only church members could vote was abolished, thus giving the vote to virtually all of the province's adult men.

THE COLONIES BECOME MORE MODERN, BRITISH, AND LIKE ONE ANOTHER

In the wake of the Glorious Revolution, the colonies became much more politically uniform as Britain pulled them more tightly into a British Atlantic world. Most colonies now had royally appointed governors. Connecticut and Rhode Island managed to keep their elected executives; Pennsylvania, Delaware, and Maryland remained under proprietors who could appoint royally approved governors. A powerful faction in Pennsylvania pushed hard against the Penn family proprietors: Benjamin Franklin spent years in London pressing for a royally appointed Pennsylvania governor, despite his later stance in the American Revolution.

The colonies' modernization was rapid. They developed complex commercial ties with Britain and with other British colonies. At the same time, many traded illegally with other European nations and their colonies, smuggling goods in defiance of the Navigation Acts. Expanding outside ties upset more isolated and conservative forces, especially in New England. Rifts formed in churches and communities, fueling suspicion and dangerous outbursts. In 1692, tensions between traditionalist Puritans in Massachusetts's Salem Village and their more commercially focused neighbors helped spark the Salem witch panic. Puritans worried that their religious mission was failing, and their suspicion of those with outside commercial ties helped bolster fears of a satanic plot against the godly.

Yet trade's transformative influence on society proved unstoppable: it was impossible to preserve the old Puritan ideal of godly communities isolated from worldly corruption in the American wilderness. In the first half of the eighteenth century, traditional religious authorities throughout the colonies were further threatened by the eruption of a populist evangelical Protestantism known as the Great Awakening. Led by such dynamic preachers as George Whitfield and Jonathan Edwards, the Great Awakening's fiery revivalist meetings challenged the more traditional churches and ministers. For many colonists, the split encouraged a broader sense of popular power against established authority.

At the same time, the colonies' cultural world expanded as they gained access to imported books and as their own literary production grew. American printing, rare until this point, became more widely established. Franklin's Philadelphia press is an important example from the early eighteenth century. Newspapers began circulating and soon became established throughout the colonies. News traveled from London and between colonies, helping create a common culture.

In short, the British colonies were developing into more diverse, modern societies. Trade across the Atlantic and between the colonies linked the colonies together while also increasing their contact with Britain. Books, printing, and the exchange of ideas helped the colonies build a shared popular culture. The colonies began to merge from a set of individual outposts, separate from the mother country and from one other, into a single British America with a more British identity—one that included the expectation that colonists would enjoy the traditional rights of Britons.

THE COLONIES' ROLE IN THE EMPIRE GROWS AND BECOMES MORE COMPLEX

As royally appointed governors gained power in the colonies, they established local networks of officeholders and supporters. This created discord between, on the one hand, the governors' followers and, on the other hand, elected politicians who were often hostile, especially because the elected assemblies retained sole power to introduce tax bills—and thus to control the purse strings. Because the governors represented Britain, such quarrels had the potential to create tension between the colonies and Britain itself. Such outcomes were actually rare, however. Most colonists were strongly loyal to Britain as a whole, and they tended to blame the governors themselves rather than their British superiors for any bad blood.

British control of American trade was also problematic. Although colonists generally acknowledged Britain's right to regulate colonial trade for the empire's benefit, many still resented the customs rules and their enforcement officials. Smuggling was rampant, and British attention to the colonies was still uneven. Trade regulations were often poorly and erratically enforced, and corrupt customs officers turned a blind eye to smuggling in exchange for a share of the profits. Any serious British attempt to crack down on smuggling would inevitably cause resentment in the colonies.

Meanwhile, the colonies were often drawn into the empire's frequent conflicts with its imperial adversaries. Beginning in the 1690s, Britain fought a string of wars in and around the Americas—sometimes against the Spanish, but more often against the French. Many Native American groups, who feared further encroachment on their lands by land-hungry British colonists, became French allies and fought against the British American colonies in wars, raids, and border skirmishes.

The last and largest of these wars—known in America as the French and Indian War (1754 to 1763) and in Europe as the Seven Years' War (1756 to 1763)—began because of British-French quarrels over the land west of the Appalachian Mountains known as the Ohio Country. Virginia sent an army under Colonel George Washington to secure the territory; his clashes with French forces led Britain to dispatch troops, and war rapidly escalated. By coincidence, at the very same time, a congress had been called to consider Native American relations and joint colonial defense. Delegates from seven colonies met in Albany, New York, just as the war was starting, and accepted a plan of colonial union proposed by Franklin. This was the first serious attempt at a colonial confederation, but Britain and the colonial governments promptly rejected it.

Britain lost its initial battles with the French and their Native American allies. But after the war spread to Europe in 1756 and ultimately escalated around the globe, Britain won allies and gained military might. By 1759, Britain had invaded Canada and taken Quebec. In 1763, the combatants signed a peace treaty in Paris; the French surrendered Canada and all lands east of the Mississippi. Britain had won an enormous victory, but with much difficulty and at great expense. British attempts to recoup some of those expenses from its American subjects would spark some of the most important events in modern history.

ERA 5: INDEPENDENCE: AMERICA GAINS ITS FREEDOM *(1763 TO 1783)*

THE FRENCH AND INDIAN WAR PRODS BRITAIN TO SEEK REVENUE FROM THE COLONIES

The French and Indian War and the global Seven Years' War that it sparked were long and costly. Although Britain successfully drove the French from Canada, the empire now had to defend the newly conquered Canadian territory—an expensive challenge made more difficult by the territory's hostile French population. Britain had begun the war to defend its North American colonies from the French, and King George III's ministers decided that the colonies should pay taxes to help cover the cost of the war.

To draw more revenue from the colonies, Parliament passed the Sugar Act in 1764. The customs duties on molasses and other imports that smugglers had so often avoided paying (partly because of ineffective or corrupt British customs officials) were now to be strictly enforced. Britain also greatly expanded officials' and courts' powers to enforce the customs regulations.

These changes outraged many colonists. Although they accepted Britain's right to regulate colonial trade for the empire's well-being, they considered the new rules overreaching, burdensome, and unfair. New rumors swirled, including one implying that Britain might begin taxing the colonies directly. Many Americans considered direct Parliament-imposed taxes unnecessary, unjust, and in violation of their rights.

But Parliament ignored the colonists' loud objections and passed another measure, the Stamp Act, in 1765. The act demanded that virtually all printed materials—from legal documents and newspapers to playing cards—be printed on stamped, taxed paper. Stamp taxes were common in England, so the king's ministers expected the colonies to accept the measure without complaint. The ministers even promised that all revenues raised would go toward America's defense, and they appointed colonists as stamp masters to distribute the stamped paper.

Parliament went still further when it passed the 1765 and 1766 Quartering Acts, which required local colonial governments to provide supplies and barracks, or quarters, for British soldiers stationed in their respective colonies. Americans viewed the measures as another tax—and thus as one more violation of their rights.

The ministers, Parliament, and King George III had made a terrible miscalculation. They saw the sums raised through the stamp taxes as fair contributions to the colonists' own defense. But for most Americans, the *amount* of money was never the issue. The colonies already paid heavy taxes to support their local governments and to pay down the colonies' own debts incurred in fighting the French and Indian War. Many paid these local taxes proudly, even boasting of the patriotic burden they were willing to shoulder in support of government and defense. The issue at hand was *how*, and by whom, taxes were imposed.

THE COLONIES REJECT BRITISH TAXATION AND RESPOND TO THE STAMP ACT

According to British legal tradition, taxes represented the people's free monetary gift to the king for the support of his government. Therefore, taxes could only be granted with the people's consent, in person or through their representatives. Although few men in Britain could vote, members of Parliament were seen as representatives of the whole nation. But no colonist could vote in any parliamentary election; Americans had no voice there, nor any control over Parliament's actions. Therefore, Americans had not consented to the new taxes, and Parliament's members were making a "free gift" of money that was not theirs to give.

Americans famously rejected taxation without representation. But the issue went far beyond money. If Parliament could take Americans' money without their consent, what could it *not* do? If the colonists paid the tax, they would be accepting Parliament's right to govern them however it pleased—without an American say in its actions. For most colonists, subjection to such rule—power without check—amounted to despotism and slavery, depriving them of basic British liberties. Although they still accepted the idea that Parliament should have some role in governing America, they argued emphatically that such a role must not include taxation.

The colonists erupted in fury over the stamp tax. Because almost all documents now required stamps, the tax was impossible to avoid, so Americans decided to prevent Britain from collecting it. Angry crowds destroyed stamped paper and forced stamp masters to resign, while local courts allowed business to continue without the purchasing of stamped sheets. Such popular leaders as Patrick Henry in Virginia and Samuel Adams in Massachusetts helped rally "Sons of Liberty" against Britain's new policies—though not against British rule itself. Meanwhile, Benjamin Franklin and other prominent Americans in London pressed the British government to repeal the Stamp Act.

Colonists also organized boycott movements against British manufactured goods, which were crucial to Britain's wealth. Some threatened Stamp Act supporters and destroyed their property. Nine colonies united to protest the act by sending delegates to a Stamp Act Congress in October 1765.

British policymakers were alarmed by colonial agitation, and came under pressure from British merchants fearful of America's nonimportation agreements. The British government was eager to find a way out of the crisis, but it refused to recognize any American claim that would limit Parliament's powers over the colonies. In March 1766, the ministry and Parliament repealed the Stamp Act—but on the premise that the law was unwise and inconvenient as opposed to unjust. To ensure that the colonists understood this distinction, Parliament passed the Declaratory Act, a measure that asserted Britain's *right* to control America "in all cases whatsoever."

Americans were jubilant over the repeal of the Stamp Act. They saw the Declaratory Act as a face-saving gesture only, and believed that Parliament had recognized its errors and was trying to correct its missteps. However, Britain was still determined to draw money from the colonies. A new minister thought an external tax on imports would bypass American objections. Yet although colonists would accept import duties meant to regulate trade, they were *not* willing to pay duties contrived to raise revenue without their consent.

CRISIS BUILDS TOWARD REVOLUTION

A year after repealing the Stamp Act, Parliament passed the Townshend Acts. Americans were now forced to pay taxes on tea, glass, paper, and other imports. The colonists, who had thought the taxation issue settled by the Stamp Act's repeal, were stunned by what they saw as a fresh attack on their liberties. Determined to avoid taxed goods and to pressure Britain, they formed associations to block British imports and produce their own clothing and other goods. John Dickinson's *Letters from a Farmer in Pennsylvania*, reprinted in newspapers and pamphlets throughout the colonies, helped focus and articulate opposition to Britain's policies.

Bursts of violent protest and attempts (led by Massachusetts) to coordinate the colonies' petitions against the acts were seen by nervous royal officials as acts of rebellion and were met with punitive British crackdowns. In October 1768, royal troops occupied Boston—a key center of protest—to enforce obedience. But nonimportation only took firmer hold and spread throughout the colonies.

As petitions and protests brought greater hostility from London, many Americans grew more disillusioned with and dubious about distant powers entirely beyond their control. Gradually, they began to reconsider the very nature of free government. They shaped their views with help from the writings of such political thinkers as the seventeenth-century's John Locke, who argued that God granted basic rights to people through nature and that all government power—even that of kings—was granted to rulers by the people through binding compacts. When founding colonies, Americans had believed they had formed contracts with the king, thus making the king the head of Americans' own local governments. But now they began to reject any automatic subordination to Britain and any role whatsoever for Parliament in governing America.

Faith had always played a central role in American life, and religious beliefs strengthened the growing liberty movement. Most believed they were defending rights that God had granted to the people, and thus their political cause was also a sacred one. Preachers stressed that God alone could rule absolutely, and many worried that coarse soldiers and corrupt British officials would undermine public morality. Yet there was also a long-established colonial belief that America was specially favored, and that divine providence would help America prevail as a seat of liberty so long as the people upheld their faith and their morals.

Bostonians, still garrisoned with troops, chafed under military occupation. On March 5, 1770, after days of clashes, panicked soldiers fired into an angry crowd and killed five colonists. This Boston Massacre—its image quickly immortalized in a defiant engraving by Paul Revere—struck many as the inevitable fruit of oppressive British policies. Though Americans did not yet know it, Britain's ministers had already moved to repeal most of the Townshend duties (except the tax on tea, which was left to uphold Parliament's power to tax). The key issues remained unresolved, and the partial repeal satisfied few Americans. Although their boycott of British imports mostly collapsed later in 1770, they continued the embargo on still-taxed tea.

The Tea Act of 1773 allowed Britain's East India Company to ship tea directly to America, thus lowering its price and undercutting smugglers. But Americans saw the lower price as a ploy to trick them into paying the Townshend tea tax. Committees of Correspondence, which had been formed as suspicions about British plans increased, allowed the opposition to coordinate throughout the colonies. The new tea consignees were threatened, and tea was destroyed. Crisis culminated that December in Boston. Tea ship captains feared public fury and tried to turn back to sea, but the governor refused to let them leave. Townsmen disguised as Native Americans dumped hundreds of chests into the harbor, an act that future generations (though not the participants) would dub the Boston Tea Party.

At the king's urging, Parliament responded with the 1774 Coercive Acts. Boston's port was to be closed until the tea was paid for; if crown officers were to kill rioters, they would be shielded from American courts; Massachusetts's government was drastically altered to curb the people's power; and troops reoccupied Boston. Far from cowing Massachusetts, the "Intolerable Acts" (as colonists called them) enraged nearly all Americans. As calls sounded for a congress to coordinate resistance, further laws only widened the breach. The Quebec Act not only set up a wholly undemocratic government in Canada but also gave full toleration to Canada's French Catholic majority, and American Protestants feared what they saw as the tyrannical influence of the pope. And a new Quartering Act allowed troops to be housed on private property without owners' consent.

THE REVOLUTIONARY WAR: AMERICA STANDS UP FOR FREEDOM, BRITAIN FOR ITS EMPIRE

The First Continental Congress met in Philadelphia in September 1774. Some delegates urged caution, but the majority warned the people to arm and pressed a new nonimportation agreement. Britain responded with Lord North's February 1775 conciliation plan, which only offered that if America submitted to Parliament's revenue demands, North would let the colonies raise the funds themselves. In April, British troops marched from Boston to seize weapons and powder at Lexington and Concord. Alerted by Paul Revere and others in a prearranged warning network, local militia Minutemen met the troops, pushed them back to Boston, and laid siege to the British-occupied town.

In June 1775, the Second Continental Congress asked Virginia's George Washington—prominent landowner, politician, militia commander, and veteran of the French and Indian War—to lead American forces around Boston. These forces would constitute the core of a new Continental Army. Even as Congress issued a statement that justified taking up arms, moderates drafted the Olive Branch Petition, which pleaded for a peaceful alternative solution. George III refused even to receive it. Trying to head off a British invasion from Canada, American forces launched a dismally unsuccessful strike on Quebec. But in March 1776, after months of siege, Washington forced the British to evacuate Boston. He expected the next British blow at New York.

Many Americans remained strongly loyal to Britain—their mother country—despite its attacks on their liberties. They had been reluctant to turn on the king or to consider independence. But the escalating war pushed a number of them to reconsider. *Common Sense*, a January 1776 pamphlet by English émigré Thomas Paine, impressed many with its direct attack on George III and on monarchy itself. Although some colonists still resisted, Congress took up the subject of independence in June 1776. With help from Franklin and John Adams, Thomas Jefferson drafted a declaration. On July 2, Congress voted for independence. And on July 4, the Declaration of Independence was adopted by "the United States in Congress assembled." In laying out the God-given rights of all men and the right of all societies to create their own governments, the declaration would help form a cornerstone of American beliefs and influence throughout the world.

As America formally claimed independence, Britain stepped up its effort to bring the rebellious colonies to heel. The American Revolution began in earnest, and it proved difficult for the new United States. Britain could rely on hired German mercenaries and Native American allies who feared American expansion into their lands. And although most Americans backed independence, there were still many Loyalists (insultingly called *Tories*—an old word for the supporters of absolutist kings) who wanted to defend British power. By late 1776, the British had driven Washington's forces from New York. Washington struck back at Trenton and Princeton, and salvaged his men's morale. But the British took Philadelphia the next summer, and Washington withdrew to hard winter quarters at Valley Forge.

Meanwhile, a large British army tried to cut off New York as it moved from Canada into rural New York. American forces there did far better, and they decisively defeated the British at Saratoga in October 1777. This victory was crucial because it convinced France to join the war on America's side. Whereas some French officers (like the Marquis de Lafayette) admired America's cause, its absolutist king despised the revolutionaries and joined the cause only to undermine Britain. Suddenly, the colonists had a strong ally with a powerful army and navy. The British feared French attack and left Philadelphia in summer 1778, as Washington's army pursued them into New York.

Britain shifted its efforts to the South, expecting Loyalist support and help from slaves. In exchange for loyalty, the slaves were offered freedom (although many would ultimately be abandoned by the British). In 1780, while Washington's men suffered in winter quarters near New York, fighting flared in the South. Loyalist and Native American forces led frequent raids. There were British victories, but the overextended British were forced to retreat to the coast. In spring 1781, Lord Cornwallis's main British force entered Virginia. The French fleet headed for the Chesapeake, and Washington and the French army followed. French ships cut off Cornwallis while the Americans and French laid siege to his position at Yorktown. In October 1781, Cornwallis was forced to surrender his entire army.

In battling for a vast territory on hostile soil three thousand miles from home, Britain had faced an enormous task from the outset. And with the defeat of Cornwallis, the nation lost its will to fight. Early in 1782, Parliament voted to abandon the war and open negotiations. The specific terms—which dealt with borders, fishing rights, and more—took months to resolve, but Britain had accepted that its former colonies were now the independent United States of America. The Treaty of Paris was signed in 1783, and British forces left their last foothold in New York. The colonists' rebellion had truly become an American Revolution, establishing an independent United States determined to build a new way forward—one led by a government founded on the consent of its citizens.

ERA 6: WE THE PEOPLE: BUILDING AN AMERICAN REPUBLIC *(1776 TO 1789)*

DEMOCRATIC EXPERIMENTS: THE ARTICLES OF CONFEDERATION AND THE STATE CONSTITUTIONS

Americans faced enormous challenges during the Revolutionary War. They were waging a complex war against a powerful enemy over vast territory. Soldiers often suffered poor conditions and received only promissory notes as payment. Some even threatened to mutiny. Amid these crises, Americans were constantly confronted with a difficult question: Who was in charge? Congress was in overall control of the war effort and the main Continental Army, but its powers were poorly defined. It had few means to raise revenues and no way to force individual states to cooperate.

America needed an overarching government to unite its thirteen new states. Thus far, the only attempt to create an American confederacy had failed: Benjamin Franklin's 1754 Albany Plan had been rejected by the colonial governments. In 1777, Congress completed the Articles of Confederation, establishing itself as the permanent legislative body—composed of state delegates—for the United States. There was no president or bicameral legislature (a legislature with two houses, each balancing the power of the other), and the individual states managed virtually all of their own affairs.

When Congress had agreed on the articles, it sent them to the states for ratification. But just as they did for most major acts of Congress, the articles demanded unanimous support for ratification. The thirteen states each had their own interests and priorities, and unanimity was difficult to achieve. Several states claimed western lands on the basis of old colonial charters; others refused to ratify until those land claims were yielded to Congress. A 1781 compromise finally allowed ratification, but the land cession agreement soon broke down. It was a sign of struggles to follow.

The revolutionary crisis had left people deeply suspicious of powers beyond local control, and the Confederation government was left deliberately weak. Congress could not impose direct taxes and was largely limited to dealing with foreign affairs. Every state had one equal vote, and unanimous agreement was required for any major action or for an amendment to the articles. The articles, in short, created exactly what their name implied: a confederation of individual states, as opposed to a national government.

Meanwhile, states each had to create their own new governments. Most had to replace obsolete colonial charters, which granted key powers to royally appointed governors or royally authorized proprietors. Even as the Revolutionary War raged, states began to experiment with elected republican systems by passing a variety of new constitutions.

Like the Articles of Confederation, the new state governments generally kept central power weak. Most authority was placed in the elected assemblies. The executive branch had little power: governors typically served for short terms and could only run once, because frequent elections were seen as an important check on government abuses. Over time, though, people's fears of centralized government were trumped by their realization that government needs strength to function and move forward. The early constitutions were eventually replaced or heavily modified, but the first experiments were crucial steps as Americans learned to build elective, representative systems.

The Articles of Confederation had some success. For instance, Congress finally managed to take control of the western lands that some states had claimed, despite the disintegration of the 1781 deal. Though it took a long time, Congress organized the new lands into nationally controlled territories. One of the final acts of the Congress established by the Articles of Confederation was the Northwest Ordinance of 1787, which set up a major section of territory for settlement and eventual statehood. The ordinance followed a 1784 proposal from Thomas Jefferson and banned slavery in the Northwest Territory.

These successes, however, were overshadowed as the disadvantages of a weak central government under the articles became clear. Congress had no power of direct taxation and could raise revenues only through trade duties and fees. And with unanimous votes required to do or change virtually anything, it proved immensely difficult for the states to agree on significant matters. As states went their separate ways, foreign powers saw America as divided and weak.

Dissatisfaction and calls to revise the articles and expand the government's powers grew, but still Congress could hardly agree on any positive steps. The situation was worsened by Shays' Rebellion (from 1786 to 1787), during which debt-ridden farmers rose up against the state of Massachusetts and attacked a federal arsenal in Springfield. Congress was unable to respond effectively, and the rebellion was finally put down by the state government. The need for revision was clear, and calls for reform increasingly sounded.

Around the same time, in September 1786, a convention of state delegates met in Annapolis, Maryland, to discuss interstate commerce. While there, they urged Congress to call a new convention in Philadelphia to consider changes to the articles. Several states agreed and appointed delegates. Members of Congress tentatively endorsed the plan in early 1787, envisioning a convention that would only consider revisions to the existing articles.

Fifty-five delegates from twelve states assembled in Philadelphia that spring and summer. Notoriously uncooperative Rhode Island, which had often blocked action in Congress, did not attend. It refused even to discuss changes that might leave it with less influence than larger states.

Although many delegates played key roles in the convention debates that followed, particularly important participants included James Madison of Virginia, a learned student of government who greatly influenced the proceedings; Benjamin Franklin of Pennsylvania, now eighty-one years old, a peacemaker and elder statesman; and Alexander Hamilton of New York, who pushed for a strong government—almost an elected monarchy that would look more like Britain's. The delegates elected Revolutionary War hero George Washington of Virginia as the convention's president. His reputation instantly enhanced the legitimacy and magnitude of the proceedings.

THE CONSTITUTIONAL CONVENTION OF 1787

The convention in Philadelphia was designed to propose revisions to the Articles of Confederation. Those revisions would then be submitted to Congress and the state legislatures for consideration. But the delegates quickly went further. Meeting under a pledge of secrecy (debates were recorded mainly in a private journal kept by Madison), they were soon discussing plans to replace the articles with an entirely new plan of government. The assembly moved beyond its original purpose and would be called the Constitutional Convention.

As the delegates debated a new federal system, the convention's key challenge was to balance increased central authority with the individual powers of the states. The Virginia Plan, which was largely Madison's work, was favored by the bigger states. It stated that each state's representation in the federal legislature would be proportional to population, and would thus grant the largest states the greatest power. The smaller states responded with the New Jersey Plan; although it accepted many of the Virginia Plan's tenets, this plan gave states equal representation, which they had held in Congress under the articles. The result was deadlock.

A compromise proposal from the Connecticut delegation finally broke the stalemate. Under the Connecticut Compromise, the legislature would be bicameral, as Madison had urged. In the lower house, each state's representation would be proportional to its population. But in the upper house, each state would have an equal vote. The delegates decided that the lower house, which they named the House of Representatives, would be popularly elected every two years. This would help ensure representatives' accountability to the people. In the upper house, each state would select two senators for six-year terms. Only the popularly elected lower house could introduce tax bills, thereby upholding the principle of taxation with representation.

During the sweltering Philadelphia summer, in an airless room closed off for secrecy, the delegates worked through a string of contentious issues. The government would consist of legislative, executive, and judicial branches—a new Congress, a president, and a Supreme Court that would check and balance one another to prevent abuses of power. But how would the president be chosen, and how long would he serve? How much power would Congress have over commerce, or to levy taxes? How could the new Constitution be amended? Would slaves—who could not vote—be counted as part of the population in assigning representation to the states?

Compromises gradually emerged. The president would serve a four-year term, and could be reelected. He would be chosen by an electoral college: each state would have electors equal to its total number of senators and representatives, and each state government would decide how to choose its electors (for example, by popular vote, or by the state legislature). The new Congress would control foreign and interstate commerce, and it would be able to impose taxes. The amending process was made deliberately difficult to avoid frequent and disruptive changes. Unlike the articles, however, the new system would require only three-quarters of the states to agree on any amendment.

As already noted, some questions proved difficult: Should slaves be counted as part of a state's population? To give their states more representatives and consequent weight in Congress, southern states wanted them counted. Northern states—which had far fewer slaves and had, in several cases, moved to abolish slavery—did not wish to see the South gain so much influence. Therefore, they did not want slaves counted at all. An awkward compromise finally emerged, granting much of what the slaveholders demanded: three-fifths of a state's slave population would be counted in determining its representation.

Slavery itself was a contentious issue. Many Americans were uncomfortable with the institution, even if they were unwilling to give it up. The new Constitution avoided the words *slave* and *slavery* entirely. One clause required all states to return fugitive slaves, but referred to them as persons "held to service or labor"; the three-fifths clause distinguished between free people and "other persons." The document also prohibited any federal interference with the African slave trade until after 1808, but described it only as the "Importation of such Persons as any of the States . . . shall think proper to admit." The Constitution thus protected the rights of slaveholders without openly endorsing the institution of slavery. It was a delicate balance.

THE BATTLE FOR RATIFICATION AND THE CALL FOR A BILL OF RIGHTS

The convention had met in strict secrecy; its debates would actually remain secret for decades. Madison's notes were not published until 1840, four years after his death. By mid-September 1787, the convention was ready to present its plan. Americans were suddenly confronted with an entirely new model of government and nationhood—a far stronger central government with multiple balanced branches, elected both directly and indirectly. Though states would still have significant internal power, the Constitution was to become the "supreme Law of the Land." The people now had to decide whether they would accept or reject this radical proposal.

Some members of the old Congress protested that the convention had exceeded its powers, but most soon agreed to submit the new document to the states. The Constitution included rules for its own ratification. To ensure that ratification was a decision of the *people*, not only of current state governments, each state was to elect a special ratifying convention. Those normally allowed to vote by the various states, generally adult males who met a minimum property requirement, were allowed to elect the conventions (a remarkable degree of popular participation by the standards of the time). Once nine states had ratified it, the Constitution could take effect.

Supporters of the new Constitution—that is, advocates of increased federal power—came to be known as Federalists. They insisted on the need for a strong, centralized national authority that could manage U.S. affairs without being blocked by a few local interests (as had so commonly happened under the articles). The proposed system's opponents, who came to be called Anti-Federalists, were more swayed by memories of the American Revolution. They feared the loss of local control and thought that the new federal government would be too far removed from the people; they worried that it could come to threaten liberty as Britain had before independence. Federalists answered that unfettered local democracy, without broader checks and balances, would fragment the United States and allow factional majorities to tyrannize minorities.

Many states were deeply divided over ratification. Some ratified easily, even unanimously. Delaware was first, ratifying unanimously in early December 1787; Pennsylvania ratified a few days later by a two-to-one margin, followed by several more states. But some states witnessed far greater battles. Rhode Island rejected the Constitution, and would long refuse to reconsider. Debate raged not only in the ratifying conventions but also in the popular press. For months, newspapers and pamphlets were dominated by essays on the Constitution's virtues or dangers. For several months between 1787 and 1788, there appeared in New York the period's most distinguished and widely circulated series of essays: *The Federalist*, an influential defense of the Constitution by James Madison, Alexander Hamilton, and New York politician John Jay.

A major Anti-Federalist concern was the new Constitution's failure to explicitly guarantee basic rights. Federalists found such guarantees unnecessary, because the new government's powers were strictly limited; some even feared the idea and worried that lists of specific rights could lead to the trampling of any rights not mentioned. But Federalists were prepared to compromise, and their promises to add a Bill of Rights once the Constitution took effect swayed enough opponents to win major ratifications. In Massachusetts, such arguments won over the influential Samuel Adams and helped secure a close vote in favor. Several conventions attached to their ratification vote recommendations for specific amendments.

The ninth state, Maryland, ratified in April 1788 and allowed the Constitution to take effect. But everyone knew the system would fail without the support of such important states as New York and Virginia. Virginia's Federalist forces, led by Madison, were challenged by Patrick Henry's Anti-Federalists, but Madison's promise to pursue a Bill of Rights helped secure a narrow vote for ratification in June. Hamilton led the Federalists in New York, winning a narrow victory in July. (The twelfth state, North Carolina, did not follow until November 1789, when the new Congress proposed a Bill of Rights. Rhode Island would not ratify until May 1790.)

The old Confederation Congress prepared to transfer power to the new government, which would be based in New York City. Although Patrick Henry and other fiery Anti-Federalists pushed for a second convention, the states proceeded late in 1788 to choose their senators and elect their representatives. Early in 1789, the states selected their presidential electors. George Washington, without doubt the most revered man in America, was unanimously chosen by the electors. John Adams of Massachusetts—chief author of his state's constitution and Confederation Congress diplomat—was chosen as vice president. It was time to put the new system into practice.

ERA 7: DEMOCRACY MADE REAL: AMERICA PASSES THE TORCH *(1789 TO 1800)*

CREATING THE NATIONAL GOVERNMENT

The new federal Constitution was pieced together in a series of complex compromises. Many important clauses were written in broad, general terms to satisfy different priorities and to give the new government much-needed flexibility. As a result, important questions about the nature and extent of federal power were often left open to considerable interpretation.

The first great task facing the newly elected Congress and president was the creation of a working system from the Constitution's general outline. Basic issues still had to be resolved, such as the fundamental rules on which the two houses of Congress would operate. For example, the Senate met in secret session for its first five years, a practice that Americans would later consider inconceivable.

The Constitution assumed there would be "executive departments" but did not define them; it stated only that the president's nominees for executive offices would require Senate confirmation. Congress was left to decide what departments were necessary and to create them through legislation. The idea that the heads of the various departments would form a presidential cabinet largely came from President George Washington, who began to consult with and depend on the counsel of department leaders.

There was even a lengthy dispute over the president's formal title. Some senators and Vice President John Adams favored elaborate concoctions, such as "His Highness, the President of the United States of America, and Protector of the Rights of the Same." But such suggestions smacked of royalty and were deeply unpopular with the public and many congressmen, who preferred the simple "President of the United States" and "Mr. President." The controversy's main effect was to damage Adams's standing with Washington, and to help block vice presidents—whose only official duty under the Constitution is to preside over the Senate—from participating in Senate debates.

During his presidency, Washington's greatest achievement was leading the government through these early trials. His firm, steady, and dignified leadership, coupled with the near-universal high regard in which Americans held him, helped overcome divisions and hold the government together as it gradually assembled itself.

In September 1789, as soon as the executive departments were established, James Madison turned his focus to the amendments he and other Federalists had promised in the ratifying conventions. Congress submitted twelve amendments to the states, ten of which were ratified by 1791. The resulting Bill of Rights guaranteed freedom of speech, freedom of the press, and freedom of religion; the right to bear arms for militia service; freedom from unreasonable search and seizure; the right to a jury trial; and freedom from cruel or unusual punishments. The ninth amendment, addressing Federalist concerns about the dangers of listing only certain freedoms, protected rights that were not specifically enumerated; the tenth reserved to the states or the people all powers that were not specifically granted to the federal government by the Constitution.

Congress then had to establish the federal judiciary. The Constitution specified only that there would be a Supreme Court and "such inferior courts" as Congress established. Even the number of Supreme Court justices was (and today remains) left to Congress. Yet the exact role of the Supreme Court remained unclear. It was not until 1803, in *Marbury v. Madison* under Chief Justice John Marshall, that the court ruled an act of Congress unconstitutional. This began a long process by which the court established its power to review the constitutionality of both federal and state laws.

THE FIRST PARTY SCHISM

The new government was created carefully and methodically, but a completely unplanned phenomenon also emerged: the rise of political parties. Different groups of politicians and citizens inevitably had divergent visions for the country's direction, and many began dividing into factions. President Washington tried to discourage factionalism by promoting compromise and accord, but the differences were too great. Two nascent parties were soon identified with two rival members of Washington's cabinet: Secretary of the Treasury Alexander Hamilton and Secretary of State Thomas Jefferson.

Hamilton's faction, which believed in strong federal power, called itself the Federalist Party (this should not be confused with the Constitution's Federalist supporters, who split their loyalties between the new parties). The new Federalists aimed at a powerful central government that would promote industry and commerce, and in turn create moneyed classes. These classes would invest in government debt and fund government operations, including permanent and potent military forces. In essence, they aimed for an elected, representative version of wealthy and powerful Great Britain.

The Federalists' rivals were known as the Democratic-Republicans, or simply Republicans, and Jefferson was widely seen as their leader. They embraced a strict constructionist vision, pressing for a far weaker federal government whose powers were limited to those explicitly granted by the Constitution. They wanted state and local governments to retain considerable power because they were closer to the people and thus more democratic. The Republicans, or Jeffersonians, also envisioned an agrarian society of independent small farmers, as equal in wealth and influence as possible. They feared that extensive commerce and industry would foster inequality between owners and laborers, leaving the latter unable to resist the political will of the former. They particularly resented financial speculators (or investors) who reaped profit at others' expense while never producing goods of their own.

The party divide was heavily sectional (that is, regionally divided between the different sections of the country). Federalist support was strong in commercially developed New England and the mid-Atlantic region, whereas the agrarian South, and its plantation-owning elite, was primarily Republican. Sectional priorities and economic interests thus further exacerbated the increasingly bitter party divide.

Conflict erupted as early as 1790, when Hamilton offered a fiscal program to strengthen America's credit and economic standing. Some tenets of his plan, such as one honoring the Confederation's debts to foreign powers, were uncontroversial and widely accepted. But his insistence that the new federal government honor the states' Revolutionary War debts sparked a crisis. Much of that debt, including pay still owed to soldiers, had been bought up by speculators at a fraction of face value. The Jeffersonian South vehemently objected to increasing federal power and raising taxes to enrich speculators (mostly northern) with money properly owed to others.

In the end, a compromise was reached. A strong lobby wished to move the nation's capital from New York to Philadelphia (which served as the capital from 1776 to 1787). Jeffersonians, however, did not want the government based in either city, because both were so tied to powerful commercial interests. Hamilton, Madison, and Jefferson reached a deal: Jeffersonians would support Hamilton's debt plan if the capital were moved to a patch of reclaimed swampland along the Potomac that was far removed from northern commercial cities. The government would move to Philadelphia only while construction of the new federal city, soon named in honor of Washington, was under way. The government would finally move to Washington, DC, in 1800.

THE NEW NATION'S PARTIES AND POLITICS

The debt compromise did nothing to relieve the fundamental split between the parties. Despite President Washington's efforts to mediate, partisan conflict only deepened, especially as members of the press aggressively began to take sides. In 1791, seeking to stabilize the currency and promote development, Hamilton persuaded Congress to charter a national Bank of the United States. Jefferson insisted that the Constitution did not authorize such an act, but Hamilton countered that Congress's "implied powers"—those necessary to meet the Constitution's stated aims—allowed the bank's creation. Washington signed the bill, but the bank remained deeply unpopular among Jeffersonians.

The parties also broke sharply over the French Revolution that erupted in 1789, especially when the new French government deposed and executed King Louis XVI in 1792. Federalists, on the one hand, feared France's atheistic and populist radicalism; they also wished to maintain close ties with Britain, which was soon at war with revolutionary France. Many Jeffersonians, on the other hand, admired the French cause despite its growing violence. They were wary of British influence, and considered Britain's enemy their friend.

Washington kept the nation neutral, but in 1793 a new French envoy, calling himself "Citizen Genêt," tried to bypass the government and appeal directly to the people for support. He and the French cause proved widely popular. The "Citizen Genêt Affair" widened the party breach, even though Jefferson, Madison, and others soon found his excesses embarrassing. Genêt's faction meanwhile fell in France; called home to face trial, he took asylum and became a U.S. citizen. In the wake of Genêt's meddling, Washington shifted toward Hamilton's anti-French position, and Jefferson resigned as secretary of state.

Despite deepening partisan feuds, the new government proved its strength. At Hamilton's urging, Congress had enacted an excise tax on distilled liquors. This tax, along with trade duties, served as the government's main source of revenue. Western Pennsylvania distillers rebelled against the tax in 1794's Whiskey Rebellion. Unlike the Confederation government, which had not been strong enough to quell Shays' Rebellion in 1786–1787, Washington's government was able to put down the rebels. And it did so with strong public support: because the tax had been passed by the people's representatives, few saw rebellion as a legitimate response. Rebellion was valid only before the American Revolution, when the people had lacked any say in Britain's actions.

Relations with Britain also brought controversy. Even after independence, America and Britain clashed over the continued presence of British forts on the northern U.S. border. Seeking to isolate revolutionary France, the British also began to seize American ships and even press American sailors into the British navy. The threat of war loomed, but America was heavily dependent on British imports (duties on which provided a major source of federal revenue). In 1794, Washington sent Chief Justice John Jay to negotiate.

Jay managed to defuse the crisis and negotiate a treaty, but he tacitly acknowledged America's dependence on British trade. Although he secured a British guarantee to abandon its forts along the border, he acquiesced to Britain on many points. Republicans were outraged and stirred up popular clamor against the treaty, but Federalists swallowed their own doubts and defended it as tactically wise. The Senate narrowly ratified the Jay Treaty. But debate had been very divisive, and the dispute further alienated the parties from one another.

In 1796, Washington retired after two terms; he thereby set another important precedent, as no president would win a third term until 1940 (after which time a constitutional amendment would make the traditional two terms in office the legal limit). Washington's famous 1796 "Farewell Address" (published, rather than delivered as a speech) explained the rationale for his retirement and warned against permanent alliances with Europe's feuding powers. He also cautioned strongly against the dangers of partisanship and warned that sectional divisions were especially perilous.

But even Washington could not suppress the schism. The party split differed from the divide in the American party system that emerged in the nineteenth century, in which two parties competed in successive elections to shift policy in one direction or another. The first party schism was a battle over the fundamental nature of the country—each party believed that only one could survive and ultimately prevail.

THE REVOLUTION OF 1800

The presidential election of 1796 was the first truly contested race, and it became an openly partisan battle. The Constitution made no allowance for party candidates: as the Electoral College then stood, the top finisher became president, and the candidate who placed second became vice president. Adams, who had served as Washington's vice president, won the election. But the Jay Treaty had strengthened the Democratic-Republicans: Jefferson, Adams's chief opponent, finished a close second and thus became vice president. Jefferson, the de facto opposition leader, would have a very limited role in the Adams administration.

Under Adams and the pro-British Federalists, relations with France quickly deteriorated. Like Britain, France interfered with American shipping to war-torn Europe. Adams dispatched ambassadors, but French negotiators (identified as X, Y, and Z in diplomatic reports) demanded a hefty bribe to engage in negotiations. The "XYZ Affair" caused a scandal, and negotiations collapsed. Hawkish Federalists pressed for war, which Adams resisted. As a result, an undeclared quasi-war erupted at sea from 1798 to 1800. Adams eventually defused the crisis through diplomacy—and stoked the fury of Hamilton and other war hawks.

At home, however, Adams was more amenable to strong measures. With his approval, the Federalist-dominated Congress passed the Alien and Sedition Acts in 1798. Some prominent Republicans were recent European émigrés; the Alien Act and other related measures made it much more difficult to win citizenship, and allowed the president to expel politically suspect aliens. The Sedition Act made it a crime to oppose the execution of federal laws or to publish "false" writings that brought the government into disrepute. This was used to target Republican newspapers, and Republicans knew that the act was set to expire just when Adams's term would end.

Republicans were furious at these partisan attacks on personal liberty and free expression. Resolutions passed in the legislatures of Kentucky (drafted by Jefferson) and Virginia (drafted by Madison) assailed the Alien and Sedition Acts as unconstitutional and insisted that the states had the right to judge the validity of federal laws. Northern states, most of which were still Federalist, objected that only the federal courts had that authority. In response, Kentucky insisted that states not only could judge but also could nullify, or strike down, federal laws they deemed unconstitutional. Kentucky stopped short of challenging the federal union of the states, but notions of state power and nullification would prove potent, and divisive, in coming decades.

The unpopular Alien and Sedition Acts helped undermine the Federalists in the election of 1800. But as the party system became more fixed, the flaws in the electoral process were further exposed. Each elector cast a vote for two different candidates for president. Now there were not only party candidates but also party *tickets*, complete with presidential and vice presidential candidates. The Republicans finished first, with seventy-three electoral votes to Adams's sixty-five. But each of the seventy-three Republican electors cast one of his votes for Jefferson and the other vote for Jefferson's running mate, Aaron Burr. The result was a tie, and the ambitious Burr refused to step aside.

In the event of an electoral tie, the House of Representatives was to decide the election (with each of the sixteen states' delegations getting a single vote). But the newly elected Republican House had not yet taken office, and the outgoing Federalists were determined to thwart Jefferson. With two states evenly divided, neither candidate could secure the nine states needed for a majority. However, Hamilton thought Burr was potentially dangerous. So, despite his hatred toward Jefferson, he finally threw his support to his rival and broke the deadlock. Jefferson was declared president on the thirty-sixth ballot, and Burr assumed the vice presidency.

Ugly though the process was, the new government had passed a crucial test in the 1800 election. The system had survived a serious crisis with neither violence nor disruption, and Jefferson was inaugurated without incident. This peaceful transfer of power from one party to the other marked a momentous achievement for the new nation, coming to be known as the Revolution of 1800.

ERA 8: GOING WEST: OPPORTUNITY AND PERIL ON AMERICA'S FRONTIER *(1800 TO 1830S)*

A YOUNG AND FAST-EXPANDING NATION

The electoral stalemate of 1800 was disruptive for the young United States, and everyone agreed that such a crisis must never happen again. The electoral system had to change to allow for party tickets before the next election. In 1803, Congress passed the twelfth amendment, which gave each elector separate votes for president and vice president. The system had thus passed another test: the amendment process worked and would provide an effective framework for making changes in the future.

The 1800 election marked a political watershed. Both the Federalists and the Democratic-Republicans had believed that only one party could survive. At least for the immediate future, they were right. After the turbulence and public suspicion of the Federalists' aristocratic elitism that wracked the 1790s, most Americans shifted their allegiance to the more populist Jeffersonians. The Federalists lost Congress as well as the presidency in 1800. As the country expanded, they were increasingly confined to New England and fell into permanent decline. The Federalist vision of an America closely modeled on Britain's fiscal and military state was clearly the losing perspective, and would gradually all but vanish.

Yet the pure Jeffersonian vision—an agrarian America with a weak central government, limited industry, and a small military—would not suffice either. As its commerce and industry grew rapidly, the new nation was changing irreversibly. The Democratic-Republicans, who had a growing monopoly on power, were forced to adapt. Although many party members remained hostile to the building commercial boom, other factions began to support pro-growth government policies and to represent commercial interests.

The young nation also began expanding west, just as Native Americans had long feared. The U.S. population was rapidly growing, and most of the country was still dependent on farming (an economic reality that would hold for over a century), so Americans' appetite for more land was insatiable. During the colonial period, Americans had looked east (toward Europe, and Britain in particular) and had viewed the West as a sort of backcountry. Now the image of an expanding American frontier became increasingly tantalizing. Soon, Americans would begin to see a divinely ordained right and need to expand the nation across the continent—by the 1840s, they would come to call it "Manifest Destiny."

West of the Mississippi River, the continent was still in foreign hands. In 1800, French emperor Napoleon Bonaparte won back the vast Louisiana Territory (which had been under Spanish control since the 1760s), and intended to revive France's colonial efforts in America. French ambitions alarmed President Thomas Jefferson. Fearing loss of access to the Mississippi River, he sought to buy New Orleans from France in 1803. To the astonishment of the American negotiators, Napoleon—mired in European troubles and reconsidering new colonial ventures—instead offered to sell the entire Louisiana Territory. Jefferson's emissaries, ignoring their instructions to make a much more limited purchase, immediately agreed.

Jefferson was in a bind. He had long insisted on a strict constructionist view of the Constitution, which said nothing about purchasing foreign territory. But the acquisition would double the size of U.S. territory with one stroke. For Jefferson, whose vision of a nation of independent farmers depended on land, this prospect was irresistible. (The Federalists had always taken a loose constructionist view. But they feared that an even greater westward expansion would further damage their dwindling northeastern base, and so they assailed Jefferson's move on strict constructionist grounds.) Jefferson quickly arranged an expedition (from 1803 to 1806) under Meriwether Lewis and William Clark to explore the new territory and lay the ground for future settlement.

Jefferson was also prepared to be flexible on foreign affairs. Even as he sought to reduce government spending and debt (for example, by scaling back the military forces that John Adams had expanded), his foreign policy grew more aggressive. Like George Washington, he was keen to avoid "entangling alliances" with European powers—that phrase, often attributed to Washington's "Farewell Address," is in fact Jefferson's.

But independent American strength was another matter. North Africa's Barbary States had long exacted tribute by threatening American ships. Washington and Adams had continued to pay the ransom. Tripoli, one of the Barbary powers, increased its demands and finally declared war in 1801. Jefferson responded forcefully, and dispatched warships to the Mediterranean in 1803. Americans blockaded Tripoli, and Tripoli was forced to make peace in 1805. Even though other Barbary States continued to demand tribute, the American victory was significant in that the United States had shown that it could exercise power abroad.

AMERICA DEFIES THE EUROPEAN POWERS

Conflict with Europe was also brewing. As the Napoleonic Wars dragged on, both Britain and France tried to block neutral ships from trading with their enemies. Yet compared with the French navy, the British fleet was far more powerful. It seriously threatened American commercial shipping. Britain not only ramped up its seizures of American ships after 1805 but also pressed American sailors into its navy by claiming they were Royal Navy deserters.

The conflict revived many of the issues that the unpopular Jay Treaty of 1794 had left unresolved. The United States attempted to negotiate with Britain, and threatened to block British imports from entering America. (Though such boycotts had been tried in the Revolutionary War era and were considered successful, their impact on Britain had never been as powerful as Americans believed: if faced with a U.S. embargo, Britain could simply sell its goods elsewhere.) Britain was unbending, and negotiations failed. In 1807, the British warship *Leopard* opened fire and killed several sailors aboard the U.S. Navy's *Chesapeake* near the Virginia coast. Sailors on the *Leopard* claimed they were searching for British deserters.

Jefferson responded with the Embargo Act of 1807, which essentially banned all trade (that is, both imports and exports) with foreign nations. Britain was the intended target, but America emerged as the measure's real victim. Denounced by Federalists and commercially oriented Republicans alike, the embargo was widely evaded by rampant smuggling. Public pressure forced Congress to ease the embargo, but the British government refused to make concessions. Pressure for war mounted. In 1812, President James Madison—Jefferson's ally and successor—asked Congress to declare war. Despite opposition from New England and other eastern commercial states that favored a negotiated settlement to protect trade, southern and western support pushed the vote through Congress. The War of 1812 had begun.

The war began badly for the United States. American forces launched a poorly planned, inadequately armed invasion of Canada. Despite the fact that British resources were tied down in Europe, America made a weak showing. The United States did have notable successes at sea—for example, the famous exploits of the *Constitution* and a major victory on the Great Lakes that blocked a British push from Canada. But the 1814 defeat of Napoleon allowed the British to commit greater forces to America. British troops pushed into the mid-Atlantic and burned Washington, DC. Nonetheless, American forces made a crucial stand at Baltimore, stopping the British advance. A huge battle flag, flying over Baltimore's Fort McHenry at dawn, showed that the city had withstood the British assault, inspiring eyewitness Francis Scott Key to write "The Star Spangled Banner."

Despite these sporadic successes, America's resources were strained, and its citizens were bitterly divided by the war. New England, in particular, remained violently opposed. Efforts at peace talks began, and both sides finally signed the Treaty of Ghent in late 1814. With news of the treaty still en route, General Andrew Jackson won a major American victory at New Orleans in January 1815, blocking British attempts to seize the Mississippi River. Ultimately, the Treaty of Ghent resolved very few of the issues that had sparked the war. But the end of the Napoleonic Wars in 1815 allowed Britain to relax its harassment of American ships, and tensions between the two nations gradually eased.

Despite the war's inconclusive ending and the overall poor performance of American land forces, Americans were emboldened by the naval victories and Jackson's New Orleans triumph.

In 1816, a naval expedition under Stephen Decatur forced the remaining Barbary States to end their attacks on American ships. The United States would never pay foreign tribute again. By 1823, President James Monroe was prepared to declare the entire Western Hemisphere a uniquely American sphere of influence. Many of Spain's Central and South American colonies had recently rebelled and declared independence. The Monroe Doctrine also indicated that the creation of new European colonies or interference with the newly independent Latin American states would be considered an act of aggression toward the United States.

THE ECONOMY TRANSFORMS AS COMMERCE EXPANDS

The young American republic was marked by dizzying commercial development. New urban factories turned out textiles and other manufactured goods, while ever-expanding rural territory and the growing plantation system produced masses of crops. There were markets both at home and abroad: Europe needed goods and raw materials to fight the Napoleonic Wars, then demanded more imports to rebuild the continent at the wars' end.

A major requirement for growth was the construction of modern roads and canals, which would allow efficient movement of goods across the country's huge distances. Such projects depended heavily on private and government investment. The Erie Canal, for example, opened in 1825 to connect Lake Erie with the Hudson River, and was built by the state of New York at government expense. This project, and others like it, provided entirely new avenues for crops and goods to reach urban centers and trading ports. Commercial development dramatically increased in once-isolated inland communities.

Despite the political unease felt by some Democratic-Republicans, commercial growth was unstoppable. As the Federalists faded and the Republicans' political hold became unbreakable, elements of the party came to represent the nation's commercial and pro-development interests. Tension between the party's different factions increased as the demand for economic investment intensified. Despite considerable political resistance, the federal government slowly began to promote such internal improvements as roads and canals in the 1820s. This policy would remain a major point of controversy in the coming decades.

Another source of political dispute was the still-controversial national bank. Although many continued to believe a nationally chartered bank was unconstitutional, the bank helped fund expansion and stabilize the currency, and it offered money for borrowing and investment. A divided Congress had let Alexander Hamilton's First Bank of the United States expire at the end of its charter in 1811. But without a central body to coordinate national economic policy, the War of 1812 sparked a currency crisis. Congress was forced to create a Second Bank of the United States in 1816, complete with another twenty-year charter.

The Supreme Court under Chief Justice John Marshall was crucial in establishing the federal government's power to promote economic development. In 1819's *McCulloch v. Maryland*, the court upheld the constitutionality of the national bank against a challenge by the state of Maryland. Marshall's decision endorsed Hamilton's "loose construction" and "implied powers" arguments of the 1790s, which insisted that Congress could enact whatever laws were necessary to achieve the Constitution's broad aims. This was an enormously influential decision, in that it cemented the growing power of the federal government. In its other decisions, the Marshall court consistently backed broad federal power to aid and develop commerce.

Economic change also presented many Americans with new perils. Rural farmers had long relied on local farming and barter economies. But industrializing cities and the growing European market for American exports increased demand for food and raw materials. Farmers were asked to supply those goods in exchange for cash, and now they needed that cash to fulfill their own needs and wants. Tied into new trading networks and a vast money-based market economy, rural areas were thus exposed to new and frightening risks if the larger economy stumbled.

And stumble it did. Fevered growth and heavy borrowing from the national bank spurred risky investment in insecure up-and-coming ventures, and the complex economy became dependent on unpredictable exports and bank policies. The Panic of 1819 illustrated for rural farmers how vulnerable to outside forces they had become. Many of them were now mired in crippling debt. They blamed the Second Bank of the United States for these new problems (mismanagement in the bank had contributed to the 1819 panic), demonizing it as a monstrous predator on ordinary citizens. The old Jeffersonian prejudice against "speculators" took on new urgency and fueled a wave of popular fury, laying the groundwork for a populist political backlash.

ERA 9: FREEDOM FOR ALL: AMERICAN DEMOCRACY BEGINS TO TRANSFORM *(1820S TO 1840S)*

THE NEW PARTY SCHISM AND THE JACKSONIAN ERA

By 1820, the Federalists were virtually extinct—in that year's presidential election, they did not even field a candidate. Four years earlier, the overwhelming victory of Democratic-Republican James Monroe had ushered in the Era of Good Feelings, a supposedly nonpartisan period of Republican dominance. Yet with the collapse of the Federalists and their vision of a more aristocratic America, the Democratic-Republicans inevitably grew more diverse. The party now included Americans from many regions who had competing priorities. And because there was no opposition party, members were not motivated to strive for unity within their own. Republican factions formed, and members of Monroe's cabinet battled over policy and influence (much as they had during George Washington's presidency).

As the national government became more heavily invested in promoting internal transport routes, the deepest political divisions revolved around the federal government's role in fostering economic growth. One faction supported protective tariffs and government-funded internal improvements. Henry Clay, an influential Kentucky congressman (and later senator), called this the "American System." But others in the party held a more traditionally Jeffersonian populist line. They feared the growth of federal power at the states' expense; they resented the economic crises, which they blamed largely on speculators; and they assailed the banks—especially the ever-controversial national bank—for providing those speculators with loans.

The dramatic expansion of voting rights fueled the growing partisan split. Since the Revolutionary War, Americans' notions of popular rights had gradually changed. As the frontier moved west in the early nineteenth century, new states increasingly rejected property requirements for suffrage (the right to vote). Federalists had argued that power should be restricted to a more educated and prosperous elite, but their decline was echoed by a rapid expansion of suffrage in the older states. By the 1820s, most states had given virtually all white males the vote. On the world stage, this was nothing short of extraordinary: in Britain, the democratizing Great Reform Act of 1832 still left fully 80 percent of men without the vote.

As popular power grew, the means by which American presidents were elected also changed. Since the republic's beginning, states had differed on how they chose electors (that is, selection by state legislatures versus election by the voters). By the late 1820s, voters chose their electors directly in all but two states. The president was, in essence, now popularly elected by all adult white men. The transformed political landscape came to be known as Jacksonian Democracy in honor of Andrew Jackson, the Tennessee frontiersman, politician, and War of 1812 hero who led and symbolized the populist movement.

In the absence of an opposition party, the 1824 election pitted four rival Republicans against each other. Jackson finished first in both popular and electoral votes, but fell short of a majority in the four-way race. Members of the House of Representatives were required to choose between the top three finishers; Henry Clay finished fourth and threw his support behind John Quincy Adams of Massachusetts, who finished second nationally but secured the backing of the House. When Adams named Clay secretary of state, rumors swirled that the two men had made a corrupt bargain.

Widely seen as illegitimate, Adams's election further fractured the party. Jackson, whose supporters now called themselves the Democratic Party, decisively defeated Adams in an 1828 rematch. Whereas Adams—from the commercially active Northeast—had favored a strong government role in economic development, the aggressively populist President Jackson challenged that role. He targeted speculators, blocked federal spending for internal improvements, and vetoed the renewal of the national bank on the grounds that it was unconstitutional. The bank expired in 1836.

Yet despite his insistence on limited federal powers, Jackson used his own executive powers with ruthless force. He bullied the other government branches and appointed his personal friends and allies to federal offices (the so-called spoils system). He also fiercely defended westward expansion by any means necessary. Determined to push Native Americans out of the way, Jackson aggressively backed Congress's Indian Removal Act of 1830. He ignored a Supreme Court decision that upheld the sovereignty of Native American nations, and he aided states' efforts to remove Native American peoples from the South. The difficult and deadly migration of the Cherokee and others to the Oklahoma Territory was called the Trail of the Tears by the dispossessed tribes.

Jackson's opponents called his policies wrong-headed and his use of power tyrannical, and the opposition press branded him "King Andrew the First." In the face of his growing Democratic Party, pro-development Democratic-Republicans began to form their own rival party in the early 1830s. Led by Clay and his allies, the Whig Party took its name from a British term, widely used in the American Revolution, that referred to opponents of unchecked monarchical power. The Second American Party System, the real start of the permanent two-party system that would come to define American politics, had arrived.

A MORE PERFECT SOCIETY: SOCIAL CHANGE AND THE REFORM MOVEMENTS

In the 1820s and 1830s, the new nation was gripped by a surge of Protestant evangelical fervor. The Second Great Awakening, like the first a century earlier, was marked by revivalist meetings and proselytizing churches that sought to save American souls (particularly those along the western frontier). Baptists, Methodists, and other evangelical sects grew rapidly, and new movements emerged. For example, upstate New York's Burned-Over District (named for the revivals that swept over it like wildfire) was the birthplace of Joseph Smith's Mormon movement.

Revivalist leaders wanted to achieve a perfect society through moral reform. This was a particularly urgent aim for many old-stock Americans, who were concerned about the morals of the growing waves of immigrant laborers. Germans arrived in large numbers in the 1830s and 1840s, and Ireland's potato famine drove many Irish to move to America in the late 1840s. In eastern cities, the surging immigrant population changed the political landscape. Democrats courted their votes, whereas anti-immigrant, nativist parties warned of the dangers posed by the newcomers' supposedly inferior stock. Revivalist reformers believed that they were charged with improving immigrants' morality.

Coupled with a broader post–Revolutionary War push to expand and improve social justice, revivalist beliefs drove a host of reform movements. The temperance crusade battled alcohol and the social ills surrounding it. Immigrants were considered particularly vulnerable to degrading saloons and especially dangerous when they were under alcohol's influence. Other efforts sought to expand public education opportunities, including those for women. Still other reformers worked to transform the American prison system, hoping to create model prisons, or reformatories, that would rehabilitate instead of merely punish those who were incarcerated.

The reform movements also sparked the country's first concerted push for women's rights and suffrage. Led by Elizabeth Cady Stanton, women's activists held a convention at Seneca Falls, New York, in 1848. Its "Declaration of Rights and Sentiments" was carefully modeled on the Declaration of Independence, and insisted on the self-evident truth "that all men and women are created equal." The women's rights movement grew and became a long-standing element of the country's reform efforts. Although it had little immediate effect on women's status, the movement also promoted other reforms of the period and laid a strong foundation for the successful women's suffrage push of the late nineteenth and early twentieth centuries.

The North's growing abolitionist movement would have the greatest immediate impact. Even before the Revolution, some Americans (particularly Quakers, who also became heavily involved in the women's rights movement) had challenged the morality of slavery. But the Revolution pushed the issue to the forefront: Could a free people continue to enslave others? The Second Great Awakening fostered a heavily religious abolitionist movement, which denounced slavery as a moral evil and demanded its immediate elimination throughout the United States. Though some southerners certainly had doubts about slavery, the organized abolition movement was almost entirely a northern phenomenon.

Condemnation of slavery did not necessarily imply concern for blacks' rights. Most abolitionists viewed blacks as natural inferiors in need of protection, whereas others regarded them with blatant contempt and hostility. Many backed so-called colonization: a plan to resettle freed slaves in Africa that was already promoted by such ambivalent slave owners as Thomas Jefferson and James Madison in the 1810s. One early effort created the African state of Liberia as a home for emancipated slaves. Relatively few abolitionists advocated anything approaching racial equality. True abolitionism, demanding the full and immediate abolition of slavery, was always a minority position—even in the North. Yet the movement was powerful, helping focus the North's attention on the growing grip of slavery in the South. In turn, southerners grew alarmed as they pondered northern intentions to interfere with the cornerstone of their labor system.

AFTER ITS POST-REVOLUTION DECLINE, SLAVERY GAINS STRENGTH

In the wake of the Revolutionary War, doubts about slavery were particularly strong in the North, where the system was less entrenched and could more easily be dismantled. Many southerners—including Presidents Washington, Jefferson, and Madison—also expressed concerns. Yet few plantation owners were actually prepared to emancipate their slaves: they simply did not know how to live without them. They also wondered what would happen to large populations of freed slaves in a white society.

The North began to act against slavery even before the Revolution ended. Mainly in the South, many slaves heeded British calls to cross the lines and fight for their freedom. But several thousand, mainly from the northern states, fought on the American side in exchange for liberty; free blacks also fought for the American cause. Their example—fighting alongside white Americans in a broader struggle for freedom—made it particularly difficult for the northern states to defend slavery.

Pennsylvania, with its strong Quaker antislavery sentiment, was the first state to act, passing a gradual emancipation law in 1780. The 1780 Massachusetts Constitution stated that all men are created free and equal. In 1783, Massachusetts's highest court ruled that slavery was a violation of that guarantee, and slavery in Massachusetts collapsed. Gradual emancipation laws, like those passed in Rhode Island and Connecticut, were more typical, ordering that all slaves born after a given date would become free once they reached a given age. Slavery was more firmly entrenched in New York, but that state too passed a gradual emancipation act in 1799 (though its slow workings delayed slavery's final end in the state until July 4, 1827). New Jersey was the last northern state to act, enacting gradual emancipation in 1804.

Even in the upper South, where slavery was deeply rooted, emancipation was seriously considered. A Virginia state convention only narrowly defeated gradual emancipation proposals in 1832; had emancipation won, the region's future would have been profoundly different. As it happened, emancipation's defeat marked a turning point. Powerful, prominent Virginia would remain part of the slaveholding South. And southerners, who were terrified after the bloody insurrection led by Virginia slave Nat Turner in 1831, now tightened their control over the slave population. They restricted movement, meetings, education, and voluntary manumission (the freeing of slaves by their masters) by individual slave owners.

In the deeper South, some had also questioned slavery in the wake of the Revolution. But few planters, or even political leaders who harbored doubts about human bondage, could accept the total demise of their labor system. Most southerners were unwilling even to consider the idea. For a time, it seemed nature might force the question: by the 1790s, soil degradation had begun to undermine traditional cash crops and reduce the value of slave labor. But by 1800, new technologies like Eli Whitney's cotton gin made the once labor-intensive harvesting of cotton—which was in heavy demand in northern and European textile mills—highly profitable.

Thus, even as slavery was phased out in the North, and as Virginia hung in the balance, the institution became an even more integral part of the southern economy. In 1808, Congress abolished the trans-Atlantic slave trade. Though there would later be calls in the South to reopen the trade, many slave owners supported the ban. American slave populations were increasing rapidly through natural growth. As the demand for slaves grew and cotton plantations quickly spread south and west, planters knew that the ban on new imports would increase the sale value of their own surplus slaves.

Even as manufacturing and commerce expanded in the rest of the United States, the South became more reliant than ever on its plantation system. At the same time, it lagged behind the rest of the country in terms of industrial development. In the North, abolitionist voices like those of William Lloyd Garrison and his influential newspaper, *The Liberator*, were growing louder. Most northerners were not abolitionists, but they felt threatened by slavery's implications for white society. Although they did not push for an end to slavery in places where it already existed, they were determined to stop it from spreading. The North was turning firmly against slavery, just as the South was rallying behind its "peculiar [that is, unique] institution." Collision was inevitable.

ERA 10: A HOUSE DIVIDED: NORTH VERSUS SOUTH *(1820 TO 1859)*

A LINE IN THE SAND: SLAVERY IN THE TERRITORIES

Most northerners were never abolitionists: they did not demand an immediate end to slavery in the South or focus on slaves' suffering. Nonetheless, many of them turned strongly against slavery—not on moral grounds, but because of its impact on whites. A majority believed that slavery degraded free labor, lowering all laborers to the status of slaves. They looked angrily at the South's undemocratic slaveholding aristocracy, with its outspoken contempt for all working men:

indeed, some planters openly equated white laborers with slaves. Many feared this lordly class of southerners would seek to dominate all Americans. As the South clung more and more fiercely to its slave system during the first decades of the nineteenth century, more northerners came to see slavery as a direct threat. Antislavery sentiment escalated rapidly.

Although they did not represent mainstream northern opinion, abolitionists helped stoke such attitudes. Their tracts and newspapers circulated widely, graphically publicizing the brutality of slavery and its degrading social impact. Adding to their influence were a growing number of black abolitionists, many of whom had experienced slavery firsthand; they bitterly challenged the still-popular notion of colonizing freed slaves in Africa, and firmly pointed out that slaves were Americans, not Africans. Frederick Douglass, having escaped from bondage to come to the North, became prominent in the 1840s and 1850s. Books by Douglass and others revealed the horrors of enslavement to a wide audience. Most northerners saw abolitionists as fanatics—yet the abolitionist portrait of slavery stuck in many minds.

Though typical antislavery northerners did not demand southern emancipation, they were determined to keep slavery from expanding. The nation had turned its eyes westward: by the mid-1840s, Americans had begun to talk of their "Manifest Destiny" to expand all the way to the Pacific. The crucial issue was not slavery in the South, but the status of the burgeoning western territories. The North's increasingly powerful antislavery movement was fixed on one goal: keeping the territories as "free soil" for free white labor. Slavery—and in the view of most whites, all blacks, whether slave or free—had to be excluded absolutely: most free-soilers bore deep racial hostility to blacks. So, indeed, did many white abolitionists: though they denounced slavery as a moral evil and decried the suffering it caused, most viewed blacks as natural inferiors in need of protection, not as potential equals.

The status of the territories also had immediate political implications, for it was key to the balance of power in the federal government. Many northerners feared the aristocratic "slave power" exerted in Washington, DC, by the slave states—particularly in the Senate, where the equal allotment of two seats to each state blocked the North's rapidly growing population from giving free states any advantage. Keeping slavery out of the territories would mean many new free states and no further slave states, guaranteeing a solid free-soil majority in both houses of Congress.

Slaveholders, however, were just as determined to keep the territories open to slavery. There were commercial reasons: new territories with expanding plantations meant an ever-growing market for slaves and a permanent boost to their market value. But there were also more fundamental motives. Southerners, seeing slavery as the foundation of their society, felt besieged by the North's surging antislavery movement. They feared that new free states—with no new slave states to balance them—would undermine southern power in Washington and allow antislavery interests to dominate, strangling slavery everywhere. The West quickly became each section's battleground.

Sectional divisions were not, of course, entirely consistent or predictable. Some northerners sympathized with the South and its slave system—motivated by racial prejudice, by an aristocratic outlook, or by cultural or commercial ties with the South. Urban immigrants were particularly likely to reject antislavery views, fearing that free blacks would compete for the low-skill jobs on which they themselves largely depended. Such attitudes helped make the northern wing of the Democratic Party (which attracted many immigrants) a frequent ally of the slaveholders, making immigrant neighborhoods dangerous for the North's free blacks and helping give antislavery and anti-immigrant parties common cause.

At the same time, some southerners—particularly poor farmers in the backcountry, where slavery barely penetrated—looked at the slave-owning elite with distrust and hostility. Much like the northern Free-Soilers, they resented the aristocratic pretensions of the "slaveocracy" and believed that slavery degraded the standing of all laborers. Like many antislavery northerners, most of the South's antislavery whites were nonetheless violently antiblack, fearing competition from black labor and seething at comparisons between their own status and that of an "inferior race."

THE SECTIONAL DIVIDE GROWS

The sectional split was already plain in the first decades of the nineteenth century, and the status of the territories was quickly emerging as the flash point. In 1819, Missouri—part of the territory gained in the Louisiana Purchase—sought to join the Union as a slave state, triggering a battle over the future of slavery in the West. There were then twenty-two states—eleven slave and eleven free. Free-state populations not only were larger but also were growing more quickly: their influence in the House of Representatives was greater and was poised to grow further. The slave states were determined at least to maintain equal power in the Senate.

In 1820, Congress struck the Missouri Compromise. Missouri was admitted as a slave state. At the same time, Maine (until then a part of Massachusetts) was admitted as a free state, to preserve the equal balance between slave states and free states. In the future, the compromise declared, new states above the 36°30′ line of latitude (Missouri's southern border) would be free states, and those below the line would be slave states. The issue, for the moment, seemed settled.

But sectional tensions continued to rise as the North and South eyed one another with growing suspicion. In the 1820s, northern industrial interests pressed for higher protective tariffs on British and European imports to shield American manufactures from outside competition. But the South, dependent on crop exports to Europe and with few industries to protect, painted protectionism as a northern plot against southern interests—even against the South's slave society. A small number of radical southerners began to suggest secession from the federal union if northern policies won out.

In 1828, pro–Andrew Jackson, antitariff forces in Congress plotted to discredit tariffs (and embarrass pro-protection President John Quincy Adams before the 1828 election) with a bill so extreme that no region could support it. But to the horror of the plotters, protectionist forces chose to uphold the tariff principle even with an unattractive bill, and the so-called Tariff of Abominations passed. Stunned, several southern legislatures denounced the law as unconstitutional. John C. Calhoun of South Carolina, Adams's vice president, anonymously published his "South Carolina Exposition and Protest," in which he asserted the right of affected minorities to challenge majority rule—and the right of states to nullify federal laws.

The crisis worsened under President Jackson, who defended the tariff's constitutionality even while working to soften it. Calhoun, now Jackson's vice president, began openly promoting nullification. A gentler 1832 tariff changed little; a South Carolina convention declared the tariff acts void and barred collection of duties within the state. Jackson, though urging further tariff compromise, threatened to answer nullification with military force; Calhoun resigned as vice president and moved to the Senate. In 1833, Congress passed a compromise tariff—and the Force Bill, which authorized military action against the nullifiers. South Carolina backed down and accepted the new tariff (to save face, it also declared the Force Bill nullified). Tensions temporarily eased, but sectional conflict was reaching alarming heights.

Faced with a rising stream of northern antislavery petitions in the mid-1830s, Congress overwhelmingly voted that it lacked any authority over slavery, and passed a gag rule barring the reading of such petitions. Former president Adams—now a Massachusetts congressman—led an annual battle against the gag, finally defeating it in 1844; ominously, the congressional vote increasingly fell on sectional rather than party lines, with northern Democrats beginning to split from their southern colleagues to vote with Adams and the northern Whigs.

But it was the new territories that remained the key battleground—especially as the nation's western possessions grew and rapidly expanding railroad networks raised the prospect of faster western settlement. In 1836, American settlers in Texas declared the territory independent of Mexico and sought annexation to the United States. Being below the 36°30′ line, Texas would become a slave territory under the 1820 Missouri Compromise, and northern Whigs strongly opposed annexation. In 1845, ignoring threats from Mexico and antislavery objections, Congress finally voted in favor of annexation.

The dispute over Texas erupted into war with Mexico in 1846. Nurturing blatant territorial ambitions, many in Washington welcomed the conflict. American forces captured Mexico City in 1847, forcing Mexico to cede vast southwestern lands, including California, in 1848. Inevitably, the huge new acquisitions opened a fresh battle over slavery's expansion. As early as 1846, northern congressmen pushed the Wilmot Proviso, barring slavery from any territory the United States might gain in the Mexican-American War. Southern interests killed the measure, but the principle would be repeatedly pressed by northern congressmen in the coming years. Southern forces, led by Calhoun, declared their section under attack. In the face of growing northern strength, they insisted on the inviolability of state power.

THE DIVIDE BEGINS TO REND THE COUNTRY

By 1850, the crisis over the territories had become an obvious threat to the federal union of the states. Kentucky's Henry Clay returned to the Senate; desperate to rein in the conflict, he proposed a series of compromise resolutions meant to forge a permanent peace. California would be admitted as a free state, but the rest of the territory won from Mexico would be open to slavery; slavery in the District of Columbia—a common target of antislavery opposition—would be protected; and a stronger fugitive slave law would be passed, enforcing the Constitution's requirement that free states return runaway slaves.

The Compromise of 1850 barely passed Congress; each element had to be voted on separately, with majorities cobbled together from different interest groups. At best, the resolutions offered little more than a truce. Calhoun, though near death, denounced the entire scheme, essentially demanding a southern veto over federal measures. Meanwhile, northern states were infuriated by the new fugitive slave law, openly defying it (even declaring it nullified) and actively protecting runaway slaves. The so-called Underground Railroad, a network of sympathizers who helped slaves escape the South, was never as organized or as coherent as later legend made it out to be—nonetheless, it grew more so in the 1850s after the passage of the Fugitive Slave Act.

In another attempt to defuse the impending crisis, Democratic senator Stephen Douglas of Illinois (who also hoped to profit from railroad construction by encouraging settlement) promoted a new principle of popular sovereignty, by which a majority of settlers would choose their territory's status as slave or free. Congress passed Douglas's Kansas-Nebraska Act in 1854, overturning the Missouri Compromise—and the status of Kansas and Nebraska, above the 36°30′ line, would be decided by their settlers. But many southerners were determined to block northern antislavery settlers by force.

Since at least 1840, there had been efforts to organize an antislavery political party. The Liberty Party ran presidential candidates in 1840 and 1844, with little impact. The stronger Free-Soil Party followed in the 1848 and 1852 elections; attracting disaffected northern Whigs and Democrats, it ran second in some northern states. By the early 1850s, the Whig Party was disintegrating, divided between North and South over slavery while struggling with anti-immigrant nativism and other issues. In 1854, a new Republican Party was organized, thus capitalizing on northern anger at the Kansas-Nebraska Act. The new party quickly absorbed the Free-Soil Party, most northern Whigs, the nativist parties, and the North's antislavery Democrats. Southern Whigs meanwhile crossed to the Democrats, who were left as the South's sole effective party.

Sectional tensions were swelling everywhere. Harriet Beecher Stowe's 1852 novel *Uncle Tom's Cabin*, a sentimentally tragic account of slave life, became an enormous northern best-seller by the mid-1850s, helping deepen northern hostility to the South's "peculiar institution." The Kansas-Nebraska experiment had swiftly degenerated into chaos: free-soil Kansas settlers were overwhelmed by organized pro-slavery forces from Missouri. By 1856, the territory, enmeshed in guerilla warfare, was lamented as "Bleeding Kansas." When abolitionist Senator Charles Sumner of Massachusetts denounced southern politicians' efforts to impose slavery on Kansas, he was savagely beaten on the Senate floor by Congressman Preston Brooks of South Carolina; the South's gleeful celebration of Brooks's attack shocked the North even more than the assault itself.

The new Republican Party came to dominate the North, sweeping northern congressional seats in 1856. The Republicans were the main challenger to the pro-southern Democrats in the 1856 presidential election, carrying eleven northern states (though losing the election). The crisis over Kansas, meanwhile, only worsened. Efforts to force through a pro-slavery constitution culminated at Lecompton, Kansas, in 1857, succeeding through a combination of intimidation and fraud. The tame acceptance of the rigged Lecompton constitution by Democratic president James Buchanan and his congressional allies—determined to appease the South at almost any cost—enraged even Douglas, who considered it a betrayal of the popular sovereignty principle. Another attempt at compromise had devolved into sectional turmoil.

In 1857, the Supreme Court, dominated by southerners, ruled in *Dred Scott v. Sandford*, the case of a slave who claimed his freedom after his owner took him into free territory. The court did not merely deny Scott's claim—it ruled that slavery could not be barred from any territory without destroying property rights, making the Missouri Compromise unconstitutional. It also ruled that blacks could not attain U.S. or state citizenship and, in even more absolute terms, that under the U.S. Constitution blacks had "no rights which the white man is bound to respect." The North, racist though it was, found the ruling shocking. Many feared the court might next force slavery even on the free states—and such a case, challenging free states' right to deny a slave owner his property, was in fact making its way through the appeals process to the Supreme Court.

Some northern radicals—a fringe of the abolitionist movement—were now prepared to turn to violence. John Brown, a religious zealot who had committed violent atrocities while battling pro-slavery forces in Kansas, led a raid on Harpers Ferry, Virginia, in 1859, hoping to spark a general slave insurrection. The raid, put down by federal troops under Colonel Robert E. Lee, failed utterly, and Brown was hanged for treason by the state of Virginia. The South, always terrified of "servile insurrection," looked on Brown with horror—but many in the North, though unwilling to condone his methods, admired his stance; at the very least, many would not entirely condemn him. Southerners were more alarmed by the northern reaction than by Brown's actions themselves, and they became further convinced that antislavery agitation endangered their very survival.

ERA 11: BLUE VERSUS GRAY: CIVIL WAR AND RECONSTRUCTION *(1860 TO 1877)*

SECESSIONISTS AND UNIONISTS

By 1860, the sections were near rupture. The outgoing president, Democrat James Buchanan, had tried to appease the South and settle the dispute over the territories by colluding with the Supreme Court on the Dred Scott decision and by supporting Kansas's rigged pro-slavery constitution. But in spite of such concessions, the breach only widened. The Democrats' 1860 presidential nominating convention split into northern and southern factions: northern Democrats nominated Stephen Douglas, whereas southern Democrats chose Buchanan's vice president, John Breckinridge, as their candidate and demanded unlimited expansion of slavery into the territories. Another group, the Constitutional Union Party, fielded John Bell of Tennessee, who pledged to unite the North and South.

The only group with a solid power base was the young Republican Party, which dominated the northern states with a platform that embraced westward expansion into free-soil territories. At the Republican convention, delegates argued over well-known (and controversial) potential candidates. Abraham Lincoln of Illinois emerged as their compromise candidate. He was a rising figure in the new party, having garnered national attention when he challenged Douglas for his Illinois Senate seat in 1858. The two had engaged in a series of widely followed debates on slavery in the territories, and Lincoln's cogent arguments and powerful speeches had made him a strong voice for the antislavery Free-Soil movement as it fought to keep slavery out of the territories.

Lincoln swept the solidly Republican northern states, crushing Douglas. Yet southern ballots did not even list his name. Because the rest of the country was divided, Lincoln won the four-way race with 40 percent of the vote. Lincoln was fiercely opposed to slavery, believing that it must eventually disappear. But he was confident it would die on its own—probably within another century—if it were blocked from expanding. Lincoln vowed not to interfere with the southern system, so long as slavery was barred from the territories. And although he defended the humanity of blacks and their basic right to freedom, he in no way argued for social or political equality. For much of his presidency, in fact, he favored proposals to colonize freed slaves in Africa.

Lincoln's careful assurances did nothing to calm most southerners, who saw him as a dangerous fanatic out to destroy them. He was, as they loudly objected, a president who had been elected without a single southern vote. Dark rumors swirled throughout the South: Lincoln and his "black Republicans" would send in the army, hand all property to the slaves, and force white women to marry black men. Although most southerners did not own slaves, they resented outside interference with their local affairs and way of life—and they were terrified by the supposed Republican plots to impose "Negro rule."

South Carolina had repeatedly threatened to secede from the Union since the nullification crisis of the 1820s, in which it had first proclaimed a right to invalidate federal laws. As soon as Lincoln was elected, the state called a convention for the following month. Delegates declared the new president "hostile to slavery" and voted unanimously to secede from the Union. By February 1861, eight states—the entire lower South—followed suit. They agreed to form the Confederate States of America, with a constitution that would permanently enshrine slavery. The states in the upper South did not yet follow, but they warned the North not to attack the new Confederacy or attempt to force the seceding states back into the Union.

Struggling to reassure the secessionists, outgoing president Buchanan backed a constitutional amendment that would protect slavery in all territories below the 36°30′ line. President-elect Lincoln strongly opposed the idea. He was prepared to support an amendment that would protect slavery solely in the southern states where it already existed, but southerners were dissatisfied. A last-ditch peace conference met in Washington that February, but agreement was impossible. Meanwhile, southern states demanded the handover of federal forts within their territory. Buchanan refused, but was unwilling to use force to defend the installations. Charleston's Fort Sumter in South Carolina was besieged, and southern batteries drove off federal resupply vessels.

Many northerners, however, were ready to fight to preserve the Union. They worried that if a losing minority—the arrogant and aristocratic southern slaveholders—could reject the results of a legitimate election, democracy was dead. Its demise would signify the failure of the American Revolution and its great experiment in popular self-rule.

At the same time, southerners believed that in fighting for local control and state-level democracy, *they* were defending the Revolution's legacy against the tyranny and aggression of an outside power—and they were ready to battle for those freedoms. Both sides readily invoked George Washington and the founding generation. Many northern Democrats also opposed war against the South, blaming Lincoln and the Republicans for the crisis; the most extreme faction openly supported the southern cause (Republicans would derisively call them "copperheads" after the poisonous snake). Even pro-war northern Democrats sought only to restore the Union as it was, and would tolerate no broader moves against slavery.

Lincoln refused to accept secession, and he would not give up Fort Sumter. Determined not to fire the first shot, he sent ships in early April to peacefully resupply the fort—forcing the secessionists to decide whether they would open an armed conflict. On April 12, 1861, South Carolina opened fire on Fort Sumter, which was soon forced to surrender. Lincoln now called for seventy-five thousand volunteer soldiers to quell the rebellion. Virginia and three other states declared Lincoln's order an act of aggression against the South. Although several of these states harbored strong unionist movements, majorities now voted to secede and join the Confederacy. Four border slave states remained in the Union, although several had to put down their own secession movements (federal troops helped keep Maryland in line, lest Washington, DC—between Maryland and Virginia—be surrounded by Confederate states).

THE WAR FOR THE UNION: 1861–1862

The American Civil War had begun. The North's larger industrial base and population were huge military advantages. But it was fighting for the more abstract aims of preserving the Union and protecting democracy. The South, in contrast, was fighting on its own soil to protect its independence—the stakes were concrete and very high. It hoped to make a Northern victory so costly that the Union would lose its will to continue. Both sides expected a quick victory.

The Union hoped to starve out the Confederacy with a naval blockade that would cut off its crucial cotton exports to Europe (known as the Anaconda Plan). Union forces sharply curtailed the South's outside trade, but Confederate blockade runners kept the sea routes open and smuggled out cotton while they imported weapons and supplies. The blockade was not enough to decide the war.

In July 1861, Union troops marched on the new Confederate capital at Richmond, Virginia. However, Southern forces soon bested them at Bull Run, driving them back to Washington in confusion. The Confederates had shown they would not be easily beaten, yet the Union showed no signs of giving up. This war would be neither brief nor easy.

Confederates sought recognition and aid from Britain and France, with whom they had strong trading ties. "King Cotton," they hoped, would bring Europe aboard—and many upper-class Britons would have been delighted to see America's democratic experiment fail. (In contrast, however, the middle and working classes, including those in the cotton-dependent textile trade, were often sympathetic toward democracy and the Union.) Britain debated whether it should support the Confederacy, and nearly came to blows with the United States in late 1861 when a Union warship seized Confederate emissaries from a British steamer. Europe, however, was strongly opposed to slavery. Indeed, despite demands from many Southerners to reopen the African slave trade, the Confederate constitution banned it—in a diplomatic gesture to Europe. Yet the European powers ultimately refused to openly align with the Confederacy.

After their humiliating defeat at Bull Run, Union forces continued to gather and train troops, so as to take advantage of their enormous manpower and industrial resources. By early 1862, Union troops had seized coastal enclaves along the Carolinas and Gulf of Mexico, and they had begun to push down the Mississippi River from the North. In April, the Union took New Orleans and won a bloody, close-run victory at Shiloh, Tennessee. In the coming months, Union forces tried to push farther down the Mississippi and north up the river from New Orleans. Setbacks would leave the front stalemated until the end of the year, but Union troops began to push south toward the strategic town of Vicksburg, Mississippi.

The Virginia expanse between Washington and Richmond was the key military theater. After Bull Run, the Union's Army of the Potomac was put under General George B. McClellan, who molded it into a professional force. But once he began his push on Richmond, McClellan proved painfully hesitant, exaggerating Confederate strength and refusing to press his advantage. And he soon faced a dangerous new opponent: General Robert E. Lee, commander of the new Army of Northern Virginia. Lee, a former U.S. Army officer, had refused Lincoln's offer to command Union forces. When Virginia left the Union, he immediately followed. Though he was reluctant to endorse secession, Lee's first loyalty was to his state.

Lee invaded Maryland in September 1862, hoping to threaten Washington and force the North out of the war. After a fierce and bloody battle at Antietam, Lee had to abandon his Northern invasion and retreat to Virginia. But the Union's victory was hardly decisive: McClellan failed to commit his full forces or to pursue Lee's retreating army. In November, Lincoln permanently removed him from command. But the battle nonetheless proved critical. Until now, Britain and France had been thinking about recognizing the Confederacy and pressing a negotiated peace. Lee's defeat made them lose confidence in Confederate strength. The appearance of Union strength also allowed Lincoln to take a step he had been contemplating for months: making an attack on slavery into a fundamental aim of the war.

THE WAR AGAINST SLAVERY: 1863–1865

The North had entered the war in singular pursuit of defending the Union, not of attacking slavery—the Union even contained four slave states that bordered the Confederacy. But slaves were now fleeing to Union lines in search of freedom, and in summer 1861, the United States declared them contraband (confiscated enemy property). In spring 1862, Congress abolished slavery in the District of Columbia and throughout the territories, the Homestead Act opened western land to settlers for minimal fees, and Congress soon financed a transcontinental railroad to further open the West. These measures fulfilled popular Republican pledges and solidly established the West as free soil. In July, Congress declared all rebel-owned slaves behind Union lines to be permanently free. But Lincoln was already planning to go further.

By summer 1862, Lincoln was seeking to target the entire Confederate slave system, which would undermine the Southern war effort and make it impossible for antislavery Europeans to support the Confederacy. And though the four unionist slave states continued to reject even compensated emancipation, Lincoln also had a growing sense that the war must settle the issue of slavery once and for all. His cabinet feared that a bold move would look desperate while Union arms were struggling, and it urged him to wait for a victory before acting. Victory came at Antietam, and Lincoln issued a preliminary Emancipation Proclamation just days after the battle. The final version, issued on January 1, 1863, declared all slaves in rebel territory free. Union-occupied areas were excluded (as were the border slave states that stayed in the Union)—but Congress had already moved to free rebel-owned slaves behind Union lines.

Union troops could now liberate entire slave populations as they advanced, and slaves in the Confederate interior would be encouraged to resist their masters. The proclamation also urged freed slaves to enter Union armies, an opportunity that free blacks and so-called contrabands had sought since the war's beginning. Recruitment of black regiments (though under white officers and at reduced pay) began in early 1863. At that time, the Union was implementing a highly unpopular draft to raise troop levels; now the Union had a million black men eager to fight. Furious Southerners vowed to enslave all black prisoners and execute their white officers. Lincoln promised retaliation against Southern prisoners, and the Confederate policy was shelved.

White Union troops were often hostile to black soldiers, and generals often used them for manual labor. Some Northerners, especially Northern Democrats, rejected the war on slavery entirely, and lashed out against blacks: in July 1863, New York workingmen and immigrants rioted against the draft law and killed dozens of blacks. Yet the war also changed minds. Lincoln slowly abandoned his earlier support for colonization of freed slaves. When given the opportunity, black troops performed with bravery and distinction. Their performance impressed many Northerners; more began to wonder if the Northern cause should extend beyond preserving the Union and look to end the moral evil of slavery. Although racist attitudes still pervaded the North, many people were forced to confront prejudices that had long gone unchallenged.

As Northern perspectives evolved, war raged. Lee continued to hold off the Army of the Potomac in Virginia into early 1863. But Union forces, led by General Ulysses S. Grant, advanced down the Mississippi and laid siege to Vicksburg in May. In June, Lee's army pushed through Maryland into Pennsylvania—again seeking a decisive blow with a second invasion of the North. The Army of the Potomac met Lee at Gettysburg. Fighting on their own home soil, Union forces finally dealt a devastating blow to Lee during the first three days of July. Although Union troops were too exhausted to pursue and destroy his army, Lee was forced to retreat. Gettysburg marked a turning point in that going forward, Lee would be on the defensive as he worked to hold back and wear down Union forces.

The same day Lee retreated from Gettysburg—July 4, 1863—Vicksburg fell to Grant. The entire Mississippi River was soon in Union hands, and the Confederacy was cut in two. In early 1864, Grant assumed command of all Union armies and pressed into Virginia with a series of costly battles. But unlike his predecessors, Grant refused to retreat even after he suffered heavy losses. He maintained pressure on Lee and pushed toward Richmond. To the west, Union armies had pushed south into Georgia; in May 1864, General William T. Sherman began a drive toward Atlanta.

The 1864 election was the South's last hope. But preserving democracy was the Union's chief cause, and Lincoln was determined to hold the election even during wartime. His challenger was George McClellan, his one-time general. If elected, McClellan was expected to concede Southern independence and negotiate peace. The brutal war, capped by Grant's slow and bloody Virginia campaign, had deeply strained the North. Sherman took Atlanta in September, however, and gave Northern morale a timely boost. Lincoln won 55 percent of the popular vote, and he dominated the electoral vote. Soldiers who had once adored McClellan now supported Lincoln—they refused to see their sacrifices thrown away. Grant continued his relentless push toward Richmond, while Sherman began a drive to the sea across Georgia and South Carolina, devastating the towns through which he passed.

By early 1865, the South was imploding: wracked by shortages and internal unrest, its slave system was eroding from within. Some desperate Confederates even urged that slaves be recruited as soldiers in exchange for their freedom. In the North, Republicans now dominated Congress. In January 1865—after furious debate and pressure from Lincoln—Congress passed the Thirteenth Amendment, which banned slavery in the United States. This would have been unimaginable four years earlier when the war began. Richmond fell on April 2, 1865; seven days later, Lee surrendered his army at Appomattox, Virginia. Within a week, Lincoln was assassinated at Washington's Ford's Theater by a small conspiracy of Confederate sympathizers led by actor John Wilkes Booth. But the Union pressed on, and remaining Confederate forces soon surrendered. The Civil War was over.

THE RISE AND FALL OF RECONSTRUCTION

Now the United States was left with the massive challenge of Reconstruction, which would involve rebuilding the southern states and readmitting them to the Union. The states ratified the Thirteenth Amendment by December 1865, including many southern states, which understood they had no choice: slavery was dead, and readmitted Southern states would have to accept that fact. Yet the government was divided. Congress was dominated by Republicans determined to remake the South. The new president, Andrew Johnson, who had served as Lincoln's 1864 running mate, was a pro-Union Tennessee Democrat—antislavery, but virulently racist. His hatred of slavery had stemmed from his hatred of aristocratic slave owners. With those same plantation magnates now paying him homage, he quickly shifted ground. And he shared their aim of keeping the black population harshly subordinated.

Lincoln had envisioned lenient terms for readmission of the South, and Johnson followed through with enthusiasm. He swiftly returned political power to ex-Confederates in exchange for oaths of allegiance. Major property owners and other prominent ex-Confederates were required to apply to him personally, but Johnson readily granted pardons as the once-hated plantation lords humbly appealed. By the end of 1865, virtually the entire Confederacy had returned to the Union, under governments run by the former rebels. Although many northerners were unsatisfied, Johnson declared the Union restored.

In the final months of his life, Lincoln had been moving toward bolder positions on race. He had contemplated granting full citizenship to African Americans—a concept utterly repugnant to Johnson. In 1865, southern states began to impose Black Codes. To control former slaves, these laws imposed harsh restrictions: blacks were denied freedom of movement, could not leave their former masters' employment without permission, and could be sentenced to "penal servitude" for vagrancy (that is, leaving their respective plantations without a pass). Johnson enthusiastically backed such laws, which precisely matched his racial ideas—and which restricted free blacks almost as much as had their previous enslavement.

During this early Presidential Reconstruction, the heavily Republican Congress was not in session. When its members assembled in December 1865, they immediately turned on Johnson and began to implement "radical" Reconstruction. In early 1866, Congress overrode Johnson's veto and empowered the new, military-backed Freedmen's Bureau to protect the rights of southern blacks. Determined not to cede power to former rebels, the Republicans sought instead to enfranchise the South's large—and inevitably Republican—black population. In July, Congress passed the Fourteenth Amendment. Dismantling the Dred Scott ruling, the amendment granted full citizenship to all Americans, and allowed the federal government to protect citizens' rights against state interference.

Although Johnson campaigned aggressively against Republican radicals, northern voters viewed his lenient Reconstruction plans as a surrender that squandered the Union's costly victory. In the 1866 elections, Republicans took even firmer control of Congress. Again over Johnson's veto, they placed the South under martial law and ordered the army to enroll new voters. Many of these new voters were African American, whereas many ex-Confederates were barred from voting. New state constitutions were enacted that protected black rights while limiting the power of ex-Confederates. In the coming years, due to large black electorates allied with pro-Union whites, a number of African Americans were elected to public office—even to seats in the U.S. Congress and Senate.

Congressional Republicans, who were easily able to override Johnson's regular vetoes, worked to strip the unwanted president of his powers. Even the army, still commanded by Grant, was placed virtually outside of Johnson's control. When a new law barred him from removing cabinet members without Senate permission, Johnson denied its constitutionality (the Supreme

Court later agreed) and fired the Lincoln-appointed secretary of war. In 1868, the House impeached Johnson for defying its laws, though the Senate fell one vote short of convicting him and removing him from office. Aided by half a million newly enfranchised African American voters, the far more sympathetic Grant was elected president that fall.

Southern white anger remained a dangerous problem. Vigilantes, including members of the new and violent Ku Klux Klan, terrorized blacks, northern officials and activists (whom they derided as parasitic carpetbaggers), and their southern allies. Trying to safeguard Reconstruction, Congress passed the Fifteenth Amendment in 1869, guaranteeing the right of African Americans to vote. But ex-Confederates were regaining power. Southern states officially accepted the Fourteenth and Fifteenth Amendments, but only the army kept the South in check—and the army could not stay forever. Anti-Reconstruction southerners—called Redeemers, as they strove to restore the white antebellum order—gradually won control. And in 1874, amid a struggling economy, corruption in Grant's cabinet, and growing suspicion among northerners of "radical" pro-black policies, Democrats took the House of Representatives.

Fierce southern resistance and waning northern will had undermined Reconstruction, and the 1876 election delivered the final blow. With the southern black vote already widely suppressed, Democrat Samuel Tilden won the nation's popular vote. But Republicans, who still controlled three southern states, manipulated the count to give Rutherford B. Hayes the Electoral College by a single vote. After months of conflict, Democrats agreed to accept Hayes's election. But in exchange, they demanded the final withdrawal of troops from the South and the acceptance of its Redeemer governments. The Compromise of 1877 restored white control to the South, and the status of African Americans there would quickly sink. Yet the Fourteenth and Fifteenth Amendments remained, and they would be invoked again in the future.

ERA 12: RESISTANCE AND RECOVERY: REBUILDING A WAR-TORN NATION *(1870S TO 1890S)*

INDUSTRIALIZATION, IMMIGRATION, AND EXPANSION

An estimated seven hundred fifty thousand Civil War soldiers died in combat, and many more succumbed to poor sanitation and camp disease. Although the South suffered less than half of the war's fatalities, its smaller population made those losses more severe. Further, because the majority of the battles were fought on Confederate soil, the South endured more home-front shortages, disrupted agriculture, civilian casualties, and overall devastation. The North also suffered massive loss of life, but its larger population and undamaged industrial base made it well poised for recovery. Indeed, the North was already moving into a post-war boom as the South battled through Reconstruction.

Westward movement—boosted by the 1862 Homestead Act and expanding railroads—continued to accelerate. American farm production surged. But foreign production also increased, flooding world markets and cutting demand for American exports. By the mid-1880s, crop prices had slid, and many farmers were plunged into debt. In the cities, post-war industrial mechanization took firm hold. Earlier in the nineteenth century, inventors had experimented with interchangeable parts—simple mass-produced components that could produce virtually any product. Now factories churned out such products on assembly lines, and skilled artisans were no longer necessary. The new factory system pushed them aside in favor of unskilled laborers who were willing to work for low pay in dismal and dangerous conditions.

Meanwhile, large monopolies called trusts took control of entire industries. The magnates who led these trusts amassed unprecedented fortunes. In the 1870s and 1880s, Pittsburgh's Andrew Carnegie greatly improved the manufacture of steel and soon controlled much of the country's steel production. The discovery of oil just before the Civil War created a new and fast-booming industry, displacing whale oil as the country's chief lighting source; John D. Rockefeller's Standard Oil Company was formed in the 1860s and controlled 90 percent of the U.S. oil refining industry by the 1880s. The trusts targeted smaller rival companies with incredible ruthlessness, removing them by whatever means necessary, including smear campaigns, beatings, and even bombings. As competition was eliminated, laborers' wages were driven lower—but workers had few alternatives.

Across the Atlantic, Europe was also under strain. As its population grew, there were too few farming opportunities for too many would-be laborers. They moved to the cities for work, but factories there also had limited jobs to offer. With little to lose, many were driven to seek new opportunities in America. Until this point, the U.S. immigrant population had consisted mainly of Western Europeans. Now, as the population in eastern and southern Europe swelled, Catholics and Jews increasingly immigrated to the United States. America's well-established Anglo-Saxon majority responded with hostility as new waves of culturally alien immigrants crowded the cities' tenements and dominated the low-wage employment market.

Other routes to wealth proved more difficult than Americans had anticipated. Many had rushed to California after the discovery of gold there in 1848. After the war, even more fortune seekers moved westward in pursuit of precious metals. But rich and easy finds were rare, and forced increasingly complex underground mining. Although a few entrepreneurs became fabulously wealthy, the vast majority of miners worked dangerous, low-wage jobs deep under the earth.

The American West enticed those who wished to escape the crowded eastern cities. Many were lured by open, available land and jobs in western mining towns (although farming, overproduction, and the corporatization of mining made neither a sure bet). Post-war railroad construction finally linked the coasts and opened the vast U.S. interior to the rest of the fast-growing nation. Like factories, the railroads needed cheap labor and attracted more immigrants. On the West Coast, railroads relied heavily on Asian immigrants—who endured prejudice from and tension with the white population as well as open legal discrimination.

The westward push also sparked violent campaigns against Native Americans. The Plains Indians' nomadic culture depended on vast spaces and the West's enormous buffalo herds—both of which were incompatible with white settlement and railroad expansion. The U.S. government tried to force Native Americans onto fixed reservations, but even the treaties granting such lands were readily violated whenever the government wished the tribes moved elsewhere. A Native American alliance led by Sitting Bull and Crazy Horse destroyed a U.S. cavalry force under General George Custer at Little Bighorn, Montana, in 1876, but the United States soon gained the upper hand. The Dawes Severalty Act of 1887 aimed to push native people into farming, ending native groups' land claims in exchange for U.S. citizenship and personal land grants. But the land was poor, and speculators often tricked Native American families into losing it.

The final large-scale Native American resistance effort, the religiously inspired Ghost Dance, arose on the western reservations in the late 1880s. It promised to remove white settlers and restore the Plains Indians' traditional culture. American troops were sent to squelch the movement. In late 1890, troops captured a large group of Lakota Sioux and brought them to Wounded Knee, South Dakota. When the soldiers tried to disarm the Native Americans, shots were fired. The soldiers launched a furious attack; even their officers lost control, and many of the Native Americans, including women and children, were massacred. The slaughter effectively marked the end of active Native American resistance in the West, and left a bitter, enduring wedge between Native Americans and the U.S. government.

THE STRAINS OF THE GILDED AGE

The last decades of the nineteenth century were hard. Farm prices dropped, and the American economy grew more susceptible to international crises. Urban wage labor surged, but for low pay and in poor conditions; and with immigration also increasing, there were often fewer jobs than prospective workers. Republicans and Democrats battled in a series of hard-fought elections, feuding over protective tariffs, immigration, civil service reform, and veterans' benefits. Both parties were corrupt and internally divided; often, they focused on little more than factional gains and the interests of their most powerful supporters. Urban political machines all but controlled working and immigrant communities, providing protection in exchange for votes. Many Americans felt ignored by the political process entirely.

A handful of industrialists—branded "robber barons" by their many critics—had ruthlessly amassed vast wealth. Self-made men, these determined, aggressive, and hard-working businessmen exemplified the opportunity so many sought in America; the corporations and infrastructure they pioneered were crucial to the country's rapid industrial expansion after the Civil War. But their success came at a high price for many: most of their numerous laborers worked for low wages and in poor conditions, and rival businesses were cold-bloodedly suppressed or destroyed.

Satirist Mark Twain dubbed the era the "Gilded Age": gold-plated rather than golden, with a thin, glittering veneer that masked the seething troubles beneath. By the 1880s, some of the corporate giants, led by Carnegie, began to contribute large sums to philanthropy, endowing libraries, museums, and other institutions. Carnegie came to preach a "gospel of wealth," arguing that vast fortunes must be used to better society. Such efforts somewhat improved the magnates' image and made dramatic contributions to public culture and the arts—but conditions for their employees scarcely changed.

A rising labor movement sought to improve wages and working conditions. Many found inspiration in such radical European ideas as Marxism and Socialism, which insisted on communal ownership of property (that is, Communism) or, less radically, on a larger government role in promoting social welfare. One group, the Knights of Labor, helped organize influential labor strikes in the 1880s. Industrial leaders pushed back, limiting labor's gains. In May 1886, as a multi-city strike pressured industry for a standard eight-hour workday, anarchists rallied in Chicago's Haymarket Square to protest deadly police attacks on strikers. When police tried to subdue the protest, someone threw dynamite into the police ranks. The Haymarket Riot helped discredit labor organizers by casting them as dangerous radicals.

Later that year, Samuel Gompers formed the American Federation of Labor (AFL). As the AFL merged groups from across the country to increase political pressure for reform, clashes between labor and industry only worsened. In 1892, Carnegie refused to recognize a steelworkers' union. When his Homestead, Pennsylvania, factory went on strike, the company brought in private detectives to suppress the workers, and the strikers opened fire. With support from the state militia, the union was defeated. Carnegie's reputation was tarnished, but steel unions were effectively blocked until the 1930s. In 1894's Pullman Strike, unions shut down railroad networks, and the federal government directly intervened. Declaring it illegal to interfere with interstate commerce and the U.S. mail, the government sent troops to suppress the strike and restore order. Now facing direct federal suppression, labor had suffered another blow.

In rural areas, a new populist movement gained ground as farmers fell further into debt. Farmers' unions and political organizations lashed out at banks, eastern businesses, and railroads. They demanded inflationary silver-backed currency (as opposed to a pure gold standard) to increase the money supply and drive down the value of their debts. The Populist (or People's) Party ran a presidential candidate in the 1892 election, and although the party finished a distant third with just a handful of electoral votes, it succeeded in familiarizing Americans with its grievances. The silver issue, in particular, gained traction. International financial moves had reduced the country's gold reserves, and now many Americans looked to "free silver" as a popular check on the eastern big-money magnates.

The free-silver movement was especially popular among Democrats. In 1896, Nebraska's William Jennings Bryan was nominated by both the Democrats and the Populists. Delivering a rallying call for free silver at the Democratic convention, Bryan famously proclaimed that the people must not be crucified on a "cross of gold." Bryan broke with the tradition of candidates' saying little before the election, instead actively campaigning across the country. Despite dominating the West and South, Bryan lost the election. Republicans had successfully painted him as a dangerous, anarchy-loving extremist. Bryan ran again in 1900, but populism's large following fast faded. The agrarian movement, like the labor movement, was left angry and largely powerless.

Although the trusts dominated oil, steel, beef, sugar, whiskey, and other industries across the United States, political pressure yielded a few victories. In the late 1880s, western and southern states began to pass antitrust laws that sought to limit the huge monopolies. The states, however, had no power over interstate commerce. An 1890 federal law, the Sherman Antitrust Act, banned conspiracies "in restraint of trade." But the courts ruled that the act did not apply to most multistate conglomerates. Instead, they used the law to brand the unions as conspiracies against trade. The trusts emerged largely untouched, whereas the unions were deeply hampered. Further action would be needed to address growing public discontent.

THE NEW SOUTH AND THE RISE OF JIM CROW

After Reconstruction, with the former slaveholding aristocracy largely restored to power, the South sought new routes to prosperity in a world without slavery. Southern leaders poured their energy into industrialization, and the region modernized and became more integrated with the national economy. The "New South" was untroubled by labor agitation and thus attracted some northern industrialists. Yet despite the growing industrial boom, low pay and unproductive farms created a sharp divide in wealth. A few leading men became extremely rich. At the other extreme, many southerners were desperately poor. Rural and urban poverty would become a chronic southern problem.

With few exceptions, African Americans were pushed to the bottom of the economic pile. As slavery collapsed, most southern blacks had dreamed of independent land ownership and true freedom from others' control. Such dreams proved illusory. Although Congress overturned the 1865 Black Codes, with their virtual reimposition of slavery, any dramatic post-war gains quickly faded. Black rights were rarely recognized, and the withdrawal of federal troops made antidiscrimination laws unenforceable. Social and economic advancement was thwarted by oppressive discrimination. And although blacks fared the worst economically, they bore the brunt of poor whites' resentment.

Once slavery ended, planters needed to replace the labor force. Their attempt to keep hold of their former slaves through the Black Codes had failed, but by the late 1860s, a new pattern was emerging: sharecropping. Under this system, families were allotted their own plot on a plantation's land, farming it themselves in exchange for a small share of the profits from the crop. Both black and white laborers were forced into sharecropping, but African Americans often found it to be their only option. This was not slavery: individuals could not be sold, and families could not be divided. But it fell far short of full economic freedom.

More direct threats to freedom also lurked. Sharecroppers were forced to buy food and supplies from plantation owners at exorbitant prices. This often forced them into debt, and planters demanded labor in return. This peonage (or virtual enslavement based on unpaid debts) was technically illegal. But poor farmers—black or white—had little access to legal assistance, and they easily fell victim to the powerful and well connected.

African American political rights barely survived Reconstruction. By 1876, the black vote was widely suppressed, and the situation only worsened as federal troops permanently withdrew and the white so-called Redeemer governments took hold. The Fourteenth and Fifteenth Amendments were evaded with poll taxes and literacy tests, undermining blacks' citizenship and voting rights. Poor southern whites, and immigrants throughout the country, were also disenfranchised by such methods. But the discrimination against blacks was systematic and widespread. Vigilante groups, such as the Ku Klux Klan, enforced exclusion and repression through lynching, intimidation, and other acts of terror.

By the 1890s, black suffrage in the South was effectively dead, and the Republican Party had all but vanished from the region. White social pressure routinely forced blacks into segregated spaces, and they were almost entirely excluded from public education, juries, and virtually everything else. As public transit offered Americans new travel options during the 1880s, blacks were legally restricted to separate cars. African American resistance met with little success, and discrimination became even more systematic as employers and unions barred blacks from skilled professions. By the 1890s, all ex-Confederate states had legally imposed segregation, a system that came to be known, after a caricatured black character in pre–Civil War minstrel shows, as Jim Crow.

In upholding southern segregationist legislation, the Supreme Court turned a blind eye to black disenfranchisement. In the civil rights cases of 1883, the court rejected discrimination complaints and struck down a Reconstruction-era civil rights law: the justices ruled that the Fourteenth Amendment protected citizens only against discrimination by the state, not by individuals. In its 1896 *Plessy v. Ferguson* decision, the Supreme Court ruled in favor of state discrimination as well, upholding Louisiana's segregated railroads. The court held that the maintenance of separated yet equal facilities for blacks and whites fully satisfied the Fourteenth Amendment's guarantee of equal protection under the law. This "separate but equal" doctrine would form the legal framework of segregation for the next six decades.

ERA 13: THE NEXT BENCHMARK: AMERICA IS A GLOBAL LEADER *(1890S TO 1920)*

THE UNITED STATES LOOKS OVERSEAS

Since George Washington's presidency, the United States had pursued an isolationist foreign policy that avoided what Thomas Jefferson called "foreign entanglements." Although the 1823 Monroe Doctrine had asserted U.S. strength and declared the Western Hemisphere a uniquely American sphere of influence, it mainly aimed to keep Europeans out of the region. But the nation's foreign policy began to shift even before the Civil War, showing the first signs of a broader global reach.

In 1854, a naval expedition under Commodore Matthew Perry forced Japan, which had for centuries been closed to most foreigners, to open its borders to Western trade. In 1867, the United States purchased Alaska from Russia and commenced occupation of Pacific islands, such as Midway. In the 1870s, the United States began to exert influence over Hawaii and to devote significant resources to the construction of a powerful modern navy. By the late nineteenth century, the nation's economy was strong, and its foreign dealings were fast increasing. Many Americans began to see their nation as a natural global power.

The events that truly catapulted America onto the world stage began in Spanish-held Cuba, one of the last European footholds in the New World. In the mid-1890s, Cuba rebelled against Spanish control. Spain's brutal crackdown on Cuba, coupled with sensationalist coverage in William Randolph Hearst's *New York Journal*, earned the Cubans considerable American sympathy. Spain offered concessions, but unrest continued, and relations with the United States deteriorated. Prominent U.S. politicians saw an opportunity to expand American influence in the Caribbean, and early in 1898, the battleship *Maine* arrived at Havana Harbor in a show of American force. On February 15, the *Maine* exploded, killing more than two hundred of its crew. Although the explosion was probably accidental, Americans—goaded by Hearst's "yellow press"—believed a Spanish mine had destroyed the ship. "Remember the *Maine*!" became a national rallying cry.

Alarmed, the Spanish offered further concessions, and President William McKinley sought a peaceful solution. But American pro-war pressure was powerful. McKinley issued an ultimatum that demanded Spain's withdrawal from Cuba, and he asked Congress to declare war even before Spain's reply arrived. As war erupted, America's Pacific ships destroyed the Spanish fleet at Manila Bay in the Philippines and soon seized the islands. Spain's Cuban fleet was blockaded and finally destroyed. American ground forces (which included Theodore Roosevelt's famous volunteer cavalry, the Rough Riders) quickly conquered the island. American battle casualties were few; many more soldiers succumbed to disease than to combat. By the end of 1898, the brief Spanish-American War had ended, and Spain was forced to seek peace.

Victory triggered an identity crisis: Should America abandon isolationism completely and assume its place as an imperialist power? The United States had annexed the Hawaiian Islands during the war, and a powerful lobby argued that the nation was destined for global leadership. They invoked an increasingly popular ideology of racial strength, which asserted that the Anglo-Saxon elite had a duty to "civilize" inferior races. (Inevitably, such ideas also questioned the racial fitness of the ever-rising immigrant tide.) Crudely distorting Charles Darwin's new ideas on evolution through natural selection, theories of Social Darwinism lent pseudo-scientific credence to the domination of "weaker" nations, races, or economic classes by "racially superior" elites.

Anti-imperialists meanwhile denounced conquest as expensive, unwise, and fundamentally un-American. Pushed and pulled by rival factions, American actions abroad proved inconsistent. The peace treaty with Spain granted independence to Cuba and ceded Puerto Rico to the United States; America also purchased the Philippines from Spain. Over the strong objections of the newly founded Anti-Imperialist League, the United States quashed a Filipino uprising. The government also recommended that the islands ultimately gain independence—at some future point, when the United States deemed them ready. Further, America sought influence in China, even though it made no territorial claims there. Determined to evade the European powers' competing claims to China and open Chinese markets to Americans, the United States worked to create an Open Door Policy for all foreign powers and helped suppress China's anti-foreign Boxer Rebellion in 1900.

Becoming president after McKinley's assassination in 1901, Theodore Roosevelt sought a navy capable of dominating both the Atlantic and the Pacific. Roosevelt helped engineer a revolution in Panama that created a friendly regime and allowed the United States to build a canal across the isthmus—thus linking the two oceans. The ever-ambitious president bolstered America's influence in the Western Hemisphere with the Roosevelt Corollary to the Monroe Doctrine, which authorized an American police power to intervene in Latin American countries to stop "uncivilized" behavior and protect U.S. interests. Roosevelt further enhanced American might and prestige by helping negotiate an end to the 1905 Russo-Japanese War (making him one of the first Nobel Peace Prize winners) and sending the U.S. Navy's Great White Fleet—a group of dazzlingly white battleships—on a two-year tour around the world.

SOCIAL STRAIN AT HOME AND THE PROGRESSIVE PUSH FOR REFORM

By the turn of the century, industrial leaders had reined in some of their more aggressive practices and poured money into philanthropic causes. But labor conditions were only slightly improved, and unions made little progress after the setbacks of the 1890s. The courts consistently turned antitrust laws against the unions and rejected attempts at reformist legislation. In 1905's *Lochner v. New York*, for example, the Supreme Court struck down a New York law that limited bakery workers to ten-hour shifts, ruling that the state had violated employers' right to negotiate contracts. Critics decried the decision as an abuse of judicial power, but the labor movement continued to face stiff headwinds. And as immigration increased, anti-Catholic and anti-Jewish discrimination blocked union aid to unskilled workers who faced some of the worst conditions.

Alarming social strain, pressure from traditional religious social campaigners, and the growing power of the popular press all led to calls for new and bold reforms. Whereas the "yellow" journalism of Hearst and his imitators sought mainly to sell newspapers through cheap sensationalism, others wanted to expose injustice and inspire change. Aggressive journalists—branded "muckrakers" for the dirt they uncovered—revealed rampant corruption in business and government, also drawing attention to slum conditions, failures in public education, and other shocking social ills that most had chosen not to notice.

As outrage over these widespread injustices grew, and as the courts continued to block many attempts at reform, the rising Progressive movement sought to enact change at the federal and state levels. Progressivism had an ally in President Roosevelt, a Republican, who channeled his activist policy instincts into correcting society's blatant wrongs. First, he launched a new attack on the trusts that aimed to dissolve or otherwise reform the conglomerates. In the face of increasingly widespread logging and mining, Roosevelt also pressed for the protection of natural resources and scenic wonders with the establishment of the National Park System and other pioneering conservation measures.

Meanwhile, Congress also began to promote reformist legislation. In 1903, it took a major step toward government economic oversight as it created the Department of Commerce and Labor (split a decade later into two separate departments) to regulate interstate business. In 1906, muckraker Upton Sinclair published *The Jungle*, which exposed Chicago's shockingly unsanitary meat industry. With measures like the Pure Food and Drug Act, Congress banned the sale of tainted products and mandated government inspection. Despite fierce opposition from private banks, the Federal Reserve Act established a system of government-controlled banks to stabilize the currency. Another measure granted immunity to business officials who exposed corporate abuses. And at the state level, reforms allowed the recall of elected officials and the proposal of referendums by popular initiative.

Because it was impossible to enact all reforms through legislation, Progressives sought constitutional amendments to implement more fundamental changes. One major demand was a national income tax system: a progressive tax—drawing most heavily from higher earners—would fund expanded programs to benefit the less fortunate. The courts had ruled income taxes unconstitutional, but in 1909, Congress passed the Sixteenth Amendment (ratified by the states in 1913) to legalize such levies. Progressives also sought to increase the people's power; in 1912, Congress passed the Seventeenth Amendment (also ratified in 1913), which established direct popular election of senators. The people had previously elected only their representatives, and state legislatures had chosen senators.

Many Progressives also embraced the long-standing and powerful temperance movement. Casting saloons as evil destroyers of men and of families, anti-alcohol or "dry" forces had gradually built a power base that bolstered politicians who helped them or defeated those who hindered them. By 1900, many states and counties had passed dry laws. A federal ban on alcohol was more difficult to secure, as the excise tax on liquor was one of the main sources of federal revenue. However, the income tax amendment shifted the balance and freed the government from its dependence on the excise. The dry lobby turned its power on Congress, winning passage of the Eighteenth Amendment in 1919 and securing state ratification with dramatic speed. The production or sale of most alcoholic beverages was now illegal.

Another major part of the Progressive cause was women's suffrage. At the Seneca Falls Convention in 1848, some women had begun to demand public equality. But the majority of Americans, both male and female, continued to see the home as a woman's natural place. After the Civil War, Susan B. Anthony and other activists worked to shift perceptions of women's roles. Families also needed more income, and there was a massive demand for unskilled labor; thus, more women joined the workforce, challenging traditional definitions and barriers. Local politics led the Wyoming and Utah Territories to enact women's suffrage in 1869 and 1870, respectively, which encouraged an active lobbying push across the country. Other states had held referendums on women's suffrage by the 1890s, but most failed.

The rise of Progressivism helped reinvigorate the women's rights movement. Although an 1896 suffrage referendum had been defeated in California (saloon owners feared the onslaught of so many potential temperance voters and fiercely opposed the measure), a new initiative narrowly passed there in 1911. Attitudes began to shift, and other western states followed California's lead. Politicians sensed the shift, and were eager to win the support of women soon-to-be voters. In 1918, under political pressure, President Woodrow Wilson endorsed national women's suffrage; Congress passed the Nineteenth Amendment a year later. Most southern states, worried that the reformist wave would also challenge their disenfranchisement of African Americans, opposed the amendment while virtually every other state endorsed it. American women could now exercise a right to vote.

THE LIMITS OF PROGRESSIVISM AND THE CALL FOR CIVIL RIGHTS

Despite their forward-looking achievements, Progressives had their own blind spots, centered on the issues of socioeconomic class and race. Progressives were often suspicious of the capacities and morals of the poor—especially the increasing number of poor Catholic and Jewish immigrants. Even as they worked to extend the franchise to women and improve working conditions and labor rights, many Progressives supported—or at least accepted—measures to limit the rights of the poor. Progressive-backed laws made it more difficult for immigrants to achieve citizenship, and other measures made it far more difficult for the poor to vote.

The Progressive record on race was similarly problematic. Southern Progressives supported or turned a blind eye to the many barriers (that is, poll taxes, literacy tests, and property qualifications) that denied African Americans the vote. Racial prejudice was reinforced by broader Progressive suspicions of the "ignorant poor," and southern laws that barred blacks from voting mirrored those that Progressives endorsed elsewhere to keep the poor from voting. Indeed, southern voting laws disenfranchised many poor whites as well as blacks—leaving power comfortably and unquestionably in the hands of the white elite. Southern states feared the women's suffrage push would undermine Jim Crow voting laws, yet many Progressives who backed women's suffrage were actually quite sympathetic to the South's racial restrictions.

The Jim Crow South barred African Americans from skilled professions and consigned many to a tenuous and degrading life of sharecropping and debt. Opportunities for economic advancement were scarce, and a growing number of blacks began to move to northern cities in search of greater opportunity and prosperity. But the barriers they faced in the North were nearly as serious as those they had left behind in the South. Although explicit segregation laws were rare in the North, widespread discrimination had much the same effect.

In the North, blacks were largely forced into separate—and squalid—urban neighborhoods. Living conditions were poor; those African Americans who could afford to leave these grim conditions and move into more prosperous, mainly white areas were threatened and even assaulted when they tried to do so. As migration from the South caused the black population in northern cities to swell, discrimination only deepened. Northern blacks were driven from skilled professions they had once occupied. Unions—among the few allies that most laborers had in improving their lot—often barred blacks from membership. In terms of wages, living conditions, and opportunities, black workers consistently fared worse than their white counterparts.

Isolated by society's prejudices, many African Americans viewed their communities as separate islands of refuge in a hostile world. African American leader Booker T. Washington and others urged a focus on commerce, prosperity, and self-betterment within black communities. Washington argued that if blacks built visible achievements and proved their worth through quiet, nonconfrontational accomplishments, they would ultimately win respect and acceptance from whites. But to many activists, Washington's arguments sounded defeatist, counterproductive, and even servile. They noted that even the most successful blacks endured savage prejudice.

Determined to fight for what they saw as the basic rights of all Americans, these activists—men and women, black and white—united to form the National Association for the Advancement of Colored People (NAACP) in 1909. The creation of the NAACP marked the beginning of the modern civil rights movement, which demanded full social and legal equality through legislative and judicial action. A generation of skilled young African American lawyers was integral to the NAACP's mission. One of the organization's founding leaders was Dr. W.E.B. Du Bois, a Harvard-educated African American scholar.

Du Bois produced several serious historical works on Reconstruction, in which he documented the black struggle for political equality. He was one of the first to challenge the orthodox view, which had evolved since the 1880s, of Reconstruction as an "unnatural" tragedy. The orthodox narrative stated that conniving northern "carpetbaggers" had tried to invert the natural social order by goading and misleading blacks—who were painted as simple, credulous, even bestial racial inferiors. In saving white honor, driving blacks back to their proper place and expelling the vile carpetbaggers, vigilantes like the Ku Klux Klan served as the tale's chivalric heroes.

Du Bois offered a compelling scholarly counterblast, documenting African Americans' push for political rights in the wake of the Civil War. But the orthodox caricature of evil carpetbaggers, deluded blacks, and heroic Klansmen (enshrined by D. W. Griffith's epic 1915 silent film, *The Birth of a Nation*) was firmly engrained, and would dominate America's image of the Reconstruction era for decades to follow.

ERA 14: THE GREAT WAR: RALLYING AMERICAN PATRIOTISM *(1914 TO 1929)*

AMERICA ENTERS EUROPE'S WAR

By the late nineteenth century, a newly unified and aggressive Germany had helped divide Europe into rival blocs. The British were wary of Germany's autocracy and colonial ambitions, and they looked to ally with their former enemies: France and the United States. In 1914, Britain, France, and Russia faced off against Germany and its chief ally, Austria-Hungary, the other great Germanic power. As Austria expanded into the Balkan Peninsula, nationalists from the small Balkan state of Serbia struck back by assassinating Austria's imperial heir in June 1914.

Russia warned Austria not to attack its ally Serbia, but Germany was convinced that its European enemies were waiting to pounce and supported Austria unconditionally. By August 1914, Europe was at war. Germany pushed through neutral Belgium into France, and it combined forces with Austria to press against Russia. The result was a long and bloody stalemate. Each side hoped to shorten the war by starving out the other. Britain's navy blockaded trade to Germany, and Germany used its recently developed submarine force, the U-boats, to attack Britain's maritime supply lines. In sinking merchant vessels without warning, the U-boat campaign disregarded the established rules of war.

Despite their country's growing international role, few Americans wanted to take part in a devastating war thousands of miles away. Most clung to traditional U.S. isolationism, yet Great Britain, tied to the United States by commerce and a common language, had America's obvious sympathies. The U-boat war raised the stakes by disrupting Anglo-American trade and fueling Americans' anti-German sentiment. In May 1915, a U-boat sank the British passenger liner *Lusitania* en route from New York; 1,198 people, including 128 Americans, died. The United States demanded that Germany abandon unrestricted submarine warfare. Germany feared American intervention in the deadlocked war and backed down; it agreed to offer fair warning to merchant vessels and avoid attacks on neutrals.

As war dragged on, the Germans became more convinced that starving Britain was their only pathway to victory. They wagered that they would win the war before Americans could intervene effectively on Britain's behalf. Early in 1917, Germany announced that it would resume unrestricted submarine warfare. President Woodrow Wilson, who had tried to broker peace between the European nations—and who had centered his 1916 reelection campaign on keeping America out of war—severed U.S. relations with Germany. Tensions sharply escalated when British intelligence intercepted a telegram from Germany's foreign secretary, Alfred Zimmerman, bound for the German ambassador in Mexico. Germany suggested that if the United States should join the war, then Mexico should aim to reclaim Texas, New Mexico, and Arizona.

In March 1917, the U.S. government publicized the Zimmerman Telegram. The telegram inflamed anti-German and pro-war feelings, including those in Congress. Now most Americans saw intervention as a crusade for justice and political freedom. In early April, Wilson asked Congress to declare war, emphasizing in his war message that "the world must be made safe for democracy." The United States hoped to promote a democratic post-war order throughout Europe, including in Russia—where democratic activists had recently overthrown the tsarist government and were now struggling to fight the war, even as they fended off radical Communist revolutionaries (Bolsheviks) who promised to make peace with Germany.

In late 1917, the Bolsheviks seized power and quickly pulled Russia out of the war. Germany transferred its forces west to try to crush Britain and France before America could mobilize. And as Germany had predicted, American mobilization was slow. As it had been since Thomas Jefferson's time, the peacetime army was small, requiring mass conscription to swell its ranks, and it took time to organize, train, and equip new recruits. Although Germany made gains, however, it failed to win a decisive victory before the Americans arrived. As U.S. troops bolstered Allied strength, German defeat became inevitable. Facing revolt from a war-weary populace at home and massive setbacks on the battlefield, Germany surrendered in November 1918.

During peace negotiations the following year, Wilson sought to impose his vision of a noble settlement. But the embittered Allies had borne far more devastating losses than had the United States, and they insisted on harsh punitive terms for Germany. The Treaty of Versailles stripped Germany of territory and colonies, limited it to a token military, forced it to accept sole blame for the war, and required it to pay significant reparations to the Allies. The only major concession to Wilson was the founding of the League of Nations, a multinational organization aimed at resolving international disputes. But Wilson refused to negotiate with skeptical Republicans in Congress, who led the Senate to ultimately reject the treaty and keep America out of the league.

THE WAR AT HOME: GROWTH AND GOVERNMENT, PATRIOTISM, AND REPRESSION

America suffered more than a hundred thousand deaths during World War I, but such losses were minor compared to those of the European combatants: a fraction of 1 percent of the total U.S. population was lost, as opposed to up to 4 percent of the populations of Britain, France, and Germany. America was also geographically far removed from the theater of war, so its cities and factories emerged from the war unscathed—unlike those of the European combatants. Nonetheless, the war had profound consequences for the United States and reversed long-held traditions of small government and a limited military. It also propelled the nation into an even greater global leadership role.

Progressives worked to strengthen federal power over economic affairs, including the war economy. Local control efforts were inefficient, and helped big-government advocates carry out their agenda. By 1918, federal umbrella organizations directed the war industries, controlled the production and distribution of food and fuel, managed the railroads, and decided labor disputes. Invoking powers granted by the Sixteenth Amendment, the United States also established a graduated federal income tax, and sharply increased taxes would serve as the war's main revenue source.

Under the new Selective Service Act of 1917, all men of military age had to be registered and classified fit or unfit for military service. More than twenty million men registered; for many rural Americans, it was the first time their lives were directly affected by the federal government. The classification system also offered a disturbing portrait of American public health, exposing widespread inadequacies in medicine and hygiene as well as lack of education. Three million men were found fit and called into military service, marking the largest enlistment since the Civil War.

As soon as war was declared, a federal Committee on Public Information was charged with rallying public support through newspapers, posters, and films. The publicity campaign's overt aim was to inspire patriotism, but it also helped spawn frenzied suspicion of foreigners and dissenters. All things German were vehemently rejected (for example, sauerkraut was renamed "liberty cabbage"). The federal government was given enormous power to suppress subversives—those suspected of disloyalty, such as German immigrants and labor organizations. The 1917 Espionage Act granted broad powers to pursue those suspected of hindering the war effort, and the 1918 Sedition Act—directed at Socialists and pacifists—extended the hunt to those accused of defaming the U.S. government, political system, or military.

The military's rapidly expanding needs placed enormous demands on U.S. industrial resources and helped create the fully modern, internationally dominant American manufacturing economy. The new economy required a huge influx of manpower, and as production increased and calls for more workers were issued, masses of rural workers migrated to northern and midwestern factory cities in pursuit of better-paying jobs. Because millions of men were away at war, more women were drawn into the workforce, further challenging traditional gender roles and giving another boost to the growing women's suffrage movement. With labor in such high demand, the bargaining power of unions surged (although federal crackdowns quickly targeted the unions for suspected subversive interference with the war effort).

The war also increased racial discord at home. Among the rural workers flocking to urban industrial jobs were half a million southern blacks. Wilson, the Virginia-born president, was no friend to racial integration. His academic work had glorified the Ku Klux Klan, and he promoted the then-orthodox view of Reconstruction as a crime against white society. Black leaders had supported him in the 1912 election, but Wilson soon ordered the federal government segregated.

Although many African Americans served during World War I, the military was strictly segregated, and black units were largely excluded from combat.

Social tensions did not recede at the war's end. America's labor movement had always harbored radical elements, and the Bolsheviks' new Soviet Russia spurred fears that Socialist and labor groups might foment revolution in America—particularly because Soviet propaganda was actively urging them to do so. Strikes and agitation, together with a series of anarchist bombings that targeted government officials, judges, and businessmen, helped spark a full-blown Red Scare. From 1919 to 1920, Wilson's attorney general, Mitchell Palmer, launched mass arrests of leftist and labor figures. The so-called Palmer Raids targeted those suspected of subversive views, regardless of their actions. Thousands were arrested, and although many were eventually freed, hundreds of suspected radical immigrants were deported.

As urban black populations swelled, a series of severe urban race riots broke out in 1919. They reached a fever pitch in Chicago that summer. After police there treated white violence toward blacks with indifference, African Americans fought back—and dozens of blacks and whites died before the militia finally intervened. The government and press blamed the violence on leftist agitation. As they told it, the "Reds" were plotting to push black communities into open revolution.

Facing severe discrimination and de facto segregation even in the North, disillusioned African Americans increasingly lost hope in integration and the National Association for the Advancement of Colored People (NAACP). Some were attracted by the teachings of Marcus Garvey, a Jamaican activist who moved to the United States in 1916. Unlike W.E.B. Du Bois and the NAACP, which urged a continued legal and political push for racial integration in America, Garvey preached global black unity, self-improvement, and separation from whites in a new African republic.

POST-WAR AMERICA: PROSPERITY AND NEW FREEDOMS—FOR SOME

Despite its domestic turmoil, America entered the 1920s with great international stature: its standing as one of the world's great powers was cemented. After Wilson left office, a series of Republican administrations sought a return to peacetime normality—though the administration of Warren Harding, Wilson's immediate successor, was wracked by damaging crimes among his cabinet, including the infamous Teapot Dome Scandal, in which a top official took bribes in exchange for granting oil companies access to federal lands.

The Republican presidents of the 1920s—Harding, Calvin Coolidge, and Herbert Hoover—nonetheless had a strong effect on the direction of government policy. They halted the federal government's expansion, retreated from anti-Red persecution, tried to reduce the cost and size of the military, and embraced international treaties aimed at limiting an escalating global arms race. Although many Republicans of this era were not philosophically opposed to Progressive reforms (Coolidge had championed such causes as governor of Massachusetts), they were wary of expanding federal power. Generally, they preferred to let the states handle regulation and reform.

The 1920s were, for many, a time of spectacular prosperity. As the federal government retreated from its World War I expansion, business was left largely unregulated and taxes were kept low, resulting in a boost to short-term profits. Americans poured money into the soaring stock market and reaped fantastic profits in a seemingly endless economic boom. Industries emerged to supply novel demands, and a new consumer culture began to transform domestic life. Electricity, which had been used for lighting since the 1890s and was now available virtually everywhere (except in rural areas), triggered the creation of home conveniences. Radios provided nearly instant news access, leading to the rise of mass culture in music and entertainment.

This was also the Prohibition Era: although the Eighteenth Amendment aimed to eliminate drink from American life, it merely drove it underground. Prohibition promoted vast networks of illegal production, importation, and distribution, and drew millions to speakeasies: establishments that ranged from dirty holes-in-the-wall to elegant urban clubs where Americans could buy alcohol. Speakeasy culture helped fracture gender barriers, as women flaunted new freedoms in dress and lifestyle. To a lesser extent, racial barriers also shifted as jazz, a new African American music form, swept the nation. Great black jazz musicians played at high-end clubs—even though black customers were often barred. Giddy feelings of limitless prosperity filled the air, and the atmosphere of the Jazz Age created a looser popular culture that defied centuries of more restrained cultural mores.

For many other Americans, however, the period was anything but glittering. Although the surging consumer culture boosted industrial production and wages, rural migration to the cities increased competition for jobs. With too few jobs for the number of aspiring workers, many remained mired in poverty. Unions also suffered: an oversupply of labor weakened their leverage, and widespread mistrust of their objectives lingered after the Red Scare. African Americans, as they moved north, continued to face some of the worst prejudice and exclusion. Their wages were lower, and neighborhoods remained largely segregated. Antiblack harassment and violence were routine, as was discrimination in education, social services, and transportation. Nonetheless, black communities flourished culturally. For example, New York's Harlem Renaissance revitalized black music, literature, and arts—and attracted scores of white admirers and patrons.

To many religious traditionalists, the flamboyant culture of the 1920s seemed extremely alarming, apparently defying their most basic ideas of a decent society. As Protestant fundamentalism pushed back against threatening modern ideas, Darwinian evolution became a particular target. Fundamentalists saw the notion that humans had descended from "lower" animals as a serious threat to traditional morals and beliefs. Moreover, evolution was often used at that time to promote a callous Social Darwinism, which raised further religious objections. The most famous clash occurred in Dayton, Tennessee, where the Scopes trial pitted local activists and northern liberals against the state's antievolution law. Dayton drew ridicule in the national and international presses, and the situation was often subsequently painted as a humiliation for the fundamentalists. But higher courts evaded the issue of the law's constitutionality, and the religious furor in fact terrified many educators. Evolution was all but dropped from American textbooks until the 1950s.

Immigrants also continued to flood the United States, further alarming many traditionalists. By 1920, measures to reduce the flow were in place. These measures mainly targeted Catholic and Jewish immigrants in the East and Asian workers in the West. But as the pace of social change radically accelerated in the 1920s, old-guard elites and rural conservatives pushed back even harder on immigration. Quota laws passed in 1921 and 1924 sharply limited the number of immigrants. A rejuvenated Klan assailed blacks, Catholics, and Jews, especially (though not exclusively) in the South, and few politicians were willing to challenge the Klan's strength. Although more intense press coverage and important court convictions helped diminish the Klan's power over the course of the 1920s, lynching and racial violence continued unabated.

ERA 15: PROSPERITY HAS ITS PRICE: ECONOMIC COLLAPSE AND WORLD WAR II *(1929 TO 1945)*

CRASH, DEPRESSION, AND THE NEW DEAL RESPONSE

The investment boom of the Roaring Twenties was built largely on euphoria and blind optimism, rather than actual economic expansion. Financial speculation was barely regulated, and the value of shares grossly outstripped real corporate growth. Investment relied on borrowed money, and investors could only repay if stock values continued to surge—this was a classic economic bubble. As the heedless rush continued, questions were raised: Could companies grow at a pace that would justify the enormous sums invested? Would such risky ventures even survive? By October 1929, nervous creditors began to call in loans and demand repayment. The bubble burst, and the market crashed. In just a few hours, billions of dollars in investments were wiped out.

The Federal Reserve tried to rein in wild borrowing by raising interest rates, but it was too late. The ill-timed tight monetary policy now made it impossible for debtors to raise funds and smothered business spending. The 1930 Hawley-Smoot Tariff Act sought to protect American farmers and manufacturers from foreign competition, yet as many economists urgently warned might happen, the law sparked retaliatory tariffs abroad and stifled international trade. Banks failed, and many Americans' personal savings disappeared. Consumer spending plummeted, and the economy slowed even further. Because of their ties to U.S. bank loans, European banks also collapsed. With trade, jobs, spending, banking, and investment in free fall, the entire developed world plunged into crippling economic depression.

President Herbert Hoover wanted alliances of private businesses—not the federal government—to fix the economic crisis and promote recovery. As unemployment surged to 25 percent, however, Hoover finally took steps to support the banks. Although he hoped that these measures would stabilize credit and boost consumer spending, he still opposed direct federal assistance to the millions of unemployed. He did not want to breed permanent dependency, nor did he want to burden the government with large deficits.

In 1932, the Bonus Army—thousands of unemployed World War I veterans—marched on Washington, asking that a $1,000 bonus promised to veterans, meant to be paid in 1945, be paid immediately. A bill to grant their request died in Congress, but many protesters and their families refused to leave, setting up camp in the city. Federal troops finally attacked the protesters, driving them out by force and burning their encampment. Although the violent crackdown exceeded Hoover's orders, public outcry helped seal his fate. In that fall's election, the president was crushed by Franklin D. Roosevelt. Roosevelt, a Democrat, campaigned on a platform of active government intervention, promising "a new deal for the American people."

FDR quickly secured emergency legislation to stabilize the banks and protect private deposits, and he ordered direct federal assistance to the poor and mortgage relief for homeowners. He supported new programs to expand federal hiring, and he commissioned public works projects that created millions of new jobs. The Tennessee Valley Authority, for example, was an ambitious federal project that brought electricity and industry to a large rural area. Roosevelt had also campaigned on a pledge to end the increasingly unpopular Prohibition laws. In early 1933, Congress passed the Twenty-First Amendment, repealing the ban of alcohol; state conventions bypassed dry politicians to ratify it in less than a year. Restoring the massive alcohol industry also provided another boost to the national economy.

To raise farm prices, the government paid farmers to keep their fields partially unsown; lower production did bolster prices, but it hurt sharecroppers and farm workers—especially African Americans in the South. In the Great Plains, the Dust Bowl's crippling drought and storm-blown soil erosion spurred emergency federal measures to reclaim the soil through improved farming practices. But thousands of sharecroppers and poor farmers (mostly white in this region) were forced to abandon the area, migrating to California in search of opportunity. A new federal agency, the National Recovery Administration, sought to reorganize the economy by negotiating industry codes that would control wages, prices, and production. This was another attempt, with only limited success, to raise employment by limiting production.

The New Deal marked a drastic expansion of federal power. Conservatives denounced such policies as virtual Communism, whereas Socialist and Marxist radicals found FDR's plans totally inadequate and urged Soviet-style revolution. But most Americans idolized Roosevelt because of the relief programs he created and the hope that he inspired for the future. Resurgent unions led large-scale strikes and demanded the full benefits of New Deal programs. Voters handed Democrats increasingly massive majorities, and an emboldened FDR pushed harder: the second part of the New Deal, introduced in 1935, created Social Security, a national pension system funded by taxes on employers and wages; it required the states to offer assistance to the unemployed and disadvantaged; it bolstered the right to unionize; and it used revenues from increased taxes on the upper classes to fund further job creation, in fields ranging from industry to the arts, through the Works Progress Administration.

But unemployment was still high. Many Americans were alarmed by the growing power of unions and feared that FDR's policies encouraged dangerous radicalism. The Supreme Court, dominated by older, conservative Republicans, struck down the National Recovery Administration in 1935. Two years later, FDR, afraid that the court would overturn Social Security and his other major initiatives, proposed reorganizing the court by adding six justices who would uphold his policies. The court-packing threat helped prompt the conservative chief justice to shift ground: he voted to uphold Social Security and FDR's union measures. But FDR's court-packing struck many middle-class and conservative Democrats as an alarming power grab, sparking an angry backlash. Americans would not give unlimited leeway to any leader, not even one they admired so much.

New Deal measures had boosted the economy, especially since 1935. But they were never intended to be permanent, and the government started dialing back its support. Federal jobs programs were slashed. The new Social Security taxes hit wages, but Social Security pensions would not begin until 1941, so for now, the money did not reenter the economy. Growth faltered, stocks crashed again, and unemployment surged. Unhappy voters sent more conservatives to Congress in 1938 who blocked further stimulus measures. FDR was left politically weakened, and the economy continued to struggle; for some—especially women and minorities, who had little influence in Washington—the New Deal reforms had brought few benefits to begin with. Yet, despite its failings, the New Deal had already changed the role of government forever, creating innovative protections for millions of working Americans.

TOTALITARIAN EUROPE AND GLOBAL CRISIS: ALARM, EXTREMISM, AND ISOLATIONISM AT HOME

Even before the global economic collapse of 1929, totalitarian ideologies had been on the rise in Europe. Russia's Bolshevik revolution in 1917 had set off a civil war, and Vladimir Lenin's Communists had emerged victorious, imposing ruthless dictatorship in the people's name. Later, in the 1920s, Joseph Stalin, paranoid and murderous, imposed still harsher rule on the Russians. In Italy, which had fought with the Allies in World War I but suffered devastating defeats, Benito Mussolini's Fascist movement (called "Fascist" after an ancient Roman symbol of authority) seized power after his militia marched on Rome in 1922. Fascism, a form of dictatorship based on fierce nationalism and total subordination of the individual to the state, would come to define the era.

Germany's post–World War I Weimar Republic suffered economic collapse in the early 1920s, crushed by the reparations Germany was forced to make to the victorious Allies. As hyperinflation rendered German money worthless, foreign aid from the United States and other countries helped contain the crisis. But the Weimar government won little support from the German people, and extremism rose sharply. Adolf Hitler's National Socialist, or Nazi, movement fed on resentment toward the Treaty of Versailles. Although anti-Communism was an essential component of all Fascist movements, the Nazis added a layer of obsessive racial politics. They preached German racial supremacy—a belief that Germans were descended from a purer and superior ancient stock that racial theorists called "Aryan." And they demanded the enslavement, removal, or eradication of those they deemed racial inferiors—Slavs; Gypsies; and especially Jews, whom the Nazis blamed for all evils (including both Communism *and* capitalism).

The Great Depression sapped Europe's faith in the strength of its democratic governments and gave extremist parties a massive boost. Though Soviet-backed Communists were strong, the anti-Communist Right made the most dramatic gains. In Germany, the Nazis—now the country's largest party, backed by gangs of thugs uniformed in brown shirts—gained total control of the government in 1933. The Nazi state took control of the economy, creating new jobs and sparking growth; Hitler's domestic standing was greatly enhanced. However, the Nazis also blocked Jews from their professions and denied them basic civil rights. With Aryan supremacy as their aim, the Nazis began secretly rebuilding the German military. Their goal was military control of Europe, with the Slavic East seized for German settlement, and Slavs to be reduced to a slave race. The Nazis intended to eliminate Jews from Europe entirely.

For many who saw a world wracked by economic despair and faced with rising Fascist powers, democracy looked weak, inadequate, and doomed. Fascist movements arose throughout the West, including in the United States. Some Americans admired the Nazis' militarism, racism, and anti-Semitism: such prominent figures as automobile magnate Henry Ford and populist "radio priest" Joseph Coughlin embraced the Nazis' anti-Jewish propaganda. Yet many other Americans were horrified by Nazi ideology and aggression. Hitler's racially obsessed state loomed ever larger over Europe, annexing Austria, allying with Fascist Italy, and threatening to invade its neighbors. Nazi sympathizers were met with increasing suspicion and faced a rising backlash in America.

Regardless of their feelings toward the Nazis, however, many doubted that Germany could be stopped. Prominent American and British statesmen urged appeasement, a policy that would allow Hitler to take virtually whatever he wanted so long as it avoided war. Some, like Joseph P. Kennedy, U.S. ambassador to Britain, not only deemed Hitler unstoppable but even saw him as an ally in the mounting fight against Communism. Although Communist and Fascist dictatorships were both brutal, Communism's attack on private property and enterprise particularly appalled many Americans. The Great Depression had reinvigorated American Communists, who blamed capitalism itself for the economic collapse—and whose leaders, as their opponents accurately charged, were actively directed from Moscow.

In 1938, Hitler laid claim to a German-speaking region of Czechoslovakia. Britain and France, which were still attempting appeasement, met Hitler at Munich and yielded to him. But Hitler soon annexed all of Czechoslovakia, and then shifted his gaze toward Poland. Britain and France vowed war if Hitler attacked the Poles; in September 1939, after having cynically allied with the Soviets—the Nazis' chief ideological enemy—Germany defied Anglo-French threats and invaded Poland. Great Britain and France declared war on Germany.

Most Americans wanted no part in Europe's new war. A new isolationist movement, embraced by prominent Americans, gripped the country and dominated Congress (famous aviator Charles Lindbergh was a prominent isolationist—and an admirer of Nazi ideology). In 1940, Germany overran France and battered Britain with air raids. Britain was pushed to the brink of defeat, and FDR pressed Congress to build up the U.S. military—a burst of spending that would finally revive the U.S. economy. But Roosevelt was not content to guard America while Britain fell, convinced that a Nazi victory would doom democracy.

Although FDR kept the United States officially neutral, he was determined to aid the British. As he campaigned for an unprecedented third term that fall, he gave fifty destroyers to Britain in exchange for naval bases in Canada, Bermuda, and the Caribbean—and risked isolationist fury. In 1941, he pushed the Lend-Lease Act through Congress, a measure that allowed him to sell, trade, or lease war material to any power deemed essential to U.S. security. That summer, Hitler broke his insincere pact with Russia and invaded the Soviet Union (U.S.S.R.). FDR put American hostility toward Stalin aside and extended Lend-Lease aid. He also defied the U-boat war that Germany was waging against Britain's Atlantic supply lines by shipping goods to Britain and even defending its convoys by air and sea. Germany wanted to keep America out of the war, so it avoided direct attacks on U.S. escorts—but American ships were inevitably sunk, and anger rose.

In the Pacific, tension was also mounting. An actively modernizing Japan had emerged as a rising world power: it defeated Russia in 1905, annexed Korea in 1910, joined the Allies in World War I, and eyed a colonial hold in China. Japan's economy had also suffered during the Depression, and in the 1930s, the nation increasingly came under military control. Espousing doctrines of national and racial supremacy, Japan invaded Manchuria (in northeastern China) in 1931 and China as a whole in 1937. Japan's brutal expansionism badly strained relations with the West—on which Japan had depended for oil and other essential resources. Japan aimed for complete self-sufficiency and began contemplating a Greater East Asian Co-Prosperity Sphere. Despite the name, this vision consisted of a militarist Japanese empire that would conquer resource-rich Asian nations and seize Europe's Pacific colonies.

THE UNITED STATES JOINS THE SECOND WORLD WAR

As relations with Japan deteriorated, the United States imposed embargoes on oil and other materials that Japan desperately needed. Japan viewed these measures as threats to its very existence, and became convinced that conquest was necessary to guarantee its security. In 1940, Japan joined the Axis alliance with Germany and Italy, and plotted massive invasions throughout East Asia. Japan feared that America's enormous industrial resources and manpower would overwhelm it in a prolonged war, so it hoped to stun the United States into negotiating peace. To that end, Japan launched a surprise air attack on the U.S. naval base at Pearl Harbor on December 7, 1941. America's Pacific fleet was badly damaged, and Japan surged to a string of military triumphs. Japan invaded other Asian nations, Europe's Asian colonies, and the American-held Philippines.

But the United States did not crumble as Japan had hoped. Americans responded to the Pearl Harbor attack with fury and indignation. Hitler felt convinced that conflict with the United States was inevitable, and he was determined to stop American aid to Britain and Russia. He promptly declared war—the exact outcome Roosevelt and British Prime Minister Winston Churchill wanted. Churchill and FDR had agreed, before the United States entered the war, that German Fascism posed the greatest world threat; they planned on a "Europe first" approach. Although huge naval forces were prepared for a Pacific offensive, the Allies' priority was still Germany. The United States also joined Britain in allying with Stalin's U.S.S.R. This union was often awkward: temporary necessity forced the Western Allies to ignore Stalin's own brutality, as well as his obvious ambitions ultimately to expand Soviet power over eastern Europe.

As the United States joined the war, the situation looked grim. Although Britain had repelled German air attacks and ended the risk of invasion during the Battle of Britain, Germany occupied most of the European continent and had pressed deeply into Russia. U-boats stalked Allied convoys in the Battle of the Atlantic and sank masses of ships and supplies. In the Pacific, Japan seemed unstoppable as it rolled from victory to victory.

However, the tide was slowly beginning to turn. Germany's Russian offensive stalled in the face of Soviet counterattacks and the harsh Russian winter, and a German push across North Africa—aimed at Egypt and the oil-rich Middle East—was stopped by British forces in early 1942.

Later that year, American troops landed in North Africa and helped force a German withdrawal. Although the U-boat threat remained serious, the Allies improved their antisubmarine tactics and struck back hard. Allied air forces mounted a strategic bombing campaign that targeted Germany's industrial base and pounded its cities to sap civilian morale. In the Pacific, the U.S. Navy suffered a string of early defeats but smashed a major Japanese fleet in the June 1942

Battle of Midway. And after months of incredibly brutal jungle combat at Guadalcanal, the Allies stopped Japan's advance toward Australia. These battles marked a turning point, and Japan was on the defensive from then on.

Germany imposed tyrannical control in the territories it conquered—forcing people into virtual slavery, stealing their wealth, and using its feared secret police to brutally suppress dissent. Communists, intellectuals, gays, Gypsies, and others were targeted and killed, but the Nazis' main objective was the extermination of Europe's Jews. From the rise of their regime, they had sought to strip Jews of all rights and ultimately to drive them out of Europe. But as the war expanded, Nazi leaders decided that total eradication was the "final solution to the Jewish problem." An increasingly mechanized extermination system, centered on slave labor and death camps, ran ceaselessly until the war's end. Six million Jews were murdered while millions of other Europeans were worked to death alongside them.

Axis forces were pushed slowly back in 1942 and 1943, but horrific battles were raging in the U.S.S.R. Stalin urgently sought a second front in Western Europe, which he hoped would divide and weaken German forces. But it took the United States and Britain years to build the forces necessary to invade Europe, leaving Stalin constantly furious. As the Russians stopped a German push at Stalingrad in early 1943, the Allies readied their first foray into Europe. That summer, as the Russians began a large-scale offensive, the Western Allies invaded Sicily and continued into Italy. The Italians soon surrendered and joined the Allies, but German forces swiftly took control of the country.

Finally, in June 1944, the Allies' D-Day invasion across the English Channel into Normandy opened their second full front. As the Western Allies began to consolidate their base in France and push outward, the Russians were driving toward Germany. By late 1944, U.S. and British forces were advancing toward Germany's western borders. The final German counterattack, the Battle of the Bulge, involved costly fighting that set the Americans back. But German gains were short-lived: the Western Allies pushed into Germany in 1945, while the Soviets drove across eastern Europe toward Berlin. With his forces crushed and his nation's defeat certain, Hitler committed suicide in April, and Germany agreed to unconditional surrender days later.

Meanwhile, the Pacific war became a slow grind of Allied naval and amphibious operations to drive the Japanese from their island strongholds. At the same time, Allied armies fought in China and pressed into Southeast Asia. By early 1945, the Allies had taken the Philippines, Iwo Jima, and Okinawa—thus establishing strategic bases for massive bombing raids on Japanese cities. Japan was willing to face a devastating invasion rather than surrender, but the Allies had a secret alternative: a new atomic weapon urgently developed by American and European physicists in the clandestine Manhattan Project. (Germany and Japan had also tried to develop atomic bombs, without success.) The atomic destruction of the cities of Hiroshima and Nagasaki, coupled with a Soviet declaration of war against Japan's empire, forced Japan's surrender in August.

THE WORLD WAR II HOME FRONT

Japan's attack on Pearl Harbor and Germany's declaration of war instantly shattered America's isolationist mood. Through the draft and widespread voluntary enlistment, young men everywhere were swept into war. A shared patriotic purpose united Americans, and civilians pledged to contribute to the war effort: millions donated domestic goods and willingly accepted the government's rationing of meat, sugar, and gasoline so that the military could be supplied. Children sacrificed their toys, which were recycled into military equipment.

To meet the war's demands, the U.S. economy swung into massive expansion, finally sweeping away the lingering effects of the Depression. Just as America's enemies had feared, the country's vast industrial and human potential was powerfully and rapidly mobilized. The American fleet had been outclassed by Japan's modern aircraft carriers, but now it grew at a dramatic pace that left the enemy far behind. Assembly lines churned out merchant ships, replacing losses more quickly than the U-boats could sink them; new guns, tanks, and aircraft fed the demands of U.S. and Allied forces.

The federal government took unprecedented control of the vast economic mobilization, and the government itself expanded to supervise the effort. New federal agencies managed industries' transition from civilian goods to war equipment, they regulated prices, they settled disputes between management and labor, and they controlled domestic rationing. Federal spending skyrocketed, and vast revenues were raised through taxation and the aggressive sale of government war bonds, through which citizens invested their money in the war effort, in return for interest payments after the war. Athletic icons and Hollywood celebrities helped spearhead war bond sales drives, part of the government's huge program of patriotic and morale-boosting *propaganda* (a term that had not yet taken on its wholly negative modern tone).

Federal money poured into industry and research. The war spurred dramatic advances in technology and medicine, as government agencies coordinated research projects in academic and industrial labs throughout the country. Cooperation with the British led to the refinement of radar (an essential Allied advantage in the war) and the development of antibiotics. Leading Jewish European scientists and those who opposed Fascism fled Nazi tyranny and came to the United States. Even before the war, Germany had driven Jewish scientists from its universities. Now some of the world's best physicists, such as Albert Einstein and Enrico Fermi, joined British and American scientists in the urgent Manhattan Project.

Large corporate empires benefitted greatly from the vast surge in spending and production. But the American labor force was rapidly changing. The flow of young men into the military and the massive labor needs of the war effort forced companies and government entities to look to new sources. Women not only filled secretarial and clerical jobs but also entered professions that had been closed to them until now: they welded ships and assembled aircraft and tanks. Images of the symbolic Rosie the Riveter graced recruiting posters and entered popular culture. When the war ended, society expected women to return to pure domesticity. But wartime experiences changed many women's expectations and ideas, with far-reaching implications.

The war's urgent labor demands also forced doors open to minorities. The migration of southern African Americans to the North's industrial cities accelerated, and federal regulators pressed industries to drop discriminatory hiring practices and train blacks for skilled positions. The demography of the western United States also began to shift, as the government recruited vast numbers of Mexicans into the country as guest workers (temporary farm laborers). As the urban black and West Coast Mexican populations swelled, there were outbursts of racial violence and widespread discrimination. Meanwhile, the military remained racially segregated. As the United States fought against racially bigoted regimes abroad, many Americans noted the blatant disconnect and argued for reform at home.

Populations linked to enemy nations were at the greatest risk of direct government discrimination. German and Italian immigrants were branded enemy aliens and faced restricted freedoms; some were imprisoned or deported. The many U.S. citizens of German and Italian descent were mostly left alone. On the West Coast, Japanese Americans faced accusations—often founded on blatant prejudice and encouraged by neighbors' schemes to seize Japanese American property—of disloyalty and sabotage. More than one hundred thousand Japanese living on the West Coast, over half of whom were U.S. citizens, were interned in federal camps (although men could win release to join the U.S. military, and many served with distinction). The Supreme Court upheld internment in 1944. The United States would formally apologize and offer reparations to surviving Japanese American internees in 1988.

ERA 16: THE NEW AMERICAN DREAM: FREEDOM FROM TYRANNY *(1946 TO LATE 1950S)*

THE SOVIET UNION AND THE EMERGING COLD WAR

The West's necessity-driven World War II alliance with the Soviet Union (U.S.S.R.) was neither easy nor natural. After overthrowing Russia's democratic revolution in 1917, the Bolsheviks had quickly proved themselves autocratic and ruthless. During the Russian civil war that followed, the World War I Allies had offered generally unsuccessful military assistance to anti-Communist forces (though an American relief effort, led by staunch anti-Communist Herbert Hoover, also saved millions of lives after a catastrophic Soviet famine from 1921 to1923). Vladimir Lenin had imposed Communist rule with savage determination. His successor, Joseph Stalin, created a tremendously brutal police state. In the late 1920s and 1930s, he slaughtered the *kulaks*, or landed peasantry, when they resisted his plan to strip them of their farms; fearing potential rivals, he savagely murdered thousands of fellow Soviet Communist leaders and Soviet Red Army officers; and he began to send dissenters to the feared Gulag labor camps—where millions would die at his orders.

From 1917 on, the United States remained deeply apprehensive of the Communists and their intentions—the Soviets not only blatantly brutalized their own people but also were openly determined to export their Bolshevik revolution to other nations. The Soviets actively controlled Communist parties in Western countries, hoping to incite Communist revolts. The United States was the last major power to recognize the Soviet government: seeking to open trade and increase his diplomatic options, Franklin D. Roosevelt established ties in 1933.

Even then, most Americans remained strongly hostile to Communism and suspicious of the U.S. Communist Party (CPUSA), which was—as many suspected—largely directed from Moscow. Stalin's coldly practical 1939 alliance with the fanatically anti-Bolshevik Nazis—which included a secret agreement to divide Poland between Germany and Russia—hardly improved the Soviet image in the West; nor did the CPUSA's overnight switch from anti-German to pro-German propaganda as soon as the pact was announced. But when the Germans threw aside the two-faced treaty and invaded Russia in June 1941, the Soviets allied with Britain against Adolf Hitler, and thus received FDR's anti-Nazi assistance. And when the United States entered the war, the Soviets by default became a major ally.

Yet Western and Soviet long-term aims were incompatible, and the differences could no longer be ignored once the war ended. The Soviets were paranoid, aggressive, and determined to expand their territory and influence. Stalin was driven by a mission to export Communism, and he was convinced that he faced a constant danger of a Western attack. Roosevelt, Winston Churchill, and Stalin met at the Yalta Conference in February 1945 to discuss terms of the post-war settlement. In exchange for Stalin's pledge to join the Pacific war once Germany fell, the U.S.S.R. would gain Asian territories and an occupation zone in Korea. The three leaders formally agreed that Eastern Europe would remain independent and hold free elections, but it was obvious that Stalin's ambitions would be hard to restrain.

Roosevelt, whose health was failing at Yalta, has been criticized for yielding too much—but realistically, with the Soviet forces already driving across Eastern Europe, he had few options. FDR died in April, and his vice president, Harry S. Truman, assumed the presidency. At that summer's Potsdam Conference, Truman and Stalin agreed that the Soviets would occupy eastern Germany and that America, Britain, and France would occupy zones in the western part of the country; Berlin, which was situated deep in the Russian zone, would be divided likewise. The new atomic bomb gave the Allied leaders leverage. But the Russians, with secrets provided by Communist spies in Western laboratories, were already at work developing their own bomb.

In 1945, the Western Allies and the Soviets managed some cooperation, joining together to create the new United Nations (UN)—a more potent body than the now-defunct League of Nations—to oversee occupied Germany and to try the leading Nazis in an international court convened at Nuremberg. But as Stalin used force to impose his dictatorial will on Soviet-occupied territory, the rift between East and West continued to widen. In March 1946, Churchill—though no longer prime minister—warned that an "Iron Curtain" had descended across the continent as repressive Soviet-controlled regimes cut Eastern Europe off from the rest of the world. In 1947, Truman presented an urgent containment plan, using American resources and influence to stop nations from falling to Soviet-backed Communist movements. The U.S. Marshall Plan committed billions of dollars to stabilize the war-ravaged democracies of Western Europe. The Soviets promptly denounced the president's policy, known as the Truman Doctrine, as warmongering. They branded the Marshall Plan an imperialist plot.

Some in the United States called for a more conciliatory approach to the Soviets, blaming American aggression for Stalin's paranoid moves. In 1948, Henry Wallace—who had been FDR's vice president before Truman—mounted a third-party presidential campaign on a Soviet-friendly platform. But most Americans, aware of Stalin's genuinely irrational and savage behavior, looked on Wallace with mistrust. The CPUSA, little more than a Soviet mouthpiece, endorsed Wallace—which hurt him still further in the eyes of most Americans. Wallace received just 2.4 percent of the vote. President Truman and his anti-Communist Truman Doctrine kept the support of most American liberals, and he won a second term in the 1948 election. In later years, when the true scope of Stalin's atrocities became clear, even Wallace would reject his own 1948 attitude toward the Soviets as dangerously naive.

In the face of Stalin's menacing expansionism, West Germany and U.S.-occupied Japan were swiftly rebuilt as anti-Communist bulwarks. In the rush to bury hostilities and build friendly governments, punishments for many wartime atrocities were scaled back or even shelved. In 1948 and 1949, the Soviets demanded full control of Berlin and blockaded the city's Western-occupied sectors. As a U.S.-led airlift kept West Berlin supplied, the Western allies formed a mutual defense pact called the North Atlantic Treaty Organization (NATO). The Soviets backed down, but East and West Germany were soon split between rival governments: West Germany (including West Berlin) was democratic, whereas East Germany—like other Soviet-occupied territories—fell under a Soviet-controlled dictatorship. The Soviets detonated their own atomic bomb soon after, in August 1949. The Cold War—tense hostility hovering just short of open conflict—had begun.

In China, Communists under leader Mao Zedong had sought power since the 1920s. Although Mao allied with the Western-supported Nationalists against Japan during World War II, civil war erupted again in 1946. In 1949, Mao's Soviet-backed forces drove the Nationalists into exile in Taiwan. The rise of so-called Red China fueled Western fears of a Communist wave in Asia. Korea, which had been divided between a Soviet-occupied North and a U.S.-occupied South since 1945, emerged as a flash point. The Soviets resisted UN efforts to unify Korea under an elected government, and Communist North Korea claimed control of the entire country in 1948. South Korea created a rival, U.S.-backed republic (which would itself prove dictatorial, corrupt, unstable, and unpopular).

In 1950, Soviet-armed North Koreans—supported by the Soviets and Chinese—invaded South Korea. The United States successfully called for a UN force to counter the invasion (the Russians, having boycotted the session, were not present to exercise their Security Council veto). The UN forces (which consisted mainly of U.S. and South Korean contingents) repelled the North Koreans after difficult fighting, and they made a daring amphibious landing behind enemy lines in the Battle of Inchon. But when UN troops pushed into North Korea, China entered the war. The result was stalemate, negotiation, and a permanent truce in 1953 that established a divided Korea. The Korean War illustrated America's refusal to tolerate Communist expansion, and showed the strength of both rival blocs of nations.

THE COLD WAR AT HOME AND THE NEW RED SCARE

As a Cold War mentality took hold in the late 1940s, Americans—with obvious justification—viewed Communism as a grave, direct, and imminent threat to freedom and the Western way of life. Many expected war between the United States and the Soviet Union, and many took a hard line against Communist expansion. General Douglas MacArthur—who had lost the Philippines in World War II, and then made himself a legend driving his army back across the Pacific to reclaim the islands—became an anti-Communist American hero as he led U.S. forces in Korea. President Truman fired MacArthur in 1951, after the general openly resisted Truman's orders to avoid an all-out war with China. Most people had no desire for a wider war, and MacArthur's insubordination had dangerously challenged the president's constitutional authority. Nonetheless, the public overwhelmingly sided with the aggressive general over Truman.

Truman's successor, Republican Dwight D. Eisenhower, completed the Korean peace talks Truman had begun. Having served as the top Allied general in World War II, he was mostly safe from charges of being "soft" on Communism. But anti-Communist crusading had become a core element of American politics: for many it was a sincere effort to combat a genuine threat, but it also provided a ticket to political advancement. Truman and Congress had both encouraged aggressive hunts for Communist agents and sympathizers. Labor unions—which were attacked even by some within the labor movement for putting pro-Soviet loyalties above the interests of their members—came under hostile scrutiny. In 1947, the House Un-American Activities Committee (HUAC)—which had pursued alleged Communists in New Deal organizations in the 1930s—began investigating suspected Communist Party members in Hollywood.

A year later, California congressman Richard Nixon gained national prominence for his work in HUAC's investigation of Alger Hiss, an aide to FDR at Yalta, for Soviet espionage in the 1930s (Hiss was convicted of lying about his activities, and the evidence strongly indicates that he was a Soviet spy). By 1952, Nixon was Eisenhower's running mate. Government agencies drove out employees on disloyalty charges. J. Edgar Hoover, the autocratic director of the Federal Bureau of Investigation, zealously pursued suspected Communists and Communist sympathizers, or "fellow travelers." He built massive files on liberal-leaning artists and intellectuals, civil rights activists, and others (as well as on the private scandals of political leaders, thus making himself untouchable). As the Cold War worsened after 1949, anti-Communist suspicions became a massive and consuming domestic concern.

The Soviet espionage threat was entirely real: the Venona Project (a top-secret effort to decrypt Soviet cables) revealed an extensive network of Communist spies in America. But unless other evidence was available, few could be prosecuted without revealing the clandestine code-cracking project and compromising U.S. intelligence. In 1951, in one of the few high-profile prosecutions, CPUSA members Julius and Ethel Rosenberg were tried and executed for giving nuclear secrets to the U.S.S.R.; Venona decrypts—not used in court due to security concerns—indicate that Julius, at least, was guilty. Many known spies escaped the legal process entirely.

By the early 1950s, fears of Communist infiltration threatened to drive the anti-Communist crusade out of control: the accused often had little or no connection to actual spies. Republicans and conservative Democrats accused the Truman administration—which had itself pursued aggressive anti-Communist policies—of shielding Communist agents. Hollywood, notorious for its left-wing and even pro-Soviet politics, had become the target of HUAC investigations in the late 1940s. Studio executives, fearing public backlash if they failed to act, created a secret blacklist to bar suspected Communists from employment. The number of blacklisted names rose sharply in the early 1950s; most could find escape only by "naming names"–pointing HUAC toward other suspected Communists.

Joseph McCarthy, a Republican senator from Wisconsin, became the public face of the anti-Communist crusade after 1950. With increasingly wild rhetoric, he declared that Truman's State Department was full of Communist agents–operatives who aided the Communist takeover of China and subverted the U.S. government. McCarthy's public hearings pursued current and former CPUSA members as well as leftist and Progressive organizations that he deemed to be Communist fronts. McCarthy knew nothing of the top-secret Venona decrypts, and his targets were rarely tied to espionage. Yet the Americans whom he targeted fell victim to public disgrace.

Rival politicians and others who challenged McCarthy's accusations were branded as Communists. McCarthy even accused President Eisenhower–a fellow Republican, but no friend of McCarthy's–of protecting Communists in his administration. At first, influential Republicans and conservative organizations stood by McCarthy. But changing circumstances helped undermine his influence: to the relief of the West (and of many Soviets), blood-soaked dictator Stalin died in 1953. The Korean War, America's first open battle with Communism, ended with an armistice soon after Stalin's death. As the Communist threat came to seem less urgent, McCarthy's excesses attracted greater scrutiny.

During televised 1954 hearings into alleged U.S. Army subversives, McCarthy's abusive and arrogant behavior soured his reputation. Newspapers and increasingly influential television reporting (whose investigations were quietly encouraged by Eisenhower) began to expose his lies and bullying tactics. The Senate voted to censure McCarthy that November, and his power collapsed. His zealous crusade to squelch freedom of speech and thought became infamous, and *McCarthyism* became a blanket term for ideological persecution. Nonetheless, the sense of an existential battle with antidemocratic global Communism was not an irrational concern, and it persisted as a major element of American politics and culture throughout the 1950s.

AMERICAN LIFE IN THE POST-WAR ERA

Roosevelt's New Deal dramatically expanded the federal government's role in America's economy after the Great Depression, and World War II demands expanded government power even further. The shift was permanent: with the rise of federal regulation, higher income taxes, and expanded national services and social programs, a return to the largely hands-off policies of the 1920s was impossible. Socialist "welfare states"–where basic services and economic guidance were provided by the government–arose in post-war Europe. In the United States, however, Socialist policies remained unpopular. Many pushed back against the government's growing powers, which they saw as a threat to individual liberty and initiative.

After the war, President Truman sought a balance between government oversight and private enterprise. To that end, he encouraged a partnership with the private sector that would help demobilized soldiers attain education and employment. The GI Bill, which gained passage during the war, helped former servicemen and servicewomen secure loans for home purchases and business investments, and it helped them pay for employment training and higher education. In his second term (from 1949 to 1953), Truman promoted his Fair Deal program–a policy that relied on the booming post-war economy to fund the government's growing social welfare obligations, including an expanded GI Bill of Rights that extended benefits to Korean War veterans. The Social Security system–withholding money from wage earners' paychecks to fund retirement benefits–was expanded and solidified.

Broader attempts at national reform, such as a push for a national health care system, struck many as too radical, too broad, and too reliant on further government expansion. Conservative resistance blocked these efforts. Also, demand for new housing soared. As GIs returned home after long absences in military service, a surge in pregnancies—the baby boom—brought pressure for wholesome new neighborhoods with open spaces and modern school systems. The Housing Act of 1949 aimed to build public housing, but funding was scarce. Private development proved the bigger impetus. Planned suburban developments, such as Long Island's Levittown, attracted growing numbers of buyers and triggered a boom of mass-produced suburban construction.

Government loan guarantees and tax deductions for mortgage interest payments helped builders and buyers, who began to envision a new American Dream: instead of urban renting, people aimed to own their own home in the suburbs, filling their houses with such new amenities as vacuum cleaners, washing machines, and refrigerators. The popularization of television had a particularly big impact. The technology had existed since the 1930s, but only a wealthy few had been able to afford it, and programming was limited. As TV ownership became widespread in the 1950s, it helped create a new popular mass culture that linked millions of households. Yet as popular programs offered idealized portraits of suburban families, some Americans began to feel confined by the safe expectations of uniformity on their screens.

As Americans moved from a wartime culture to the new American Dream, women came under enormous pressure to return to a purely domestic sphere. Family comedies on the new television networks emphasized tight-knight families managed by women who embraced the dual role of wife and mother. Advertising emphasized new home conveniences that reinforced women's wholly domestic position. Yet many women did not easily forget their wartime experiences. Meanwhile, the growing economy increased demand in lower-paid service professions, such as nursing, teaching, and secretarial work. These fields now actively recruited women. Even under the veneer of 1950s domesticity, tension between the pressures of home and work were building.

As employers adjusted to a more regulated economy, relations between management and labor unions improved. As Americans borrowed money and enjoyed increased incomes, standards of living continued to rise. Automobile ownership dramatically increased, allowing unprecedented personal and family mobility. Suburbs became more and more practical as work, shopping, and recreation opportunities spread farther from city centers. President Eisenhower was wary of additional increases in domestic spending, but he accepted the New Deal and Fair Deal programs that he inherited. He also endorsed infrastructure investment: a federally constructed highway network spurred further growth in the auto industry (it also bolstered national security by allowing rapid deployment of military forces).

THE RENEWED CIVIL RIGHTS MOVEMENT

Although class tension and labor agitation eased (or at least moved further from view) with the economic boom of the late 1940s and 1950s, the issue of race continued to divide Americans. The South clung fiercely to legal and social segregation, and African American migration to northern cities helped stimulate white migration to the suburbs—a phenomenon known as "white flight." Suburbs were virtually all white, whereas urban centers became increasingly black. At the same time, though, challenges to racist ideology were growing: World War II, a global campaign against racially bigoted regimes, provoked a fresh examination of old assumptions. Activists of all races demanded reform.

In 1947, baseball great Jackie Robinson joined the Brooklyn Dodgers, thereby shattering major-league baseball's decades-old color barrier—and the "national pastime" had a strong impact on national culture. In 1948, President Truman ordered the military to begin the process of desegregation. He also focused on civil rights during the 1948 presidential campaign. This helped cement black support for Democrats in the North (where, despite social discrimination, African American voting rights were largely intact), but it also risked fracturing the party. Democrats had controlled the South since the end of Reconstruction, but some angry southerners now bolted into the Dixiecrat Party—which vowed to protect the South's segregationist system. Strom

Thurmond, the Dixiecrat candidate, won only 2.4 percent of the national vote, barely more than Wallace earned in 1948—but he managed to carry four southern states. Although the Dixiecrats were short-lived, their segregationist aims endured.

Truman also worked to desegregate the federal government's own labor force. But a bitterly divided Congress stalled in other ways, failing to enact measures that were against lynching and for black voting rights in the South. Truman's Justice Department went to court to attack segregation in schools and housing. The courts began to question the "separate but equal" doctrine, the legal basis of segregation since the Supreme Court's *Plessy v. Ferguson* ruling of 1896. In 1953, President Eisenhower appointed Earl Warren (a moderate Republican) as the new chief justice. Warren's court would move in an increasingly activist direction, making strong use of judicial powers to pursue social justice. One case already pending before the court was a National Association for the Advancement of Colored People (NAACP) challenge to school segregation: *Brown v. Board of Education of Topeka, et al.*

The NAACP's case was developed by its lead lawyer, Thurgood Marshall, and was based on studies that showed the psychological harm inflicted on African American children by segregation. Marshall argued that such harm made "separate but equal" invalid and segregation a violation of the Fourteenth Amendment's guarantee of equal protection under the law. Attorneys for the segregationist states argued that deficiencies in black schools could be remedied, and insisted that flaws in implementation did not invalidate the "separate but equal" concept. In 1954, Warren's court unanimously declared segregated schools "inherently unequal" because of their demonstrated negative psychological effects. In further hearings the following year, the Supreme Court ordered local courts to oversee a consciously cautious implementation of desegregation "with all deliberate speed."

The *Brown v. Board* decision at first only affected the states named in the NAACP suit. But the ruling had, at least implicitly, struck down the legal foundation of all official segregation. Southern whites reacted with predictable fury. Southern congressmen and senators rallied behind a "Southern Manifesto" that defended segregation; the Ku Klux Klan launched new campaigns of terror and violence; and a new White Citizens' Council fought to beat back change. To many conservatives, the civil rights push also smacked of Communism: racial integration had been a prominent feature of Wallace's Soviet-friendly third-party presidential bid in 1948. But federal courts began to invoke the Fourteenth Amendment more consistently and forcefully. Black and white civil rights activists, meanwhile, risked the threat of violence to defy the Jim Crow system.

In 1955, Emmett Till—a black teenager from Chicago who was visiting relatives in Mississippi—was savagely murdered by white vigilantes, who claimed that Till had whistled at a white woman. An all-white jury acquitted the two killers, who then openly boasted of their crime. At his family's insistence, Till's brutalized corpse was publicly displayed; the shocking image helped rally demands for justice. Later that year, the NAACP recruited one of its members, Rosa Parks, to defy bus segregation in Montgomery, Alabama. The NAACP intended her arrest to challenge segregation in the courts and in public opinion. The local black community, a major source of bus revenue, boycotted the transit system. The boycott, which won the support of black communities nationwide, was led in part by the young Reverend Martin Luther King Jr., who emerged as a national figure.

In 1956, the boycotters won: federal courts struck down the segregation law, and the transit system changed its rules. But progress came slowly. By the mid-1960s, only a tiny fraction of southern schools had complied with *Brown v. Board of Education.* In Congress, most southern Democrats resisted civil rights legislation or sought to weaken it. But northern Democrats allied with Republicans to challenge the South's disenfranchisement of blacks. Eisenhower remained cautious; but in 1957, when Arkansas's governor used the National Guard to resist a federal court order desegregating Little Rock's public high school, Eisenhower placed the Arkansas National Guard under federal orders and sent in U.S. Army troops—the first such intervention since Reconstruction.

Other groups also pressed for civil rights in the 1950s. Japanese Americans fought with little success to regain property stolen from them during World War II internment (Warren, who was then the U.S. attorney general, had been prominent in arranging internment). Further, in Texas and the Southwest, the Hispanic population was growing rapidly. Temporary agricultural workers (*braceros*) often stayed beyond their program's expiration, and both legal and illegal immigrants came steadily from Mexico. They, like African Americans, faced systematic segregation. In *Hernandez v. Texas*—a case heard in 1954, the same year as *Brown v. Board of Education*—the Warren court upheld the right of Mexican Americans to equal treatment under the Fourteenth Amendment. The justices ruled that with nonwhites barred from jury service, a Hispanic defendant had not received a fair trial. The nation's courts were continuing to expand their definition of justice.

ERA 17: COMMUNISM AND COUNTERCULTURE: THE CHALLENGES OF THE '50S AND '60S *(1950S TO LATE 1960S)*

THE SUPERPOWERS FIND AN UNEASY BALANCE: DETERRENCE AND THE BATTLE FOR HEARTS AND MINDS

As Cold War tensions climaxed during the early 1950s, the United States and Russia pressed for every strategic advantage over one other. When the first atomic fission bombs were developed in the 1940s, scientists already knew that thermonuclear fusion—the sun's source of energy—could create a bomb that was far more powerful. In 1952, the United States detonated the first thermonuclear, or hydrogen, bomb (H-bomb), which was many times more powerful than those dropped on Japan in 1945. The Soviets followed suit in 1953. By that time, Joseph Stalin was dead, an armistice had been reached in Korea, and fears of immediate war had eased. Yet the growing H-bomb arsenals, and fleets of long-range bombers to carry them, made any hypothetical war vastly more dangerous. An all-out thermonuclear exchange would endanger all of humanity.

Such a war would probably annihilate both sides: a grim reality dubbed "mutually assured destruction" (or, fittingly, MAD). The two superpowers thus embraced a doctrine of deterrence, striving to ensure that whichever nation attacked the other would not survive the victim's counterstrike; a nuclear "first strike" would thus be suicidal. Both powers began to build intercontinental ballistic missiles (ICBMs), which were difficult to destroy on the ground—and impossible to stop once launched. In 1945, the Russians and Americans had both tried to capture the engineers behind Germany's feared V-2 ballistic missile. The top German engineers took pains to avoid Soviet captivity and soon formed the heart of the American missile program. Russia had its own rocket scientists, however, and also began to produce viable ICBM designs.

Although the deterrence policy aimed to prevent a deadly direct conflict, it required constant buildup and maintenance of forces and alliances to keep a strategic balance. West Germany joined the North Atlantic Treaty Organization in 1955, and the Soviets created a military alliance, known as the Warsaw Pact, with its Eastern European satellite states. The threat of thermonuclear war also made effective diplomacy more urgent. Premier Nikita Khrushchev was then rising to power in the Soviet Union. He kept a tight hold on Eastern Europe and lashed out with fiercely bombastic rhetoric, vowing to destroy capitalism and "bury" the West. But behind the bluster, Khrushchev was a pragmatist, determined to maintain Soviet power but also to avoid a catastrophic war. The superpowers began conducting summits in 1955; the meetings aimed to limit the arms race and keep tensions under control. In 1956, Khrushchev denounced Stalin's violent crimes at a Soviet Party Congress.

East–West relations remained difficult and tense. In 1956, Hungary rose against Soviet control and appealed to the United States for help. The United States knew that American intervention in Hungary—practically in Russia's backyard—would inevitably have meant all-out war. The United States did not answer Hungary's calls for help, and thousands of Hungarians were killed as Soviet forces suppressed the revolt. The American response reflected the high stakes of political or military challenges to Russia because of the threat of thermonuclear war.

With Europe in an uneasy balance, attention shifted to "Third World" nations: developing countries that were not aligned with Communist or non-Communist blocs. Each superpower wanted to pull these nations into its own sphere of influence, providing aid and weapons and launching secret operations to install friendly governments. Determined to defend Western democracy against Communism, the United States was often willing to bolster anti-Communist Third World dictatorships to weaken Soviet influence.

In this battle for hearts and minds, appearances in the global stage were essential; each side fought to prove its superiority. The Soviets' October 1957 launch of *Sputnik*, the world's first man-made satellite, sparked a global sensation. Until this point, the United States had not made a satellite launch a major priority. Yet most Americans were stunned and humiliated by the unexpected Soviet feat. After the shock of *Sputnik*, the United States rushed to strengthen public science education and to prioritize technological investments.

The so-called space race would remain a propaganda battlefield for more than a decade. At first, the United States struggled to match Soviet efforts—and Americans knew that a rocket that could launch a satellite could also deliver a nuclear warhead anywhere on Earth. Khrushchev boasted of his country's ICBM production, and American politicians began to fret about a "missile gap." In fact, top officials knew from secret U-2 spy plane missions that the Soviets had few missiles, and actually lagged well behind the United States—a fact that Khrushchev carefully tried to conceal behind his boastful bluster.

In 1959, Khrushchev toured the United States to ease fresh tensions over Berlin. But relations soured again the following year, when Russia shot down an American U-2. President Dwight D. Eisenhower publicly denied conducting secret spy flights over Russia. His advisors assured him that the plane's pilot must have died when the plane was shot down and that the Soviets would be unable to prove the truth to the world. But the pilot, Gary Powers, had in fact survived and been captured; under interrogation, he admitted to committing espionage. The exposure of Eisenhower's lie embarrassed the United States, and the episode strained diplomacy between the superpowers.

Meanwhile, a Communist presence was taking hold only ninety miles from Florida. In 1959, Cuba's U.S.-backed dictator was overthrown by Fidel Castro and his rebels. But Castro soon emerged as a brutal, ruthless leader. Declaring himself a Communist, he turned to the Soviets—who were eager to gain a foothold so near to the United States. Before he left office, Eisenhower authorized a Central Intelligence Agency (CIA) effort to train anti-Castro exiles for an invasion of Cuba. President John F. Kennedy (who narrowly edged out Richard Nixon in the 1960 election) carried out the plan in April 1961. Anti-Castro forces landed at the Bay of Pigs, but the Cuban people failed to rise against Castro as the CIA had expected. As the invasion quickly floundered, the United States decided to pull back and cancelled the promised air support, and the American-supported exiles were badly beaten. The new Kennedy administration was humiliated and turned to secret efforts to topple Castro—or to kill him.

COLD WAR TENSIONS UNDER KENNEDY AND JOHNSON

In June 1961, Kennedy met Khrushchev in Vienna. The summit went poorly: Khrushchev, embarrassed by the steady flow of defectors from East Berlin into West Germany, demanded that the entire city be turned over to East Germany outright. Kennedy found him bullying and irrational; Khrushchev saw Kennedy as weak, despite JFK's refusal to yield on Berlin. In August, East Germany hastily constructed the Berlin Wall and alarmed Westerners by abruptly separating East Berlin from the West. Cold War tensions were rising again. The Soviets were also building up Cuba's strength, equipping Castro's forces with weapons and secretly sending large numbers of Soviet troops.

Khrushchev hoped to protect Castro from another American invasion, and in 1962 he placed nuclear missiles in Cuba that were capable of striking the United States. JFK had strongly warned the Soviets not to take such a step. That October, American U-2s found the missile bases—a discovery that sparked the most dangerous crisis of the Cold War. Although the United States had similar missiles in Turkey that were aimed at Russia, a failure to respond to Khrushchev's move would have been politically impossible: the acceptance of secretly installed Soviet missiles so close to U.S. shores would critically weaken the United States in the eyes of its allies and of nonaligned nations. Resisting his advisors' pressure for a military strike, JFK placed Cuba under naval quarantine and publicly demanded that the missiles be withdrawn. As U.S. warships confronted Soviet vessels on the quarantine line, any misstep could have escalated into all-out war.

Khrushchev was deeply alarmed, and he was just as determined as Kennedy to avoid a nuclear exchange. Khrushchev pressed against his own militarist advisors to find a peaceful solution. Even after Russia shot down an American U-2 over Cuba (without Khrushchev's authorization) and killed its pilot, both Kennedy and Khrushchev held back. Finally, after thirteen days of crisis, the leaders struck a deal. Publicly, the Soviets vowed to withdraw their missiles in exchange for an American pledge not to invade Cuba (this pledge was never actually given, because Castro—furious that the Soviets had agreed to withdraw the missiles without consulting him—refused to accept the terms of the deal). Secretly, the United States promised Russia to remove its missiles from Turkey (by this point, these weapons were already being replaced by newer submarine-launched ballistic missiles).

The world had survived its closest brush with nuclear catastrophe. For several days, a thermonuclear war had seemed imminent—and both superpowers had learned a sobering lesson. A direct phone link was established between the White House and the Soviet Kremlin to improve communication during future crises. Diplomacy improved; in 1963, Kennedy and Khrushchev signed the Nuclear Test Ban Treaty, which prohibited all above-ground nuclear tests. The treaty sought to protect the world from nuclear fallout and to limit the quest for more powerful bombs. Nonetheless, the superpowers continued to wage their battle for global influence. With both sides more wary than ever of direct confrontation, the focus shifted still further toward propaganda efforts and battles in the Third World.

The space race remained an important part of this struggle for global prestige. In the early 1960s, the U.S. space program stood in the shadow of seemingly endless Soviet firsts. But the Soviet advantage was weaker than it appeared. The Russians sent the first human, Yuri Gagarin, to space in April 1961. But America's technology was advancing rapidly, despite its relative lack of headline triumphs. Seeking a race the United States could win, Kennedy proposed to land a man on the moon by the end of the decade. Russia could not outdo America over the long haul; the Soviet lunar program was ultimately abandoned, whereas *Apollo 11* landed a man on the moon ahead of schedule in July 1969. Later *Apollo* missions developed into more serious scientific efforts, but Cold War rivalries lay at the program's heart.

In the ongoing battle against Communist expansion, the Southeast Asian nation of Vietnam became the focal point. Vietnam had been a French colony since the nineteenth century, but Communist and nationalist uprisings drove the French out in 1954, leaving the country divided into a Communist North and a Western-aligned South. Eisenhower feared a domino effect—that nations throughout Asia would fall to Communism if the North Vietnamese prevailed—and actively supported South Vietnam's government, despite its rampant corruption. Although he was wary of major military entanglement in the Southeast Asian jungle, JFK increased military support for South Vietnam. In 1963, the United States quietly backed a military coup that overthrew and murdered South Vietnam's unpopular ruler.

JFK's successor, Lyndon B. Johnson, escalated efforts to strengthen the vulnerable South Vietnamese. In 1964, a U.S. destroyer was attacked off the North Vietnamese coast; LBJ pushed the Tonkin Gulf Resolution through Congress, which essentially gave him a blank check to use force as he deemed necessary. By 1965, South Vietnam's government was near collapse, and Johnson had a dilemma. Despite a Communist insurgency in the South, which was backed by the North, most South Vietnamese clearly opposed a Communist takeover. Yet the South lacked effective government, which meant that the worsening fighting would fall mainly on the United States. Johnson was convinced that a defeat for the United States would weaken its position throughout the world. Thus, he continued to step up combat operations and deepen U.S. involvement, bombing Communist positions and steadily increasing U.S. ground troops.

REFORM AT HOME: THE CIVIL RIGHTS REVOLUTION AND LBJ'S GREAT SOCIETY

In the wake of *Brown v. Board of Education* and the successful Montgomery, Alabama, bus boycott, the push for civil rights and racial equality gained greater momentum in the early 1960s. The pressure for change came mainly from grassroots activists. In 1960, black students—who were soon joined by white sympathizers—sat at segregated department store lunch counters in North Carolina and demanded service. Such nonviolent sit-ins soon began throughout the South, with activists insisting—ultimately successfully—that the states accept court rulings against the segregation of buses, transit stations, and more. Equality advocates and student groups used buses to carry out mixed-race "freedom rides" across the South, facing down violent and dangerous segregationist backlash.

The strengthening civil rights campaign put JFK in an awkward bind. Since the 1930s, the Democratic coalition had included many New Deal liberals, who favored civil rights reform. But since Reconstruction, the party had also relied heavily on its massive southern base. And southern Democrats, the backbone of the region's white power structure, remained heavily pro-segregation. Kennedy, however, began to take bolder steps. In 1961, he sent federal marshals to protect the freedom riders; in 1962, he used National Guard troops to force desegregation of state universities in Mississippi and Alabama. That same year, Congress passed the Twenty-Fourth Amendment (ratified in 1964). The amendment abolished the poll tax, which had long been used to prevent southern blacks, as well as many poor whites, from voting.

The following year, antisegregation rallies in Birmingham, Alabama, led to brutal police crackdowns and antiblack violence. National demands for reform increased, and JFK began pressing for stronger civil rights legislation. That August, activists staged a massive march in Washington, DC, that climaxed in Martin Luther King Jr.'s eloquent "I Have a Dream" speech. In November, Kennedy was assassinated, and LBJ assumed the presidency. A master of legislative maneuvering and deal making during his years in the Senate, LBJ looked toward an even bolder reformist agenda. In 1964, he secured an expanded Civil Rights Act (which also offered women protection against discrimination) by bypassing southern Democrats and securing the support of moderate Republicans.

Meanwhile, the Republican Party also faced internal discord. That fall, a rising conservative movement dedicated to drastic reductions in government power (except for when it came to aggressive military policy) nominated Barry Goldwater, an Arizona senator, for president. To many Americans, Goldwater was a dangerous extremist: he seemed poised to use nuclear weapons in Vietnam and willing to threaten New Deal programs, such as Social Security. And although he was personally opposed to segregation, he rejected the Civil Rights Act as a dangerous federal intrusion on state power. Goldwater was crushingly defeated by LBJ, but the movement that he had ignited continued to gain strength. William Buckley, an editor and publisher, and actor-turned-politician Ronald Reagan were rising stars in the movement, and they gained prominence and power in the Republican Party.

Crucially, Goldwater's opposition to federal civil rights laws had helped him win five states in the Deep South (his only victories outside of his home state and the first Republican victories in the region since Reconstruction). Clearly, white resentment was fracturing the Democrats' former "Solid South." Fully aware of the threat to the old Democratic coalition, LBJ nevertheless continued to press for additional reforms. The Voting Rights Act of 1965 gave the federal government broad new powers to protect African American voting access in the South. At the same time, activists kept up popular pressure. King led a series of marches from Selma, Alabama, in support of black voting rights, and televised images of police brutalizing peaceful demonstrators helped galvanize national support for civil rights demands.

Defying the increasingly vocal opposition of small-government conservatives, LBJ was determined to expand federal power even further to advance his social justice aims. Before the 1964 election, he had already declared a "war on poverty," a push for economic development and job creation. After his landslide 1964 victory, Johnson called for programs to promote a "Great Society." Medicare funded medical care for the elderly, and Medicaid did the same for the poor. Other programs sought to renew decaying cities and promote low-income housing, expand support for education and cultural programs, increase the minimum wage, strengthen environmental protections, and continue to expand civil rights guarantees.

Johnson hoped to increase the New Deal's social supports to help those whom the prosperity of the 1950s and 1960s had left behind. The Great Society tried to create opportunity and help people help themselves, investing federal resources to assist Americans in achieving prosperity. Johnson argued that such efforts would bolster the prosperity of the entire society. But these expansions of federal power were expensive and controversial—especially when the 1960s economic boom faltered and the heavy taxes needed to fund the programs seemed too burdensome to many Americans. Nonetheless, some Great Society programs—particularly Medicare, which had been urgently denounced by the new conservative movement as a fundamental threat to American freedom—became firmly entrenched alongside Social Security as popular supports for the elderly and the poor.

THE '60S: WAR, COUNTERCULTURE, AND CONFLICT

As the 1960s advanced, a host of controversies deeply divided the country. The growing movement for racial equality, supported by Johnson's aggressive push for federal civil rights activism, sparked massive southern resentment and split the Democratic Party. LBJ's ambitious Great Society programs drew a strong backlash from a reinvigorated conservative movement determined to roll back what its members deemed wasteful "big government" spending. A rebellious, anticonformist youth culture challenged traditional social rules and authority structures and turned against the worsening war in Vietnam. And, faced with continuing poverty, prejudice, and only limited gains, some minority groups erupted in violent frustration against society's status quo.

The 1950s culture of conformity had already sparked a youth rebellion centered on the new craze for rock 'n' roll music. With its roots in predominantly African American jazz and blues, the music—and the uninhibited dancing that often accompanied it—greatly alarmed the period's parents, just as their children hoped that it would. In reality, though, the rebellion was limited and offered little real challenge to society's norms and expectations. Yet during the early 1960s, the backlash against 1950s conformism grew more serious. By mid-decade, "New Left" politics added fuel to festering antiauthority attitudes. Inspired by the civil rights movement, young Americans—particularly college students—increasingly attacked the country's political and corporate cultures and demanded radical social change.

Defiant students shunned adult authority and traditional values in regard to clothing, sexuality, drug use, music, and lifestyle. These so-called hippies and their counterculture became a vast campus phenomenon, heavily influencing the broader popular culture. Hippies sparked daring new fads in dress, popular music, arts, and design. Pressure also rose for other forms of social change. A new women's rights movement—arguing that women's social standing had hardly changed since they won the vote in the 1920s—launched a fresh push for social equality and female empowerment beyond the home. Many men on the New Left dismissed women's issues as secondary, but the cause would gain strength in the 1970s.

The Vietnam War served as the antiestablishment movement's primary focus, coming to symbolize all the evils of violence, oppression, social injustice, and authoritarian power structures that the counterculture denounced. Young American males were required to register for the military draft and carry a draft card. Although most college students received deferments to complete their education, they expired on graduation. Campus antiwar protesters rallied, burned draft cards, disrupted classes, and occupied campus buildings.

As America's involvement in Vietnam deepened, controversy grew across American society. Most South Vietnamese still opposed a Communist takeover, yet the South—facing North Vietnamese guerillas and South Vietnam's own determined Communist insurgency—had neither an effective government nor an able military. The combat burden fell increasingly on American draftees, while the harsh fighting also brutalized Vietnamese civilians. Communist centers in both the North and the South were bombed, and villages were razed, turning the South Vietnamese people ever more against the Americans who ostensibly were there to help them. For the first time, television brought vivid images of wartime carnage straight to American living rooms. Media reports grew increasingly hostile toward the war, criticizing the destruction and widespread loss of life.

Assailed by student radicals and media criticism, the war grew less popular as its costs rose. North Vietnam's massive Tet Offensive, in early 1968, turned even more Americans against the conflict. The offensive was, in fact, a serious defeat for Communist forces: their dramatic gains were only briefly held before they were pushed back with heavy casualties, and the pro-Communist rising the North had hoped to trigger in South Vietnam completely failed to materialize. But the aggressive attack nevertheless caught U.S. forces off guard and shocked the American public, who saw that the war was far from over, despite the thousands of lives already lost. With casualties mounting, the fighting seemed endless; hopeful generals so often saw "light at the end of the tunnel" that the phrase became a target of sardonic mockery.

Protests against the war and the draft grew more explosive and widespread. LBJ's credibility and popularity plummeted, undercut from the Right by attacks on his "big government" programs and from the Left by outrage at the war. Challenged for the 1968 Democratic nomination by the antiwar Senator Eugene McCarthy, LBJ chose not to seek reelection. He soon halted the bombing of North Vietnam and vowed to seek a peaceful settlement.

Growing racial agitation only added to the rising sense of national crisis. By the mid-1960s, such radical black activists as Malcolm X denounced the slow pace of reform and offered a "Black Power" philosophy of racial separatism (in 1965, Malcolm X was murdered by rival members of his Black Muslim movement). Such groups as the Black Panthers attacked King's nonviolent, integrationist approach. Despite the steady progress in civil rights, frustration seethed dangerously in urban black neighborhoods, which were still mired in poverty and deeply suspicious of arrogant and often-abusive white police. Some urban blacks began to lash out in bursts of violence, looting, and arson.

In 1965, tens of thousands of local blacks rioted for several days in the Watts district of Los Angeles, killing more than thirty people and causing tens of millions of dollars in property damage. Similar riots broke out in Newark, New Jersey, and Detroit, Michigan, in 1967. Urban, working-class whites—many of whom lived in close proximity to the riots—grew fearful. Many failed to distinguish between the rioters and the moderates, such as King, turning apprehensively against all blacks. Many also grew dubious of traditional labor-driven liberalism, looking toward more conservative policies to restore order and prevent social breakdown. Many black activists, meanwhile, made increasingly radical demands for immediate change, dividing their communities and further weakening moderate leaders. In April 1968, King was assassinated in Memphis, Tennessee, by white supremacist James Earl Ray. In response, new and severe riots erupted in black communities across the United states, further worsening the racial divide.

Robert F. Kennedy, brother of slain president John F. Kennedy, sought the 1968 Democratic nomination on an antiwar platform, but was also assassinated. Hubert Humphrey, LBJ's vice president, won the nomination. Outside the Democratic convention in Chicago, violence erupted between police and antiwar, antiestablishment demonstrators. The agitation reflected a growing split among Democrats: radicals attacked the party as complacent and racist, whereas working-class Democrats grew ever more concerned at the radicals' threat to social order. Republicans pointed to the violence as proof of the danger posed by leftist extremists. George Wallace, Alabama's segregationist governor, also sought the Democratic nomination. But he soon abandoned the party, running a potent third-party candidacy against Humphrey and Republican nominee Richard Nixon.

Wallace's candidacy was unsuccessful, but it marked a political watershed. His defection from the Democrats reflected the hastening collapse of the old Democratic Solid South. Nixon, deliberately targeting frustrated southern Democrats, also made strong inroads in the region. And although Wallace's aggressive pro-war stance hurt him at the polls, his attacks on racial integration, the counterculture, and federal power helped him win several Deep South states. Widespread fears of domestic chaos and social decay bolstered Nixon's campaign. His promises to end the war in Vietnam also boosted his standing, and he narrowly won the election (recent evidence shows that his staff worked during the campaign to undermine Vietnamese peace talks, fearing progress would boost Humphrey's standing). But the 1960s left the country deeply divided: many Americans were frightened by racial tensions and urban riots, alienated by radical disaffection, and bewildered by rapid social change.

ERA 18: MODERN TIMES: PRESIDENTIAL SCANDALS, CONSERVATISM, AND UNREST *(1968 TO PRESENT)*

GLOBAL CONFLICT AND DIPLOMACY: DÉTENTE, CHINA, AND THE MIDDLE EAST

After the 1962 Cuban Missile Crisis and the close brush with nuclear war, direct communication between the superpowers improved. The following year, the United States and the Soviet Union (U.S.S.R.) negotiated the Limited Test Ban Treaty to end above-ground nuclear tests.

The treaty was an effort to control the nuclear arms race and to avoid dangerous nuclear fallout. But the rivalry between the superpowers continued through less-dangerous proxy conflicts, as the two sides battled for influence in the developing postcolonial nations of the so-called Third World. The longest, most divisive conflict was America's intervention in the extended war between North and South Vietnam.

Even as he struggled to resolve the war in Vietnam, President Richard Nixon moved to lessen the risk of conflict with the major Communist powers. Pursuing a policy of détente (or the easing of relations), Nixon hoped to slow the dangerous, expensive nuclear arms race through a diplomatic thaw with the Soviets. Greater cooperation resulted in the Strategic Arms Limitation Treaty (SALT), which directly limited the construction of weapons systems. This agreement between the superpowers marked a major shift in Cold War relations.

Even more dramatically, Nixon reached out to Communist China. The United States had refused since 1949 to recognize Mao Zedong's People's Republic, instead recognizing Taiwan's exiled Nationalist government as the legitimate Chinese state. Communist China also resisted Western ties and supported North Korea against United Nations (UN) forces in the Korean War. Mao's extremism in the 1950s and 1960s soured his ties even with the Soviet Union, and it made improved relations with the West completely impossible. By the 1960s, the Soviets were openly repudiating the oppressive brutality of Joseph Stalin. Mao, instead, continued to grow more radical. Purging his own party of more moderate elements, he unleashed the savage chaos of the Cultural Revolution. Western influences were denounced as counterrevolutionary; those with Western learning were in danger of harassment, imprisonment, or death. China's acquisition of nuclear weapons further increased tension with the Soviets as well as with the West.

But the full fury of the Cultural Revolution could not be sustained. Damage to factories and labor forces undermined the economy, and the terrorization of teachers and closure of schools threatened the entire system of education. China's ruling Communists began anxiously pulling back from the full extremes of the Cultural Revolution in 1969. Although Mao continued to push for a rigidly ideological society until his death in 1976, even he began to retreat from the intense xenophobia that had gripped China. By 1971, he tentatively reached out to the wider world. Later that year, the UN granted China's seat, which Taiwan had held since 1949, to the People's Republic. The potent Security Council veto, which China had secured in 1945 as one of the five leading Allied forces (the United States, the U.S.S.R., China, Britain, and France), was also transferred to the People's Republic. In 1972, Nixon paid a formal state visit to Beijing. His successor, President Jimmy Carter, established full diplomatic relations with China in 1979.

Other international problems remained. After escalating its involvement in Vietnam and failing to end the conflict, the United States and North Vietnam signed the Paris Peace Accords in 1973, which allowed withdrawal of American forces. But beyond the American pullout, the peace agreement had little effect. North Vietnam continued to press its attack on the South. South Vietnam tried to continue the fight, but it was weakly governed and wracked by internal Communist insurrection. It was defeated in 1975, unleashing savage Communist crackdowns and mass flight by South Vietnamese refugees. Instability had already spread throughout the region. In 1975, neighboring Laos fell to a Communist insurrection—and the pro-American Hmong minority was harshly suppressed. That same year, Communist Khmer Rouge rebels seized power in Cambodia. Dictator Pol Pot's regime murdered two million Cambodians in a fanatical effort to purge intellectuals, end Western influences, and force the nation back to an agrarian peasant society. In 1978, the nation was overrun by Vietnamese troops. In 1991, the UN finally reestablished the constitutional monarchy that Pol Pot had ousted.

Meanwhile, there was ongoing hostility between the Arab states and Israel. Under the leadership of Yasser Arafat's Palestine Liberation Organization (PLO), militant groups refused to recognize Israel's existence and demanded a Palestinian state in its place. In 1967, Israel launched a preemptive strike as Arab nations prepared to attack. In the swift Six-Day War, Israel seized East Jerusalem and the West Bank from Jordan, and the Gaza Strip and Sinai from Egypt. In 1973, Egypt and Syria attacked on Yom Kippur (a Jewish day of fasting and prayer). But after early setbacks and a difficult fight, Israel emerged victorious once more.

Western-Arab tensions had been high since Arab independence was denied after World War I, and many in the Middle East resented Western backing of often despotic governments in strategically important oil-producing states. But the West's support of Israel exacerbated tensions with the Arabs and caused rifts with their respective governments. After the Yom Kippur War, the Arab states recognized the PLO as the sole legitimate government of all Israeli territory and imposed an oil embargo against Israel's Western supporters. A first major step toward stability in the region was the U.S.-brokered peace treaty between Israel and Egypt in 1978. Under the terms of the Camp David Accords, Israel ceded the Sinai Peninsula—which it had taken from Egypt in 1967—and removed its settlements there. But PLO terrorism against Israel, and Israeli crackdowns in the remaining occupied territories, raged on. A 1982 Israeli invasion of Lebanon, a nation devastated by Christian-Muslim civil war since the mid-1970s, sought to deprive the PLO of a major base. However, the invasion mainly resulted in sparking further international dispute.

Increasingly influential followers of radical Islamic ideas aimed to purge Muslim nations of Western influence and create a strict theocratic system of Islamic rule. In 1979, Iran's dictatorial, U.S.-supported shah was removed by Islamic revolutionaries. Iranian radicals demanded that the shah, who was in America for medical treatment, return to Iran for trial. They seized dozens of Americans in the U.S. embassy in the Iranian capital of Tehran, holding them hostage for months; their actions were part of a wider ideology of Islamic *jihad*, a doctrine of holy war for the defense and expansion of Islam that extremists claimed sanctioned acts of terror against Western civilians. Jihadists intended to force the West to withdraw support for Israel and to replace Western-backed Middle Eastern regimes with Islamist rule. But the West persisted in supporting Israel, and tensions between the West and Islamic radicals continued to rise.

THE COLD WAR ENDS, AND EUROPEAN COMMUNISM FALLS

By the 1980s, the Soviet Union was in serious economic trouble. After World War II, Stalin had promoted large, impractical schemes to transform the Soviet landscape—forcing crops into unsuitable climate zones and severely damaging agriculture in the process. By the 1960s, the state-controlled economy was focused on heavy industry; there was constant pressure to increase output, and attention to safety and quality standards decreased. The Soviets strained to maintain control of Eastern Europe and to preserve their massive military. In 1979, they invaded Afghanistan to defend a new Communist regime against Islamist rebels. The Soviets were opposed by American-supported and -equipped Islamic Mujahidin guerrillas, who saw the war as holy jihad. The war soon turned into a quagmire that further drained the Soviets' overstretched resources.

Meanwhile, major Western powers were growing both more conservative and more militarily aggressive. Since World War II, many Western European nations had built complex state-supported social welfare systems. But over time, the expense of such policies grew, and taxation reached extremely high levels that many feared would stifle economic growth. In 1979, the Conservative Party's Margaret Thatcher became Britain's prime minister. Remaining in power until 1990, she worked aggressively to reduce massive government spending and to rein in taxes. Opponents accused her of callousness as she cut taxes and reduced government-funded social services, but her supporters argued that the cuts were necessary to prevent government bankruptcy and economic collapse. She also firmly promoted a hard line against Soviet and Eastern European Communism.

U.S. president Ronald Reagan was elected in 1980 on a similar platform of shrinking the federal government and assuming a more aggressive foreign posture. He, too, focused intensely on eradicating Communism from the world—and he brought the dominant resources of the United States to bear on the issue. Reagan bolstered support for anti-Communist movements around the globe—including that of the Islamic rebels in Afghanistan. He also pushed for dramatic boosts in military spending to strengthen America's defenses. The Soviets were overburdened, and their economy was struggling. American policymakers did not just intend to bolster the U.S. military; instead, they hoped that forcing the U.S.S.R. to match U.S. spending would undermine the Soviet economy and bring down the Soviet Communist regime.

Although America's massive military spending created enormous budget deficits, the policymakers' predictions were correct: the Soviets' efforts to keep pace crippled them. Growing economic crisis in the U.S.S.R. boosted an internal Soviet reform movement. In 1985, Mikhail Gorbachev took power. The reformist premier quickly moved to modernize the economy, liberalize internal politics, expand free speech and personal rights, and retreat from aggressive foreign ventures. He called these policies *glasnost* (openness) and *perestroika* (rebuilding). In 1987, Gorbachev began preparing for withdrawal from the disastrous war in Afghanistan. Sensing a historic opportunity, Reagan pivoted to a strategy of diplomacy. He startled many as he proposed a dramatic arms reduction treaty, which the United States and the U.S.S.R. signed that year. In 1989, the U.S.S.R. withdrew completely from Afghanistan.

Eastern Europe had also been hit hard by economic decline, particularly as the cash-strapped Soviets cut back on supports, such as subsidized oil. As Gorbachev liberalized the Soviet Union and the threat of Soviet crackdowns eased, pro-democracy movements gained strength in nations that had long been under the Soviet thumb. Poland's Solidarity movement, led by labor activist Lech Walesa and openly encouraged by Polish-born Catholic Pope John Paul II, began openly opposing Communism in the mid-1980s. Unrest rose elsewhere, and as relations with the West improved, Gorbachev loosened the Soviet hold on Eastern Europe and allowed states to shift away from Communism. In 1989, rebellious East Germans broke down the Berlin Wall. The Communist East German government collapsed shortly thereafter.

Other pro-democracy movements soon spread across Eastern Europe. In Hungary and Poland, Communist governments negotiated settlements with opposition forces and transitioned to free elections. In Czechoslovakia, public demonstrations forced the republic's Communist regime to yield; in November 1989, dissident playwright Vaclav Havel became president of a free Czechoslovakian government. Bulgaria's Communist government fell to a coup, and Romania's fell to an armed insurrection. The Soviet sphere quickly crumbled—and Soviet acceptance of these developments marked the effective end of the Cold War. Within months, the global political order changed profoundly.

The Soviet Union itself began to dissolve. The U.S.S.R. included the large Russian state and more than a dozen smaller, once-separate republics. As Soviet policy liberalized and Communism crumbled in Eastern Europe, the republics began pushing for local control—and for the primacy of their own local languages, religions, and ethnic identities. Gorbachev tried to hold the U.S.S.R. together by force, but he was gradually compelled to yield greater autonomy to the republics. In August 1991, hard-line Communists attempted a coup to reassert Soviet control. Boris Yeltsin, the recently elected president of the Russian Republic (which was the central component of the U.S.S.R.) led a popular street uprising that defeated the coup plotters. That December, the Soviet Union dissolved and was replaced by the loose Commonwealth of Independent States.

Since 1919's Treaty of Versailles, the eastern part of Europe's many disparate ethnic and religious groups had been awkwardly joined together within often arbitrary national borders. Soviet control had kept these schisms forcibly submerged. But now the collapse of Communism allowed them to resurge. Czechoslovakia split into the Czech Republic and Slovakia in 1993. Yugoslavia, an uncomfortable amalgam of Slavic peoples that had been created in the ever-divided Balkans after the First World War, had begun to fragment by 1990; bitter fighting between ethnic groups soon followed. Long-buried splits also emerged in the Russian Republic. The Muslim province of Chechnya tried to break away, sparking a harsh Russian crackdown and a cycle of violence that is still unresolved. Germany was an exception: Cold War geopolitics had split a single people, who were reunited in a single German democracy in 1990.

Pressure against authoritarian Communism was not confined to Europe. China, which had opened to the West in the 1970s, was increasingly affected by Western economic and political ideas. As Russia enacted liberal reforms under Gorbachev, popular pressure rose in China. Citizens, especially the educated young, wanted similar changes. Even China's ruling Communist Party was divided between those who resisted reform and others who favored concessions toward democratic change. The removal of a top reform-minded official sparked urban pro-democracy demonstrations in early 1989. In May, youth-led protesters captured the world's attention as they occupied Beijing's Tiananmen Square. In early June, the government sent the army to suppress the protests. Hundreds died in a crackdown that heralded a wave of arrests and executions. The pro-democracy movement was broken, but Chinese authorities were left with the difficult task of addressing widespread discontent without yielding their power.

THE CHANGING POST-COLD WAR WORLD

The post-Cold War world created a new mosaic of international challenges, and U.S. president George H. W. Bush helped form new relationships and alliances between nations. From 1990 to 1991, Iraqi dictator Saddam Hussein (whom the United States had supported during his long, bloody war against Iran in the 1980s) invaded Kuwait and menaced Saudi Arabia. The invasion threatened America's allies, global oil supplies, and the entire world economy. Bush skillfully assembled a broad international coalition against Hussein. He was also able to keep Israel—whose involvement would have alienated Arab states—from joining the war, even after Hussein launched unprovoked missile strikes against Israeli cities.

Western Europe continued a long-standing post-World War II push toward unity and economic integration. In 1993, the European Union (EU) was formed, which tightened political ties and harmonized foreign and economic policies—despite continuing conflicts over the extent of individual member nations' sovereignty. In 1999, a new single European currency called the Euro took effect (although Britain, always cautious about strong European ties, refused to use it).

Eastern Europe struggled in its transition to unfamiliar democratic institutions. Eastern European nations gradually moved toward EU membership in the early 2000s. Poland, Hungary, and the Czech Republic joined the North Atlantic Treaty Organization in 1999. Other Eastern European nations followed suit, signaling a greater shift toward unified European policymaking. The single market and unified currency have created ongoing opportunities and ongoing challenges, as the EU has tried to balance Europe's stronger and weaker national economies within a stable and coherent single system.

Despite the push for unity, nationalism and ethnic separatism persisted—particularly in the regions that had constituted the former Yugoslavia. In 1914, Serbian demands for control of Bosnia, with its large population of ethnic Serbs, had helped spark the First World War. In 1991, Serbians in Bosnia-Herzegovina launched a genocidal campaign of "ethnic cleansing" (or targeted extermination) against the Bosnian Muslim population. Their aim was to create ethnically "pure" areas, which Serbia could then annex. The resulting Bosnian civil war unleashed savage violence, war crimes, and civilian slaughter. In the southern part of Serbia itself, the province of Kosovo witnessed uprisings against Serbian rule later in the decade. In 1998, Serbia responded with a new campaign of ethnic cleansing in Kosovo, aimed at ethnic Albanians and Kosovar Muslims. In 1999, the United States led a NATO intervention: airstrikes and NATO troops drove the Serbians back, and Kosovo was placed under UN control. Kosovo declared independence in 2008, but its status remains disputed.

As the world struggled to achieve post–Cold War political balance, its economy was quickly shifting. Globalization—the trend toward an integrated worldwide economy in which production and consumption are spread across the globe—had gradually been taking hold. For instance, factories had increasingly relocated to developing nations where labor costs were far lower and regulations were far weaker. In the 1990s, the world was no longer divided into rival Cold War camps. Thus, globalization accelerated dramatically. Beyond the United States and Europe, new centers of economic growth were rapidly emerging.

India, the world's most populous democracy, focused heavily on economic development after achieving independence from Great Britain in 1947. The nation was a quickly expanding center for manufacturing and technology by the 1990s, even though its government struggled to deal with widespread poverty. Hindu India and Muslim Pakistan have remained hostile toward each other. Although the nations have not been at war since 1971, border incidents and diplomatic clashes have continued. India attained nuclear weapons in the mid-1970s, and Pakistan followed a decade later (although it did not openly test a bomb until the late 1990s). In spite of the tension, there have been periodic thaws and increases in cross-border trade.

Development has been difficult in Central and South America, which had long been under U.S. and European economic domination. In 1994, the North American Free Trade Agreement (NAFTA) cut restrictions on cross-border commerce. Since NAFTA, Mexico has produced more goods for the U.S. market and has developed close ties with the United States. But Mexico has also been severely hit by organized crime, drug trafficking, and lawlessness: there are large areas where the government barely has authority. Elsewhere in the region, post-war industrialization efforts have often failed, and heavy borrowing led to debt crises in the 1980s.

Political instability led some nations into successive dictatorships. The United States sometimes supported these dictatorships, so long as they were anti-Communist. In 1973, the United States covertly helped Augusto Pinochet overthrow an elected Socialist government in Chile, a move that ushered in fifteen years of corrupt, brutal rule. Juan Perón, president of Argentina, flirted with Fascism after World War II. In 1976, Argentina fell to a military *junta* (a group of military officers in charge of a dictatorship), which murdered thousands of dissenters. The regime's unsuccessful 1982 attempt to wrest the disputed Falkland Islands from the British—aggressively fought off by Britain under Thatcher—finally led to its demise, and a new democratic government took power in 1983. South America's rich raw material resources—particularly oil and agriculture—today serve as a springboard for future growth. However, the profits rarely reach large portions of the expanding populations, and serious ecological damage has been done. The destruction of vast areas of rainforest to create agricultural land has global environmental implications.

Development across Africa has been extremely uneven since post–World War II decolonization. For some countries, oil and other raw materials offered a path to rapid prosperity. As in South America, however, a drop in oil prices during the 1980s left many nations in debt. Some of them have successfully established democratic governments, but ethnic conflicts and political turmoil have continued to ravage the continent. During Nigeria's civil war in the late 1960s, nearly one million people died of starvation. Outbreaks of ethnic cleansing in Rwanda in the 1990s and in Darfur in the 2000s have drawn international attention but defied straightforward solutions. Poverty, HIV and AIDS, political crises, environmental decay, and continuing debt continue to impede new reform and economic development efforts.

International pressure and internal resistance helped bring down South Africa's white-dominated Apartheid regime of racial segregation. In 1990, South African President F. W. de Klerk began to repeal the country's Apartheid laws, freed Nelson Mandela—leader of the anti-Apartheid African National Congress—after twenty-seven years of imprisonment, and moved to enfranchise black South Africans. In 1993, de Klerk and Mandela shared the Nobel Peace Prize. The following year, Mandela was elected president of South Africa. His Truth and Reconciliation Commission sought to address the crimes of the old regime and avoid new divisions and further violence. South Africa, despite ongoing problems of poverty and ethnic tension, remains one of Africa's most successful democracies.

The Pacific Rim has experienced dramatic economic growth since World War II. During the post-war American occupation, Japan's growth was encouraged so that the nation might act as a bastion against communist expansion. Industry and technology had skyrocketed by the 1960s, as Japan became a major manufacturer of consumer goods and electronics. Within three decades, Japan had become one of the world's dominant economic powers. Although a serious fiscal crisis blunted its growth in the 1990s, Japan's economy remains powerful. Other nations in East and Southeast Asia—including South Korea, Indonesia, and the increasingly reformist Vietnam—have also become major players in manufacturing and agriculture and have received heavy Western and Japanese investment because of their lower labor costs. But there, too, destruction of rainforests and other natural landscapes for palm tree plantations, other agricultural products, and urban expansion has done serious environmental harm.

RECENT TRENDS: GLOBAL TIES AND CONFLICTS

One of the most dramatic recent global developments has been China's emergence as a dominant economic power. By the 1980s, China was bending its Communist economic doctrines as it invited foreign investment through free-enterprise zones. In the wake of 1989's Tiananmen Square crackdown and growing popular unrest, the Chinese government recognized that it needed to improve the lot of its younger, more educated citizens. In the 1990s, the nation relaxed its rigid economic restrictions further, allowing free markets to develop and privatizing many state-run industries. When the British colony of Hong Kong was returned to China in 1997, China maintained its globally connected investment markets. The result was an economic boom for the educated classes—even though the boom's sustainability depended on poor working conditions and meager pay for a large part of the Chinese population.

China's dramatic productivity and low labor costs have encouraged Western companies to outsource manufacturing to China, which in turn has become a major supplier of goods throughout the world. Although it has liberalized its economy, however, China has maintained its firmly authoritarian government. Other nations have criticized China for its autocracy and human rights violations. Tensions with the United States have repeatedly risen over regional power (including China's claim to Taiwan and territorial disputes with close American ally Japan); human rights abuses; and China's support for such regimes as that of dictatorial, militarist North Korea. But China and the West are now mutually dependent economically—which means that despite any ongoing disputes, at least some degree of cooperative coexistence is essential.

China's role in the world economy highlights the continuing importance of global economic interconnectivity. Modern telecommunication and the Internet have strengthened these ties even further. Workers in developed countries with high labor costs have been squeezed out of employment as many low- or semiskilled jobs move to less expensive overseas markets. Laborers in developing countries press in turn for opportunity and advancement, as pressure from foreign companies to keep wages low and productivity high often result in virtual slavery. Western popular culture—spread further by television and the Internet—has been embraced in many parts of the world, but it has also sparked backlash from cultural and religious traditionalists who feel threatened by what they consider to be decadent and immoral foreign ideas.

Cultural globalization has reinforced a sense of grievance in some Islamic communities, building on centuries of tension between the Middle East and the West. Opinions about pluralism and the wide circulation of diverse ideas have long differed: the first printing press did not appear in the Arab world until 1720, nearly three centuries after the first European press. Until the 1860s, independent newspapers were virtually unknown in the Arab world. But recently, Western technology, clothing, art, and music have been steadily embraced—and religious traditionalists have mounted significant resistance. The status of women, traditionally relegated to subordinate positions in Islamic culture, has prompted particularly serious clashes in some Muslim countries. Many women have pushed for greater social status, political rights, and equal employment, with widely varying success. The issue remains a difficult one, with women frequently facing social restrictions and even violent repression.

Conflict between Middle Eastern Muslims and the West mounted in the aftermath of the First World War, when the collapsing Ottoman Empire gave way to political and economic domination of the region by Europe and the United States. Even after direct colonial control of the region ended, Western powers continued to support dictatorial regimes to ensure their own access to vital oil supplies. Islamic militancy gained strength during the 1980s Afghan war against the Soviets, in which Islamic fighters, or *mujahedeen* (who were aided and equipped by the United States), were central. Some militant groups that were active in Afghanistan emerged as terrorist bodies with far larger aims—particularly Saudi billionaire Osama bin Laden's al Qaeda organization.

Although most Muslims around the world did not and do not endorse terrorism, the clash between Islamist militants and the West quickly emerged as one of the world's major post–Cold War fault lines. In the 1990s, terrorist groups turned their focus from Middle Eastern regimes to the West as they aimed to force the United States and Europe to withdraw entirely from the Middle East and end their support of Israel. In 1993, militants inspired by a radical Egyptian sheik detonated a truck bomb beneath New York City's World Trade Center. In the mid-1990s, bin Laden's al Qaeda established bases in Africa and plotted anti-Western attacks on U.S. embassies in Africa. Later, as the radical Islamist Taliban took control of Afghanistan, al Qaeda relocated to there. It launched attacks on New York City and Washington, DC, on September 11, 2001.

In the wake of the 9/11 attacks, the United States and several allies took military action to dislodge al Qaeda from its Afghan base. In the following years, enormous resources would go toward hunting down the organization's leaders and blocking further attacks. Meanwhile, hostilities widened. In 2003, the United States invaded Iraq after it claimed that Hussein was gathering weapons of mass destruction to use against the West. The charges against the Iraqi dictator proved inaccurate, and the war caused controversy across the United States and around the world. A resurgent Taliban continues to pose a threat in Afghanistan as U.S. forces begin to withdraw, and Pakistan—where many resent America's military presence in the region—has become increasingly radicalized.

Repeated efforts to restart Israeli-Palestinian peace talks, which had stalled, have resulted in little progress despite wide international support for a two-state peace arrangement. Palestinian groups have continued to launch terrorist attacks and deny Israel's right to exist, while Israel has continued to expand settlement in the occupied territories that are seen by supporters of a two-state solution as belonging to a future independent Palestine. The Middle East was further roiled by the Arab Spring revolts of 2010 and 2011, as protesters across the Arab world—avoiding government censorship by using the Internet—rose up against several dictatorial regimes. The outcome of those uprisings remains a great unknown, as pro-democracy activists struggle for influence against powerfully entrenched Islamist parties seeking to impose Islamic rule.

As it moves into the new millennium, the evolving global community faces challenges: terrorism and peace, ethnic conflicts and border disputes, pollution and global climate change, resource management and population growth, the global status and rights of women and regional minorities, and democratization and its opponents.

POSTSCRIPT: RECENT EVENTS (1992 TO PRESENT)

The 1990s

After decades of government expansion that began with the New Deal and continued in the Great Society, twelve years of Reagan Republicanism had significantly challenged post–New Deal assumptions about federal power. Views over the appropriate role of government in American life greatly differed as Bill Clinton took office as president in 1993. Although he secured a small increase in upper-income tax rates in 1993, Clinton fashioned himself as a new kind of Democrat—a more centrist politician who openly challenged the basic assumption of 1970s and 1980s Democrats that increased spending and government expansion were the default answers to social problems.

Rising health care costs and limited access to health insurance were recognized national concerns, however, so Clinton's administration pressed for comprehensive reform on this issue. Marking the first time a president's wife had taken a public role in policymaking, Hillary Clinton spearheaded the administration's health care efforts. But the complex, cumbersome plan that emerged drew considerable political and public opposition and was rejected by Congress. The aftermath only deepened the country's divisions over the direction of government.

In the 1994 midterm elections, disillusioned voters broke away from decades of rarely interrupted Democratic dominance in Congress and handed both houses to the Republicans. The voters clearly intended to issue a call for more limited government—a balance between Clinton's health care activism and Reagan Republicanism. But the new congressional majority interpreted its victory as a mandate for drastic spending cuts, in some cases aiming well beyond Ronald Reagan's positions and seeking to roll back New Deal protections Reagan had defended.

In 1995, the new Congress briefly shut down the federal government, denying funding in an attempt to force dramatic spending cuts. The political fallout damaged the new majority's standing, leaving the country even more divided and Washington in deeper partisan turmoil. Clinton compromised with Congress to reform the national welfare system; spending was reduced, and requirements that recipients of public assistance actively pursue work were tightened. He also helped lead the government to a balanced budget for the first time in decades, fulfilling a core tenet of Reagan Republicanism—one that had eluded Reagan because of the burden of soaring defense spending and revenue-sapping tax cuts. By the end of Clinton's second term, the country had a budget surplus.

Despite such examples of productive bipartisan cooperation, partisan hostility remained alarmingly high. The Republican Congress had quickly launched aggressive investigations of potential corruption in Clinton's background, although lengthy, controversial, and expensive inquiries yielded few results. In 1998, it emerged that Clinton—who had been accused of sexual harassment before his election—had lied under oath in a civil lawsuit about an affair with White House intern Monica Lewinsky. House Republicans impeached the president but fell well short of a conviction on any charge in the Senate. The impeachment, which was only the second in American history, was unpopular and contributed to a reduced Republican majority in the 1998 midterm elections.

The Clinton years, which marked the first post–Cold War presidency, witnessed an unstable international situation—one with fresh diplomatic opportunities alongside new threats and challenges. The world was no longer divided between two stable superpower-led camps. Freed from such control, regional nationalism surged, combining with religious and ethnic separatism that had been forcibly contained for decades. Nationalist uprisings and ethnic mass killings in Bosnia drew U.S. and NATO military intervention. Islamic militants—who resented America's powerful role in the Middle East, its backing of dictatorial governments in the region, and its long-standing support for Israel—strengthened and expanded their influence.

Radical Islamic militants had gathered in Afghanistan in the 1980s, trying to expel an aggressive Soviet invasion and relying on U.S. aid to do so. As Gorbachev pulled back from military confrontation and withdrew Soviet forces from Afghanistan, militants—particularly Osama bin Laden—turned their hostility to the West, determined to provoke Islamic religious war aimed at unifying the Islamic world under their own brand of religious rule. In 1993, Islamic militants inspired by an Egyptian cleric detonated a truck bomb beneath the World Trade Center in New York, killing six and injuring dozens.

Bin Laden and al Qaeda, his network of followers, moved to Islamist-held territory in Africa to develop their anti-Western plans. They returned to Afghanistan as that country fell to the Islamist Taliban movement. In 1998, they launched bloody bombings of American embassies in Kenya, and they planned further attacks. After the Kenyan bombings, Clinton launched a cruise missile strike on bin Laden's base that narrowly missed the terrorist leader. Yet the U.S. response to al Qaeda was haphazard: members of the intelligence services were unsure of America's overall goals and often failed to share and coordinate information.

As the century ended, America remained politically, socially, and economically divided. Although the economy had boomed under Clinton, manufacturing jobs were now moving to cheaper developing labor markets abroad. Increasing economic globalization, including NAFTA, which linked the United States with Canada and Mexico, further altered the domestic economy and complicated employment prospects, forcing many Americans to retrain for new types of jobs. Changing views on religious and social issues—especially among younger Americans—increased divisions on such controversial topics as abortion, gay rights, and immigration. Further, rapidly changing demographics shifted the racial and ethnic identity of the country: as America became more urban, more racially diverse, and more secular, many Americans—especially older people from more rural areas—feared that the traditional America they cherished was disappearing.

The 2000s

In the 2000 presidential campaign between Al Gore, Clinton's vice president, and Republican George W. Bush, a closely divided country yielded a controversial, contested result. Gore narrowly won the national popular vote. The Electoral College was decided by a disputed result in Florida, where Bush's brother was governor, and where the federal Supreme Court, on a five-to-four party-line vote, stopped the state's recount with Bush leading by only five hundred votes. Later analysis suggested that the limited recount Gore had sought—focused on specific counties with Democratic majorities—would not have changed the outcome. But controversy continues over the full statewide count, the role of state Republican officials in handling the vote and the recount, the Supreme Court's role, and the legal efforts launched by both campaigns after the election.

During Bush's first year in office, al Qaeda continued to orchestrate its long-planned efforts for a major attack. American intelligence services continued to misinterpret important evidence, and the new administration—presented with only fragmentary data—did not appreciate the seriousness of the threat. On September 11, 2001, al Qaeda terrorists hijacked four American airliners, flying two into the Twin Towers of New York City's World Trade Center and collapsing both buildings, and flying a third into the Pentagon in Washington, DC. The fourth plane crashed in rural Pennsylvania after passengers rallied to overpower the hijackers. Three thousand Americans died in the attacks.

Bin Laden viewed Americans as weak and cowardly, and fully expected the United States to collapse after the 9/11 attacks. But Americans united in powerful resolve. President Bush declared a "global war on terror" as he unleashed an attack on al Qaeda's base in Afghanistan. Central Intelligence Agency officers and Army Special Forces helped anti-Taliban Afghan militias retake the country. Although bin Laden and many other al Qaeda leaders escaped, the terrorist movement had lost its haven; targeted attacks over the coming years would deprive bin Laden of most of his top deputies. Although the organization and its loose-knit community of sympathizers would manage major attacks in coming years in such cities as London and Madrid, its capacity as a global threat had greatly diminished. Several attempts to wage another attack on the United States were thwarted.

Most Americans had supported the Afghan war. More controversially, the Bush administration now shifted its focus to Iraq. Bush argued that the Iraqi dictator, Hussein, was still pursuing chemical, biological, and nuclear weapons. In fact, Hussein had abandoned such programs after the 1991 Gulf War. But, wanting to intimidate his enemies, particularly Iran, he resisted UN weapons inspections. Neoconservatives had also gained influence in the wake of 9/11: they pushed to increase America's security and remake the dangerous Middle East by creating pro-Western, democratic regimes—by force, if necessary. Bush and his neoconservative advisors pressed for an invasion of Iraq in 2003, effectively eroding the unity America had enjoyed after 9/11. The Iraqi invasion was met with opposition from most foreign nations and limited support from Arab allies. Although Hussein's government quickly fell, the predicted weapons of mass destruction were not found. The situation in Iraq rapidly decayed as sectarian conflicts, long suppressed by Hussein's brutal regime, burst into chaos.

Critics charged that the Bush White House had failed to plan for realistic postinvasion scenarios, instead hoping to remake and democratize the region with little cost or difficulty. Iraq was soon teetering on the edge of religious civil war. Despite the heavy costs of the wars in Afghanistan and Iraq, Bush pressed for new rounds of tax cuts, particularly for upper-income Americans; the budget surpluses Clinton had left soon gave way to massive deficits. Many Americans distrusted Democrats on national defense, and Bush narrowly won a second term in 2004. Public discontent with Bush's policies grew, however, and the Republicans lost Congress in a 2006 midterm election landslide. A fresh American military effort restored some order in Iraq, but the new Iraqi government insisted on a solid timetable for U.S. withdrawal. Iraq remains riven by sectarian conflict, corruption, and ethnic divisions.

In 2007, the U.S. economy began to falter—and it slumped into serious crisis by early 2008. Government oversight and regulation of businesses had slackened since the late 1970s, and risky financial practices had become more common. Banks offered subprime mortgages (at higher-than-standard interest rates) to high-risk, low-income buyers. Both major political parties encouraged the practice: Democrats urged loans to low-income and minority buyers as a matter of social justice, whereas Republicans looked to bolster home ownership and the important housing market. Because those mortgages were backed by the homes themselves, and because the housing market was soaring, many saw them as sound investments. Financial institutions bought up these mortgages with enthusiasm, expecting to repossess the valuable houses if the borrowers defaulted on their loans. But many potential home buyers lacked the money to meet ever-rising prices, making the housing market a bubble ready to burst.

By early 2008, falling home prices had begun to erase the value of the subprime mortgages. Having overinvested in these assets, financial institutions were suddenly in grave danger. Business and consumer confidence fell, and major financial institutions failed. Financial lending was drastically curtailed, and economic growth was stifled. As businesses closed and jobs were lost, consumer spending plummeted, forcing still more businesses to shut down. As the unemployment rate rose even higher, consumer spending dipped even lower. And as the crisis rapidly escalated, opinions on the most effective response differed drastically. Despite conservative opposition to federal intervention, the government moved to bail out failing institutions and prevent a full collapse of the fiscal system. Nevertheless, the nation plunged into the worst recession in decades.

Both Bush and the Republican Party had been unpopular even before the fiscal crisis, and Democrats were favored to win the 2008 election. Indeed, that fall, Democrat Barack Obama was elected as the nation's first African American president. Despite his solid electoral win, however, Americans were still sharply divided on spending, regulation, taxation, and the president's push for a health care reform law. Conservative Republicans retook the House of Representatives in 2010, but their uncompromising small-government agenda also proved divisive and controversial, helping propel Obama to a second term—in spite of the nation's slow economic recovery.

As Obama's presidency unfolded, manufacturing jobs continued to move abroad, and the economy continued to shift. Many workers were unqualified for available positions, as was the case in the high-tech sector, in which many job positions went unfilled because there were not enough qualified applicants. Deep political, social, and religious differences persisted, and America's white majority shrank as its minority presence grew. Islamic terrorism and global instability continued to pose constant threats, even after a 2011 Special Forces raid in Pakistan killed bin Laden. Americans continued to battle over the nature and proper extent of the fight against terror, balancing security against privacy and due process. Inspired by their shared national heritage, many Americans were left searching for common ground and a new political center—while others clung fiercely to their own visions of America's past and future.

Who Is Common Core

Common Core is a nonprofit 501(c)3 organization that creates curriculum tools and promotes programs, policies, and initiatives at the local, state, and federal levels, with the aim of providing students with challenging, rigorous instruction in the full range of liberal arts and sciences. Common Core was established in 2007 and is not affiliated with the Common Core State Standards (CCSS).

Common Core has been led by Lynne Munson, as president and executive director, since its founding. In six short years, Lynne has made Common Core an influential advocate for the liberal arts and sciences and a noted provider of CCSS-based curriculum tools. Lynne was deputy chairman of the National Endowment for the Humanities (NEH) from 2001 to 2005, overseeing all agency operations. NEH is an independent agency of the federal government that funds scholarly and public projects in the humanities. Lynne was the architect of Picturing America (http://picturingamerica.neh.gov/), the most successful public humanities project in NEH history. The project put more than seventy-five thousand sets of fine art images and teaching guides into libraries, K–12 classrooms, and Head Start centers. In 2005, Lynne led the first postconflict U.S. government delegation to Afghanistan to deal with issues of cultural reconstruction. In 2004, she represented the United States at UNESCO meetings in Australia and Japan, where she helped negotiate guidelines for cross-border higher education.

From 1993 to 2001, Lynne was a research fellow at the American Enterprise Institute, where she wrote *Exhibitionism: Art in an Era of Intolerance* (Ivan R. Dee, 2000), a book examining the evolution of art institutions and art education. Lynne served as a research assistant to NEH chairman Lynne Cheney from 1990 to 1993. She has written on issues of contemporary culture and education for numerous national publications, including the *New York Times*, the *Wall Street Journal*, *USA Today*, *Inside Higher Education*, and National Review Online's *The Corner*. She has appeared on CNN, Fox News, CNBC, C-SPAN, and NPR, and she speaks to scholarly and public audiences. She serves on the advisory board for the Pioneer Institute's Center for School Reform. Her degree in art history is from Northwestern University.

Learn more about Common Core at commoncore.org.

Acknowledgments

On behalf of Common Core (CC), I would like to thank those whose time, knowledge, and passion created this invaluable resource for teachers. There are many who deserve heartfelt thanks; without their contribution, the Alexandria Plan would still be just an idea in our minds. My first thanks are to Kate Bradford and Lesley Iura at Jossey-Bass/Wiley, who advocated for publishing a new education series on history, despite the subject's having been marginalized for decades. They share our confidence that history is on its way back into classrooms.

Much of CC's Washington, DC, staff played—and continues to play—a significant role in shaping, shepherding, and promoting this work. Staff members include program manager Sarah Woodard, program assistant Lauren Shaw, and partnerships manager Alyson Burgess. Barbara Davidson, CC's Deputy Director, was fearless in her leadership of this effort.

Special thanks to the more than one hundred teachers who piloted the Plan in their respective classrooms. We are particularly grateful to Susan Hensley, elementary curriculum specialist for the Rogers Public Schools in Arkansas, for her lead role in the piloting effort. The piloters' enthusiastic and insightful feedback was an essential ingredient in our work. Also, recognition needs to go to CC's Alyssa Stinson for arranging the pilot project. Thanks also go to Russ Cohen of Schoolwide, Inc. Russ provided review copies of the more than eight hundred titles we considered for inclusion in the Alexandria Plan.

Many experts were involved in informing, shaping, and ensuring the accuracy of this work. Historian Harvey Klehr exhaustively reviewed our U.S. history era summaries to make sure we had our facts correct. CC trustee and past president of the National Council of Teachers of English Carol Jago reviewed and improved our text studies. Lewis Huffman, social studies education associate for the South Carolina Department of Education, provided keen, real-world guidance that was instrumental in making the Plan of service to teachers. Susan Pimentel and her team at Student Achievement Partners provided invaluable early advice that shaped the rigor of the Plan.

Research assistant Jennifer Foley's review of this work was incredibly beneficial. Our Plan was meticulously edited by Allison Lawruk to ensure that it was error-free and of maximum use to teachers. The materials were painstakingly copyedited by Shannon Last. Betsy Franz and Rebecca Hyman helped obtain the images that appear throughout the Plan. And Natanya Levioff drove our project deadlines to completion.

We are grateful to Ed Alton and his team at Alton Creative for their ingenious design of our website, commoncore.org. We are indebted to branding expert Christopher Clary, illustrator Amy DeVoogd, and copywriter Peter Chase for work that enhances both the website and this book.

There are three people who worked tirelessly for months on the Plan and who are most responsible for imbuing the Plan with heft, utility, and joy. Historian Jeremy Stern is not only our nation's foremost expert on state social studies standards but also a thoughtful, trenchant scholar who has the gift of writing the kind of history we all want to read. Jeremy brought extraordinary care and devotion to the crafting of each of the thirty-six era summaries that form the basis for the Plan and from which the topics for our text studies are derived.

Education policy consultant Sheila Byrd-Carmichael served as a writer and Common Core State Standards (CCSS) expert on this project. Sheila worked to ensure that the text-dependent questions and performance assessments for each suggested anchor text would allow students to meet, indeed surpass, the standards. She also brought forward essential academic vocabulary in each text study.

Lorraine Griffith is a teacher at West Buncombe Elementary in Asheville, North Carolina. She is also lead writer of all of CC's CCSS English language arts–based curriculum materials for grades K through 4. Lorraine identified the essential historical content in each of our anchor texts and made it the focus of the series of text-dependent questions that form the spine of our text studies, and of the Plan itself. Her uncanny ability to translate her passion for how great literature, history, and art can transform the learning experience for students is a gift to CC and to the teachers who use our curriculum materials.

Jeremy, Sheila, and Lorraine's depth of knowledge and passion for bringing quality resources to teachers inspired everyone involved in this project. We hope and expect that their enthusiasm will be evident to you as you begin to work with the material contained in this book.

It was a privilege for me to work alongside these inspired experts. I look forward to our next project together!

December, 2013

Lynne Munson
President and Executive Director
Common Core
Washington, DC

Index

Y

Z